Twayne's English Authors Series

Sylvia E. Bowman, *Editor*

INDIANA UNIVERSITY

Robert Herrick

(TEAS) 34

Robert Herrick

BY ROGER B. ROLLIN

Franklin and Marshall College

Twayne Publishers, Inc.   ::   New York

For My Wife
And for My Father and Mother

Tempora cincisset Foliorum densior umbra:
  Debetur Genio Laurea Sylva tuo.
Tempora et Illa Tibi mollis redimisset Oliva;
  Scilicet excludis Versibus Arma tuis.
Admisceas Antiqua Novis, Iucunda Severis
  Hinc Iuvenis discat, Fœminaq Virgo, Senex:
Ut solo minor es Phœbo, sic major es Unus
  Omnibus, Ingenio, Mente, Lepore, Stylo.
W. Marshall Fecit.   scripsit I.H.C.W.M.

ROBERT HERRICK

Preface

Any work of literary criticism is bound to be inadequate, and this critical-analytical study of Robert Herrick is no exception. It will, as it must, fail to do perfect justice to Herrick's art as a whole and even to its individual parts, the poems themselves. To understand why this should be the case, the reader should consider one of Herrick's apparently bizarre works, *"His Winding Sheet."* This wry ode, like any other successful poem, is a highly complex, multi-dimensional, semantic construct which the literary critic must somehow reduce to a relatively simple, one-dimensional, semantic construct—a prose analysis. What happens in the process of performing this reduction is that, no matter how accurate and sensitive the critic's reading, no matter how lucid his prose, something of Herrick's poem eludes him.

For example, *"His Winding Sheet,"* among its other elements, has an insight to communicate—a startling conception of death. The literary critic must try to reveal this insight, explain it, show its relationships to Herrick's other insights or to those of other poets, and perhaps indicate its relevance to what is sometimes called "real life." The critic must do all this without making it appear as if *"His Winding Sheet"* is merely a sermon in rhyme or that Herrick is merely a verse-making philosopher. And still the insight itself, or the *experiencing* of the insight through reading the poem well, cannot be completely reduplicated by mere analysis and explication.

"His Winding Sheet" also communicates certain feelings ranging from bitterness to quiet confidence. The critic must be responsive to such feelings and help the reader respond to them by pointing out the words, the images (such as the image in the title), and the figures of speech that bear emotional charges and thereby give the poem its emotional force. But he must write *about* such emotions objectively—without permitting his prose to become emotional.

Furthermore, *"His Winding Sheet"*—like all poems—re-creates an experience, in this case the experience of becoming aware that death is the end and thus, in an ironic sense, the goal of all life— and of finding some consolation in the democracy of death and of the great promise of salvation. In order that readers of poetry may more readily participate fully in such experiences, the literary critic must raise for them such questions as: What is the poem's setting? Where is it? When? Who is "speaking" in the poem? To whom? About what? What attitude or attitudes does he have towards his subject? Does any action occur? What changes have taken place by the poem's conclusion? Unfortunately, the critic knows that he can never give completely satisfactory answers nor even be sure that he has raised all of the right questions, for the poem transcends both.

In short, the purpose of the literary critic is to treat Herrick's *"His Winding Sheet"* or any other poem in such a way that the reader of his criticism will return to the poem itself and, with an increased awareness of all of its complexity, be able to read it more accurately and sensitively—and thus experience it more fully—and thereby receive from it more pleasure. Having made this contribution, the literary critic becomes superfluous; for the reader he has done all he can do. He has become obsolete—as a successful poem will never be. Nevertheless, for the critic there are always "fresh Woods, and Pastures new"—the next poem and the next reader.

Although this study of Robert Herrick is, therefore, inadequate, despite its inadequacy it does what no other comparable study has done up to now—it examines a sizable number of Herrick's poems *as poems*—not merely as slick imitations of Classical models, as fictionalized autobiographies, as literary and historical oddities, as versified dirty jokes, or as technical *tours de force*. (They have too often been read as all of these in the past.)

While this study cannot of course explicate even most of Herrick's more than fourteen hundred poems, it does attempt to deal with as many of them as can be closely read within the space allotted. These poems have been selected with special regard for their representativeness as the types of poems that Herrick was accustomed to write, just as they treat the types of subjects he was accustomed to treat, and just as they also exhibit the types of attitudes he was accustomed to hold towards those subjects.

Judgment will not be passed upon either the "soundness" of

Herrick's ideas or upon the "sincerity" of his feelings. The latter, as will be indicated further on, is impossible to determine; and the former is in the province of the philosopher. This study will only try to explicate these ideas, to show the connections between them, and to put them in the general context of intellectual history; evaluation will be up to the reader. In short, the concern here is to cast some light on the intellectual unity and on the artistic variety of Herrick's work.

This unity will be shown to be crystallized in Herrick's conception of himself as a pastoral poet and in his creation of a pastoral world, a "*Sacred Grove*," as the world of his book. For Herrick (as it was for Spenser and Drayton, Milton and Marvell) being a pastoral poet means being—not a "nature poet" or a mere purveyor of pretty ecstacies about nymphs and satyrs—but a poet who is both a critic and an artist of life: one who uses his artistry to portray an idyllic, ideal world that can serve as an overt or covert criticism of "the real world." By so doing, Herrick shows strong affinities not only with the aforementioned English pastoralists, but also with certain formal verse satirists of the English Renaissance and with certain Classical poets.

Herrick's "criticism of life" is shown to be grounded in a coherent, viable world view, one which has as its sources elements of the philosophy of Stoicism and of the Christian religion, but chiefly of Epicurean philosophy. By way of summation, this study further shows that Herrick's world view is given focus, order, and originality by his comprehensive esthetic which, for him, approaches the status of a religion. Thus, while the poet's lighter vein will not be neglected nor its importance minimized, an attempt is made to restore something of the balance that has too often been lacking in the criticism of his art. The *total* Herrick, it must be stressed, is compounded of both serious and light elements and of numerous gradations between; and since this book makes an effort to be comprehensive, it must be responsive to all of them.

To accomplish its ends, this book begins in Chapter 1 with certain classifications—Herrick's classifications of his role as poet and of the world of his poetry. The study then proceeds to classifications of his subjects, but as these relate to his major themes, and of these themes as they figure in his world view. Thus Chapter 2 treats some poems about transiency and death because the recognition of these facts *as facts* directly shapes that world view.

Chapters 3–6 explore the kinds of responses to these facts that many of the poems dramatize. Broadly speaking, such poems respond to the "negation" that is death by "affirming" a type of life (Chapter 3), a type of love (Chapter 4), a type of faith (Chapter 5), and a type of art (Chapter 6).

On the bases of these analyses, Chapter 7 seeks to "place" Herrick in his proper niche in the pantheon of English literature—not to inter him but to indicate to his readers and potential readers that this poet, whom the previous chapters have shown to be very much alive as an artist, also has a life and an importance in the history of literature.

I am grateful to Oxford University Press for permission to quote from L. C. Martin's *The Poetical Works of Robert Herrick*, which has served as the model for transcription of poems and titles in this work.

To borrow a line from Herrick himself, "*For* [those] *Transgressions which thou here dost see,*" I am, of course, fully responsible. For those which are not seen because they are not in fact present, I am heavily indebted to Mr. Thomas Heberling, Mr. Edward Roginski, Mr. David Williams, and the Reverend Mr. Robert Taylor for their assistance in editing the manuscript. Finally, I wish to acknowledge a debt to Professor Louis L. Martz, who some years ago guided my first "wand'ring steps and slow" through the "*Sacred Grove*" of Robert Herrick's *Hesperides*.

Franklin and Marshall College   Roger B. Rollin

Contents

Preface   7

Chronology   13

1. *This Sacred Grove:* The Problem of Herrick's *Hesper-*
   ides   15

2. *Putrefaction* and *This Sacred Grove:* The Theme of
   Transiency   32

3. *A Country Life* and *This Sacred Grove:* The Theme of
   the Good Life   48

4. "Cleanly-*Wantonnesse*" and *This Sacred Grove:* The
   Theme of Love   85

5. *The White Island* and *This Sacred Grove:* The Theme
   of Faith   125

6. *The Pillar of Fame* and *This Sacred Grove:* The Theme
   of Immortality   165

7. The "Criticks" and *This Sacred Grove:* Herrick's Repu-
   tation   206

Notes and References   213

Selected Bibliography   221

Index   225

ROBERT HERRICK

by

ROGER B. ROLLIN

Though recent scholarly research has
made extensive discoveries about Herrick's
century, and critical techniques for the
understanding of poetry have become more
refined, misconceptions about his work
have persisted. This is the first full-scale
study to challenge the stereotype of Herrick
as a charming but shallow "Cavalier Poet."
Although he wrote over fourteen hundred
poems, enough of them are of sufficient
excellence to justify his inclusion among
the best of English poets. While necessarily treating only the finest of these poems,
this book explicates Herrick's total achievement. Comparisons between poems reveal
not only his attitudes but his total world-
view; not only his artistic technique but his
esthetic. His capacity for seriousness as well
as for humor, for thoughtfulness as well as
wit, is shown. Related not only to the
Roman poets but to the vein of Epicureanism which underlay so much of their philosophy, Herrick is also shown to regard himself as a pastoral poet; and how this
orientation affects not only individual poems
but his *Hesperides* is discussed in detail.

This study is about some of the finest
poems in the English language, about what
makes them so, and about what entitles
their author to the immortality for which he
so ardently strove.

Chronology

1591 August 24—Robert Herrick, seventh child of Nicholas Herrick (goldsmith and banker) and of Julian Stone Herrick, is baptized in London.

1592 November 7—Nicholas Herrick, "sick in body," makes out his will; November 9—Nicholas dies in a fall from an upper window of his house.

1607 After a period of schooling—where, it is not known—Robert Herrick is apprenticed to his uncle, Sir William Herrick, a successful London goldsmith.

1613 Enters St. John's College, Cambridge, as a student of means.

1617 Transfers to Trinity Hall, Cambridge, to trim expenses and is graduated therefrom with a Bachelor of Arts degree; takes a Master of Arts three years later.

1623 Is ordained as deacon and priest of the Church of England.

1623– Most likely spends considerable time in London making
1627 the acquaintance of the wits and poets who comprise "the tribe of Ben." Learns about poetry from Jonson himself but also writes poetry on his own; by 1625 is well enough known as a poet to be publicly complimented as the peer of Michael Drayton and of Jonson himself.

1627 Serves as a chaplain to the Duke of Buckingham, leader of an ill-fated expedition to the Isle of Rhé.

1628 His mother dies; Buckingham is assassinated.

1630 Is installed as the Vicar of Dean Prior, an obscure parish in Devonshire.

1640 Returns to London and makes arrangements to publish *The severall Poems* (doubtless an early version of *Hesperides*), but does not carry out his intention at this time. According to one report—of dubious validity, for it is nowhere else confirmed—Herrick's illicit affair with a resident of his boarding house results in the birth of an illegitimate child.

1647   For his avowed Royalist sympathies, Herrick is expelled
       from his vicarage and likely returns to London to live as a
       private citizen until 1660.

1648   As the Civil War grinds to a close, *Hesperides* is published
       —marking, in effect, the end of Herrick's career as an ac-
       tive poet.

1660   With the restoration of the monarchy, Herrick petitions to
       have his vicarage at Dean Prior returned to him; the peti-
       tion is granted in the same year and he goes back to Dev-
       onshire.

1674   October 15—Robert Herrick is buried at Dean Prior; ex-
       actly where his "bones had . . . their Rest" is not known.

CHAPTER 1

This Sacred Grove: *The Problem of Herrick's* Hesperides

IN a letter which had the ulterior motive of asking his uncle (as usual) for money, young Robert Herrick, then an undergraduate at Cambridge University, wrote: "Are the minds of men immutable? and will they rest in only one opinion without the least perspicuous shewe of chaing? O no they cannot, for . . . it is an old but yet yoong saying in our age: as times chaing so mens minds are altered. . . ." [1] Although these fine words were only a youthful scholar's way of leading up to a painful request, they contain an unintended but accurate prophecy about the writer himself. For the minds of men have indeed changed with the times, and Robert Herrick's reputation as a poet has reaped some of the benefits of these alterations.

Today Herrick's poems are far more widely read than they were in his own lifetime. No anthology of English verse would be complete without at least half a dozen of them, and occasionally Herrick is accorded more space than poets with loftier reputations. He is also available to the reading public (as the Bibliography to this volume records) in three complete editions of his only book, *Hesperides*, as well as in two recent selected editions. Furthermore, the poet and his work have in the last decade been the subjects of a biography, a monograph, several scholarly articles, and of at least two doctoral dissertations. By all of this activity, Robert Herrick—gentleman, scholar, priest, and would-be immortal poet—would have been delighted. The glory he so avidly sought and which was largely denied him while he lived is now his. Even the prophecy he made in the following epigram has been fulfilled,

> THOU shalt not All die; for while Love's fire shines
> Upon his Altar, men shall read thy lines;
> And learn'd Musicians shall to honour *Herricks*

Fame, and his Name, both set, and sing his Lyricks.
                                    "Upon himself" [III] [2].

For some of his songs, "his Lyricks," have been set to music by a
modern composer and immortalized in a manner peculiar to our
own age—upon a phonograph record.[3]

I *The Critical Controversy*

In spite of all the renewed interest in him and in his poetry,
Herrick, were he alive today, would have to admit that "glory" is
sometimes a mixed blessing, for it has made him more conspicuous as well as more admired—and being more conspicuous, he has
drawn some fairly heavy critical fire. For example, F. R. Leavis,
while acknowledging the "charm" of Herrick's verse, regards his
talent as trivial at best.[4] Although the majority of Herrick's se-
verer critics do not go this far, in the view of many of them he
remains merely a delightful second-rater. Even while admitting
that his verses are well crafted, they charge that his book is generally deficient in "high seriousness," in the "continuous conscious
purpose" and in "the unity of underlying pattern" which usually
characterize the achievements of "major" poets.[5] But still other
critics assert or at least imply that Herrick has been poorly read
and woefully underrated;[6] and one goes so far as to contend that
Herrick should be ranked only slightly lower than the greatest
poets of the seventeenth century.[7] However vexing the presence
of such conflicting views may be, the controversy has the virtue of
forcing readers of Herrick in particular and students of seventeenth-century verse in general to peruse this poet with more
careful consideration than he has been accorded in the past.

The past has seldom been particularly kind to Robert Herrick.
Even his own age seems to have scanted him even though for a
time his star was on the rise. But this moment of glory, as Martin
notes, was all too brief:

Of the references to Herrick printed in the seventeenth century the
earliest is the most impressive, since it takes his abilities for proven
and puts him, at the age of thirty-four, on a footing with two of the
most distinguished of Elizabethan veterans. This was in 1625, when
Richard James in *The Muses Dirge* (on the death of James I) tries
to explain why the King had not been duly praised while he lived by
some really well-known poet:
             Some *Johnson, Drayton,* or some *Herick.*

This single line, the most flattering public compliment that Herrick is known to have received, is also part of the evidence that his contemporary reputation never stood higher than in the 1620's, before he went into Devonshire.[8]

Public references to Herrick are few and far between in the seventeenth century. Although J. Max Patrick contends that Herrick was more highly valued by his contemporaries than Martin suggests,[9] the fact remains that copies of *Hesperides* were still listed for sale by Herrick's publisher some twenty years after the book first appeared.[10] And even if it were only partial, the eclipse of Herrick's star is understandable: at the apex of his artistic career he left the center of the literary cosmos, London, and took up residence in what must have seemed a distant galaxy, Dean Prior, in rural Devonshire. Moreover, his collected poems were published at a time when the whole of England was engaged, not in poetical creation, but in wholesale destruction brought on by the greatest civil war that nation has ever known. Furthermore, Herrick was on the "wrong" side in the war—that of the defeated Royalists; and finally, Herrick's kind of verse was to some extent going out of style. Although historical evidence on this point is meager, indications are that popular taste in the mid-seventeenth century inclined more toward the "strong lines" of John Donne and to Edmund Waller's closed couplets than to the highly crafted verses of Robert Herrick.[11] None of this could have come as much of a surprise to the poet himself; as he ruefully notes in his epigram, *"Posting to Printing"*: "LET others to the Printing Presse run fast,/Since after death comes glory, *Ile not haste.*"

But even this dim view turns out to be somewhat optimistic in Herrick's own case. His death in 1674 apparently attracted little attention; even the location of his grave was in time forgotten and no monument to him was erected in his church until the nineteenth century when, after more than a century of almost complete neglect, his star hove into view once again. With the exception of the more naturalistic epigrams and some of the erotic verse, the Victorian period found Herrick's poetry much to its taste. Indeed, it was a prominent Victorian poet, Swinburne, who accorded Herrick his loftiest tribute, calling him "the greatest songwriter—as surely as Shakespeare is the greatest dramatist—ever born of English race." [12] Not everyone, however, concurred. Eminent Victorians of both the nineteenth and earlier twentieth centuries damned Herrick for lack of originality, for shallowness of emotion, for philosophical poverty, and even for obscenity. On the other hand, he was damned with the faint praise of those who were taken with his technical virtuosity.

If anything, this controversy has increased rather than abated. It is important, however, that a resolution at least be attempted— and not merely because literary history and criticism will thereby gain needed coherence but because of the quality of our reading of Herrick. Whether he has been overrated or underrated in the past, the sharp division in critical opinion indicates that he is being seriously misread by someone; and misreadings, of course, ought not be perpetuated. It is, after all, the function of literary criticism to facilitate accurate readings; for only through such readings can a work of literature be fully experienced and enjoyed. And this is the main reason why this book will focus upon Herrick's poetry—not upon his biography. The biographical facts are few, but they are too often invalidly imposed upon or spuriously extracted from his verse. Nor does this book dwell upon his reputation over the centuries, because it has fluctuated so extensively—nor upon his sources, because, for all their significance, the really important thing about them is the way in which Herrick transubstantiates them.

Herrick's poems must then be read afresh, and read judiciously; and those that seem most successful and most significant must be singled out for close critical scrutiny. Then too the possible relationships between individual poems must be explored in an attempt to discern the patterns and the texture of his work as a whole. To do so is no simple task. All else aside, the very number of his poems (there are over fourteen hundred of them) and their wide variety give pause to even the most determined reader. It is, therefore, not only desirable but necessary to find a sound critical approach to the problem of Herrick's *Hesperides*.

II *Herrick his own Critic*

Some assistance in developing a viable approach to Herrick's vast collection is forthcoming from the poet himself. For example, the poem by which he introduces us to his *Hesperides*, "The Argument of his Book," is not—as its title might suggest to a modern reader—a disputation; it is a poetic catalogue of some of the subjects he most frequently treats. Furthermore, Herrick so arranges his catalogue that it emerges as a classification of all the general areas of human experience covered by his book. With the first couplet, for example, it is made explicit that some of his poems will deal with certain natural objects; but, since it is obvious that no poet would restrict himself to only these few, the whole realm of nature becomes by implication his province:

> I SING of *Brooks*, of *Blossomes*, *Birds*, and *Bowers:*
> Of *April, May*, of *June*, and *July*-Flowers.

The alliteration of the first line enhances the effect of a formal catalogue, where everything is itemized in proper order. But though catalogues normally make dull reading, this one does not because the items listed are not things of which we normally take inventory. Taken together, these natural objects are readily associated with the palmy seasons, spring and early summer, when brooks run, blossoms emerge, birds return, and bowers are shady and pleasant: thus this first line prepares us for the second, which suggests that the poems of *Hesperides* are typically set in the idyllic time of the year, the season of rebirth and growth.

Thus far the indications are that some of Herrick's poems will be about nature and, in particular, about nature in its more benign aspects. In addition to alerting us about things to look for as we read on in *Hesperides*, this information is useful because it suggests something about the poet—that, as one who "sings" about idyllic nature, Herrick is related to an ancient and honorable line of bards, the "pastoral" or "bucolic" poets. The basis of the poetic tradition which they fostered is the opposition between the rural and the urban. To the pastoralist the rural stands for all that is good in this world: particularly for nature with its manifold blessings and the virtue and happiness of the simple life close to nature. The urban stands for all that is complex, human, and therefore decadent. Understanding Herrick's unique relationship to this tradition, as will be shown, is highly important to the successful reading of his poetry.

The second couplet of *"The Argument"* initiates a transition in the focus of the poem from the natural to the human realm:

> I sing of *May-poles, Hock-carts, Wassails, Wakes,*
> Of *Bride-grooms, Brides*, and of their *Bridall-cakes*.

Both May-poles and hock-carts are associated with natural events: the renewal of the earth in the spring and the fulfilment of that renewal in the fall. But both are also objects used to celebrate the human activities of planting and harvesting. The rituals in which the May-pole and the hock-cart figure commemorate in semireligious fashion the fundamental and profound association of man with nature that the pastoral tradition poetically affirms.

With wassails, or drinking bouts, and wakes Herrick completes the transition of his catalogue into strictly human activities. There is, however, an element of irony in his juxtaposition of wakes and weddings. In the seventeenth century the term "wake" could refer to a parish festival or to a death watch; these lines read on one level as a simple catalogue of festive occasions but on another become the very cycle of human existence which weddings, with their promise of new life, and wakes, with their contemplation of death, so clearly mark. And, as will be indicated later, these and other ceremonies are important to Herrick not only as subjects but as forms for his poems.

From his reference to nuptial ceremonies Herrick logically turns to the human elements most closely associated with them:

> I write of *Youth*, of *Love*, and have Accesse   5
> By these, to sing of cleanly-*Wantonnesse*.

"Cleanly-*Wantonnesse*" is a term apparently coined by Herrick to put his readers on notice that his amatory verse will be love poetry with a difference. Denotatively, it stands for a logical absurdity—"chaste lasciviousness" or the more general "pure misbehavior." Connotatively, however, it suggests a mode of behavior which, as Chapter 4 makes clear, is derived from the poet's eminently serious, viable world view and, ultimately, from his esthetic. At this point it is sufficient to note that Herrick's paradox implies a compromise in which the sensual side of life is both valued and sanctioned. In short, "cleanly-*Wantonnesse*" suggests the possibility of love without guilt. With one couplet then Herrick prepares the reader of his volume to expect not only love poems but an ethical theory of love. The possibilities for human pleasure that this concept opens up are complemented by the sensuously pleasurable objects catalogued in the couplet which follows:

> I sing of *Dewes*, of *Raines*, and piece by piece
> Of *Balme*, of *Oyle*, of *Spice*, and *Amber-Greece*.

Dews and rains are common and necessary pleasures, gifts of nature; the more exotic items listed in the second line are also natural objects but they are refined by man from their raw state for his pleasure and for practical or ceremonial uses. In their ceremonial functions and in their rareness they facilitate the transition of the poem from the familiar world of brooks and blossoms to the rarefied realms of the abstract, the supernatural, and the spiritual.

As is customary with him, Herrick makes his approach to the abstract and the supernatural through the natural and the commonplace:

> I sing of *Times trans-shifting;* and I write
> How *Roses* first came *Red,* and *Lillies White.*   10

The concept of time and its correlative, change or flux, are familiar enough; but Herrick, by using a phrase that is apparently of his own coinage, again directs particular attention to the familiar and endows it with an air of unfamiliarity. Both of these effects and the phenomena that lie behind them are exemplified in his reference to the flowers: roses and lillies are commonplace natural objects but by raising the possibility that they are not now what they once were, that they have changed in time, Herrick puts them in a new and potentially strange light. Change itself, as succeeding chapters will show, is a recurring theme of *Hesperides.* It is dramatized in poem after poem on the alterations of the world of nature and the cycles in the lives of men, and it becomes a factor which links the two together. But change is paradoxical; although it is familiar and apparently natural, it is also mysterious since neither its origins nor its ends are knowable. Furthermore, for man change eventually means decay and ultimately death. While spring and rebirth are never far behind the death of nature in winter, man has no really comparable assurance of resurrection. This problem, with all its attendant ironies, is continually raised in Herrick's secular verse. To resolve it, men have always turned to philosophy, to religion, or to myth, or to a combination of all three; and Herrick is no exception. But while he is able to secure in myth quick answers to the question of how flowers received their colors, the more searching question of man's fate, he finds, is less readily resolved.

The realm of the supernatural, one phase of which Herrick refers to in the following couplet, is of course above and beyond the influence of *"Times trans-shifting":*

> I write of *Groves,* of *Twilights,* and I sing
> The Court of *Mab,* and of the *Fairie-King.*

In our age we are accustomed to consigning the "little people," those creatures who appear in groves as the sun sets, into the custody of imaginative children and picturesque Irishmen; but in Herrick's age they assumed more importance. Occupying as it did a place between the human and divine worlds, the realm of faery was a convenient myth through which poets could comment upon both; in addition, it provided a unique challenge to their imaginative and technical faculties.

The final couplet of *"The Argument"* distinguishes the spiritual and infernal aspects of the supernatural and logically completes the process of classification upon which the poem has been based:

> I write of *Hell;* I sing (and ever shall)
> Of *Heaven,* and hope to have it after all.

Although Herrick alludes hardly at all to Hell in the "humane" or secular poems of *Hesperides* and largely neglects it even in that collection of his Christian poems which he calls *His Noble Numbers,* Heaven (or its equivalents) figures rather importantly in both sections of his book. The above couplet then, which implies that the poet's attention will be about equally divided between the two, is not an accurate reflection of his spiritual bent. Yet if the preoccupation with death that characterizes so many of his poems is interpreted as a preoccupation with the question of heaven or hell, these climactic lines orient the perceptive reader to the very source of the dominant tension of Herrick's *Hesperides.*

The foregoing analysis of the initial poem of Herrick's book is some indication that similarly close examinations of his other poems may also pay rich dividends. Not only does this introductory work provide an example of the poet's remarkable art and craft in its careful structure, its highly polished diction, and its original employment of so traditional a form as the poetic catalogue, but it also serves as an eminently useful orientation to a book that is both sizable and—in its multiplicity—complex. This poem puts the reader on notice from the start that in this volume, as one scholar has put it, Herrick treats "nothing less than the whole universe; his theme is, in a sense, no narrower in range than that of *Paradise Lost.*" [13] Furthermore, *"The Argument"* also suggests something about the book's persona—he who serves as the "speaker" of many of the individual poems and who (depending upon the poem) may or may not be identified with Robert Herrick himself. It suggests that the persona of this work will be a character of nearly infinite variety, an intelligence concerned with the whole great "Chain of Being" which links the natural, human, and divine worlds; a sensibility whose mood can vary from the serious to the gay—in short, a persona who can be thoughtful as well as sensuous, profound as well as trivial. These inferences should of course be tested against the evidence of Herrick's entire book, particularly since the portrait that they comprise is so much at variance with the one which the poet's detractors allege dominates his *Hesperides*—Herrick as the merely charming Cavalier. The latter image, for example, seems to be projected by another introductory poem of the volume, *"When he would have his verses read."*

Like *"The Argument of his Book,"* this poem serves to instil certain expectations in the reader of *Hesperides;* its technique, however, is instructional rather than descriptive to the extent that it stipulates the time, place, and mood most conducive to the appreciation of the poet's art:

> In sober mornings, doe not thou reherse
> The holy incantation of a verse;
> But when that men have both well drunke, and fed,
> Let my Enchantments then be sung, or read.
> When Laurell spirts 'ith fire, and when the Hearth   5
> Smiles to it selfe, and guilds the roofe with mirth;
> When up the **Thyrse* is rais'd, and when the sound
> Of sacred**Orgies flyes, A round, A round.
> When the *Rose* raignes, and locks with ointments shine,
> Let rigid *Cato* read these Lines of mine.   10

>   * A *Javelin* twind with *Ivy*.
>   ** Songs to *Bacchus*. [Herrick's notes.]

Because this poem is to an extent imitative of Martial and of Anacreon[14] (the half-legendary lyrist of wine, women and song), there is some warrant for regarding its instructions as rather less binding than the classifications of *"The Argument of his Book."* And as the phrasing of the title suggests, the poem is less a dramatization of a dogma than it is of a preference. Furthermore, while it stipulates that a festive occasion is the best context for reading and appreciating Robert Herrick's poems, it does not necessarily follow that all of these poems will themselves be festive in spirit. It is true that many verses of *Hesperides*—songs of love, of mirth, and of the good life—are eminently well suited to the mood of a carouse and that they constitute together a light and spirited vein that is much in evidence, especially in the earlier portion of Herrick's book. But at the same time a poet might well feel that his serious verse would also receive a better reading from men who are in a receptive mood because their appetites have been satis-fied and their thirsts quenched.

That Herrick does not seek to convey the impression that his verses are mere trifles is suggested by his epithets: a verse is a "holy incantation"; all of his poems are "Enchantments." They have magical or even mystical properties which give them the power to put those who hear them under a spell. On the one hand, this is a metaphor for a common psychological phenomenon—the transcendence of the self that occurs when any reader becomes highly involved in a work of literature; but, on the other hand, Herrick's lines, and in particular the word "holy" suggest that poetry, in its mystery and power, assumes for him the status and significance of a religion. While this particular concept by no means reverses the exuberant and even humorous tone of the poem, it does complicate it. By the same token, *"When he would have his verses read"* as a whole qualifies but does not negate the effects of *"The Argument of his Book."* To infer from the former that all of the complex categories of the latter are essentially meaningless and that Herrick himself regards his poems as trifles fit only for idle hours is to misread the poem and to ignore the evidence of his book itself. (The tendency, which some critics have shown, to oversimplify Herrick can be as ruinous to the proper apprehension of his work as has been the tendency to overcomplicate other poets.)

III *A Critical Approach*

However useful the hints of Herrick's introductory poems are to the reader of his book, it is too much to expect that, taken to-gether, they will serve in lieu of a systematic critical approach. Herrick's business, after all, is writing poems, not analyzing them or providing all the tools necessary for analysis. Here, however, help is available from one critic and poet who has taken some cognizance of the problem of *Hesperides*, T. S. Eliot. In an essay entitled "What Is Minor Poetry?" Eliot advances a critical principle upon which a reasonably valid and viable approach to Herrick's poetry can be constructed; it is his contention that:

a work which consists of a number of short poems, even of poems which, taken individually, may appear rather slight, may, if it has a unity of underlying pattern, be the equivalent of a first-rate long poem in establishing an author's claim to be a "major" poet. That claim may, of course, be established by *one* long poem, and when that long poem is good enough, when it has within itself the proper unity and variety, we do not need to know, or if we know we do not need to value highly, the poet's other works.[15]

To put this statement in terms relevant to Herrick, his *Hesperides*, which is a work consisting of "a number of short poems," may qualify him for consideration as a "major poet" (loosely defined by Eliot as "one of whose work we have to read a great deal, but not always the whole") if it exhibits the quality of "unity in variety" or, more specifically, "a unity of underlying pattern."[16] In other words, *Hesperides* must exhibit interesting differences in subject matter, theme, and form; but it must also exhibit coherence, a coherence that is both perceived and felt because of the existence of meaningful relationships between those subjects, themes, and forms. Taken together, its subjects should constitute a kind of microcosm, a world in miniature; its themes should coalesce into perceivable patterns of thought and feeling; and its forms should be recognizably under the control of a unique and unifying poetic imagination.

While it is possible, of course, to disagree with Eliot and to assert that no number of short poems, however high their quality, can properly be regarded as the equivalent of a first-rate long poem, the critical approach he proposes for testing his hypothesis has much to recommend it. It rests, for example, upon two assumptions which are basically sound: that a successful poem is a work of art which is to a great degree complete unto itself and which effects its communication to the careful reader with a minimum of reference to information external to itself; and that, at the same time, successful poems written by the same poet may stand in some meaningful relationship to one another, the apprehension of which can point up aspects of individual poems not perceived at the first reading, but which make subsequent readings fuller esthetic experiences. Because these assumptions and the procedures issuing from them *are* sound, and because they require that the potential "unity in variety" of *Hesperides* be tested both by reading and evaluating Herrick's poems individually, and by contemplating them to an extent collectively, these assumptions and procedures will in the main constitute the critical approach of this study.

Additional justification for adopting this approach is forthcoming from no less an authority than Robert Herrick himself. In a poem entitled *"To the generous Reader,"* Herrick, in his role as the author of *Hesperides,* makes the following charge:

> See, and not see; and if thou chance t'espie
> Some Aberrations in my Poetry;
> Wink at small faults, the greater, ne'rthelesse
> Hide, and with them, their Fathers nakednesse.
> Let's doe our best, our Watch and Ward to keep: 5
> *Homer* himself, in a long work, may sleep.

While this poem is worthy of note for its representation of Herrick's ingratiating good humor, his objectivity about his own verse, and his characteristic blend of artistic humility and pride, it also has special relevance to the present discussion; for, though its tone may be comic, its injunctions are well taken. Readers of poetry occasionally need reminding that it is humanly impossible for a poet to maintain a uniformly high degree of artistry at all times and hence a certain amount of tolerance on their part is necessary. And the final couplet suggests something about Herrick's own conception of the scope and nature of his book: since he obviously can not be relating himself to Homer as one epic poet to another, the basis of his implied analogy must be that both he and the Greek poet have written long works. The very term, "a long work," implies something more than a mere collection of short poems. It implies, as Eliot puts it, a literary whole that "is more than the sum of its parts." [17] That such is Herrick's view of his book can be inferred not only from *"To the generous Reader,"* but also from certain poems in which he dramatically defines the world that his *Hesperides* comprises.

IV   *The Pastoral Criticism of Life*

Although a thorough reading of Herrick's book turns up poems containing references to historical events and to actual places and persons, *Hesperides* can be seen in the over-all view to embody a reality of its own, a reality that is of Herrick's own making. To recognize this concept, however, is not to conclude that, among poets, Herrick is at all unusual. Art is not life, though it imitates and criticizes or idealizes life; and the works of any poet, if he is successful, present not just an orientation toward life but a re-creation of it. Thus it is that a single poem re-creates one segment of reality, transforming it in such a way that the reader is psychologically detached from the reality in which he physically exists and becomes deeply involved in the artistic reality that is the poem. And as one such poem comprises such a "reality," so a number of poems (if they are unified by a single, strong, poetic imagination that is the reflection of a unique and dominant personality) can together make up a type of total artistic reality, a poetic microcosm. Eliot, who denies that this is the case with *Hesperides*, contends that Herrick's book lacks unity and "continuous *conscious* purpose" and that the personality reflected in this book is—albeit charming—ordinary rather than unique.[18] That Eliot is wrong on both counts is a primary contention of this study.

Earlier in this chapter it was pointed out that *"The Argument of his Book"* implies that Herrick conceives himself to be something of a pastoral poet. This conception alone sets him apart from the other prominent poets of his age, in most of whose poetic careers pastoral was merely a passing fancy. Herrick, however, goes to some lengths to assure his reader that this is not the case with him. In the poem, *"To his Muse,"* for example, which immediately follows *"The Argument,"* Herrick describes his muse, who may be regarded as the personification of the poet's own artistic imagination, as a pastoral creature. He chides her for venturing into "Courts and Cities," into the poetic modes favored by the urban and urbane; and he recommends that she stick to her piping of "smooth, and harmlesse *Beucolicks,*" or pastoral poems. But the chiding is ironic, for as one critic has pointed out, "Herrick's world is decidedly complex and courtly" [19]—and just how complex and courtly, succeeding chapters of this study attempt to show.

Nevertheless, Herrick's irony does not serve to deny or even to diminish the importance of his pastoral orientation; rather it provides an insight into the nature of that orientation. There are in the pastoral tradition ample precedents for highly sophisticated as well as "innocent" *"Beucolicks,"* and here Herrick is serving notice that he does not regard himself as being restricted to either type. Furthermore, an examination of *Hesperides* shows that, far from underrating the pastoral, Herrick explores and exploits its subjects, forms, diction, images, and concepts in many of his most effective and ambitious poems. Thus it is that, in spite of the fact that many of his works are patently *not* bucolic and that some of them, such as certain of his poems on Devonshire, even appear to be "anti-bucolic," the world of his *Hesperides* can in general be classified as a pastoral world. Although Herrick has to a considerable extent created this world in his own image and according to his own uses, it still bears the unmistakable stamp of what he himself calls "the pleasing Pastorall." [20] Further evidence that this is the case is found in a trio of parallel poems addressed to Charles I; to Maria, his queen; and to their son, the Duke of York.

The first of these poems, "TO THE KING," is of interest here on the strength of one of its phrases. The poem itself is a conventional verse-compliment in which Herrick submits his "Lyricks" to the monarch in the hope that at least one will find royal favor. Playing upon the idea of monarchical succession, the poet goes on to say that, if one poem proves acceptable to the king, he may then regard it as his own; thus, as the king's own son is heir to the English realm, so that poem "shall be / The Heire to This *great Realme of Poetry.*" The italicized phrase is significant because it embodies the conception of *Hesperides* as a kingdom which is in some respects analogous to actual political kingdoms: the realm of poetry is created (by inspiration) as political realms are created (by God); it is governed (by what Eliot calls the "unifying personality" of the poet) as they are governed (by kings);[21] it has a kind of order (imposed by esthetic and intellectual assumptions of the poet) as they are ordered (by royal authority and by law); and it has above all a kind of character (determined in the selectivity of the creative process) as they have characteristics (determined by such factors as geography, race, language, and customs). Thus Herrick's metaphor holds up, and, though it is only one metaphor in one poem, it provides a valuable insight into his book as a whole. This insight is sharpened in the poem which immediately follows, "TO THE QUEENE," in which the metaphor is so developed as to suggest something more specific about the character of Herrick's Hesperidean realm.

"TO THE QUEENE" continues the vein of courtly compliment; and, like its companion-piece, it revolves about the idea of royal authority. But the compliment is more ornate, which is as it should be considering the sex of the addressee and what is revealed about the poetic realm itself. In the first poem the king is addressed as a god-man, "CESAR"; in the second the queen is similarly honored:

> GODDESSE of Youth, and Lady of the Spring,
> (Most fit to be the Consort to a King)
> Be pleas'd to rest you in This Sacred Grove,
> Beset with Mirtles; whose each leafe drops Love.

"This Sacred Grove," as Martin suggests and as Patrick confirms, likely refers to the mythical Garden of the Hesperides, the fabled grove of golden apples planted by the queen-goddess, Juno, and thus—in the context of the poem—to Herrick's book itself, the new Hesperides, a garden whose golden fruits take the shape of poems.[22] To add still another dimension, the Hesperides legend, as Northrop Frye has pointed out, is also associated with the myth of the Garden of Eden; and both of these are associated with England, itself a garden-isle in the Western seas.[23] And Patrick suggests further that Devonshire itself is a part of England's West Country, and thus some of the poems at least can be regarded as the fruits of Herrick's stay in that "garden" as well.[24] The image of "This Sacred Grove" then is manifold in its connotations, not the least of which is its delineation of the world of Herrick's book as a pastoral realm. Like another of his metaphors for his Hesperides —"this rich Plantation" [25]—"This Sacred Grove" suggests not only the rural world of conventional pastoral, a beauteous realm of trees and fields, but a world which, like that of Keats's "Ode on a Grecian Urn," possesses order and richness through its sanctification by art. But the world of Herrick's book, unlike that of Keats's poem, is a "Warm Pastoral," alive with real men and gods, and ever flourishing. Thus it is appropriate that its queen be addressed as "GODDESSE of Youth" and "Lady of the Spring," for both the age and the season suggest the vitality of this world as well as its relationship to traditional pastoral.

The last six lines of the poem serve to reinforce even further the impression that Herrick sees his book as having a bucolic character:

> Many a sweet-fac't Wood-Nymph here is seene,   5
> Of which chast Order You are now the Queene:

Witness their *Homage,* when they come and strew
Your Walks with Flowers, and give their Crowns to you.
Your Leavie-Throne (with *Lilly*-work) possesse;
And be both *Princesse* here, and *Poetresse.*   10

Wood nymphs are conventional figures in pastoral verse, but here
they take on an almost religious character. Inhabitants of a "*Sacred Grove,*" they constitute a "chast *Order*" (like nuns); and, in
their homage to Maria, their queen, they implicitly acknowledge
the existence of order and degree in this bucolic realm. But, since
this is also a poetical realm, the head of the hierarchy is not only a
princess but a poetess—with the implication that the two roles are
equal in importance—and her subjects are wood nymphs, beautiful and semidivine creatures, and thus Herrick's poems themselves. Herrick's compliments then have been economically extended not only to the queen but also to the art of poetry and,
indirectly, to the poet himself.

The concept of the monarch-poet is expanded into the concept
of the poet-monarch in the third poem of the trio, "*The Poets
good wishes for the most hopefull and handsome Prince, the
Duke of York.*" Among his other good wishes Herrick hopes that
the boy duke may eventually become prince of the Muses and
their realm, which is to wish that he too will become a poet, and
more specifically, a bucolic poet like Herrick himself:

> May his soft foot, where it treads,
> Gardens thence produce and Meads:
> And those Meddowes full be set   15
> With the Rose, and Violet.

The inference to be drawn is that Herrick envisions the realm of
the Muses as a bucolic one. This vision is graphically portrayed in
the frontispiece to the 1648 edition of *Hesperides* (reproduced in
Martin's edition of Herrick), which probably, like the rest of the
book, was set up under the poet's personal supervision. The background of this engraving, as Patrick has pointed out,[26] is composed
of a landscape containing the Hill of Parnassus (the mountain
sacred to the Muses and Apollo), the Spring of Helicon, "Gar-
dens," "Meads," and a "*Sacred Grove*"—all in all a scene that
could represent the realm of the Muses, the realm of *Hesperides,*
or both.

The frontispiece suggests graphically what the poems examined thus far suggest verbally: *"This Sacred Grove"* is an appropriate metaphor for Herrick's book because the book comprises a world that is sacred to the Muses in the sense that it is the creation of a poet with an essentially religious dedication to his art. His *Hesperides* is a "grove" not only because it bears the golden fruits that are his poems, but because a grove is suggestive of the traditional pastoral setting as a whole where, as in Herrick's book, nature or life is transformed by art and a unique world, a world with an esthetic integrity of its own, is thereby created. The conscious purpose that shapes this world and the unifying personality behind this consciousness are to be found, as succeeding chapters show, in many individual poems of *Hesperides* and in their relationships to one another.

CHAPTER 2

Putrefaction *and* This Sacred Grove:
The Theme of Transiency

SOME of the most memorable lines of verse that have come down to us from the seventeenth century are those of Robert Herrick's contemporary, John Donne, and few of those lines are more memorable than those which begin Donne's tenth Holy Sonnet:

> DEATH be not proud, though some have called thee
> Mighty and dreadfull, for, thou art not soe,
> For, those, whom thou think'st, thou dost overthrow,
> Die not, poore death, nor yet canst thou kill mee.

This ringing challenge, however, is summarily retracted by Donne in a later poem, his *"Elegie on* [Mistress] Boulstred," whose opening couplet affirms: "DEATH I recant, and say, unsaid by mee / What ere hath slip'd, that might diminish thee." It is noteworthy that much of Donne's poetry runs the gamut between these two points-of-view; and, when it comes to his prose—as one scholar has pointed out—his writings are heavily dominated by "terrible sermons on death, full of the poetry of charnel-house and worm." [1] All of this leads to the conclusion that "There is truth in the often-repeated charge that Donne was preoccupied with sin and death; he confesses his melancholy temperament (calling it 'a disease of the times'). . . ." [2]

While the preoccupation with death is not exclusively a tendency of Donne or of other writers in the seventeenth century, it is decidedly characteristic of them. From the soliloquies of Shakespeare's Hamlet to the meditations of Sir Thomas Browne to the cry of Andrew Marvell's persona, "But at my back I alwaies hear / Times winged Charriot hurrying near," the literature of the period is pervaded by the presence of death. Whether or not it was, as Donne claims, "a disease of the times," it is plain enough that seventeenth-century Englishmen were predisposed by their religion, by their education, and by their circumstances to meditate frequently and long upon death. Owing in part to the very primitive states of medicine and sanitation, the average life span was short. And this very brevity was emphasized by a Christianity whose prevailing theme was that life was a preparation for death; that holy dying was attainable only through holy living; and that, since the only true life lay beyond the grave, death was something to be continually confronted in the mind and eventually welcomed to the flesh. Whatever the extent of their faith and knowledge, Englishmen of the seventeenth century could no more avoid contemplating the grave than men of the twentieth century can avoid contemplating the mushroom cloud. Death was a part of a man's way of thinking and feeling.

I *The Occasion of Death*

At this point it might seem as if the discussion is far afield from the poetry of Robert Herrick, for Herrick's popular reputation today associates him above all with life, with beauty, with love, and with all their attendant pleasures—with everything, in short, but death. But while it must be stressed that this *is* one aspect of Herrick, and a side that is crucial to the character of his book, the fallacy that this is his *only* side should be apparent to any careful, thorough reader of his *Hesperides*. As one scholar has cautioned, "Herrick is hardly to be appreciated unless he is seen to be aided by two muses, one jocund, the other diviner, inspiring him to sing of 'death accursed,' and of the victory over death."[3] We have noted that the first poem of his book calls attention to the inevitability of change and death; at this juncture it is also worth noting that the first twenty-five pages, for example, of Martin's edition of *Hesperides* contain twenty other poems that deal with these same serious subjects. Finally, that Herrick himself is aware of what amounts to his preoccupation with death is indicated in the poem *"On himselfe"* [IX] which is, in a sense, the antithesis of *"The Argument of his Book."*[4] Placed at approximately the halfway mark of *Hesperides,* this poem catalogues some of the work's chief subjects, subjects which Herrick, in a melancholy mood, alleges he will no longer treat. Of these subjects, death is singled out in the climactic final couplet: "Ile sing no more of death, or shall the grave / No more my Dirges, and my Trentalls have." There is then considerable evidence to indicate that the impression that "Herrick is all delicacy and delight . . ." is, to say the least, an over-simplified one.[5]

Some of the poems of Herrick's *Hesperides* that deal with death are "occasional" in nature; that is, they are ceremonial poems written not so much about the idea of death as about a particular death, whether real or imagined. Such an occasion to Herrick sometimes calls for an epitaph, like his tender poem entitled "*Upon a Child*" [I]. The first two couplets of this epitaph call to mind a corollary of the concept of "*Times trans-shifting*," the theme of the brevity of human existence:

> BUT borne, and like a short Delight,
> I glided by my Parents sight.
> That done, the harder Fates deny'd
> My longer stay, and so I dy'd.

In the abruptness and clipped alliteration of "BUT borne" Herrick communicates the sense that something has been cut short, has been ended almost as soon as it had begun; and this sensation is reinforced by the six short monosyllabic words of the line and by the rather abstract simile. And yet the verb "glided" connotes tranquillity and even naturalness. Children are familiar creatures and delights to be treasured, but this particular child is given special value because it is like some rare, beautiful bird seen in flight: it is glimpsed only for a moment and then is lost forever. So delightful a creature might seem entitled to a "longer stay," but the mysterious plan which governs the universe, symbolized by "the harder Fates," is irrevocable. Nevertheless, these lines do not leave us with the impression that the persona, who is of course the child himself, either regards his as a special case or would rail against his fate if he could. Rather the tone here is one of calm acceptance of the natural and inevitable—"and so I dy'd."

In keeping with one of the traditions of the epitaph, the poem's last four lines are addressed to the reader as if he were a passerby who had stopped to peruse the tombstone; he is enjoined to involve himself in the event of this untimely death, not only by pitying the child's parents, but by actually empathizing with them. This empathy will be made manifest by his performance of a traditional ritual:

> If pittying my sad Parents Teares,   5
> You'l spil a tear, or two with theirs:

> And with some flowrs my grave bestrew,
> Love and they'l thank you for't. Adieu.

This direct appeal to the reader aids in confirming the impression
that Herrick's poem is ultimately something more than a simple
commemoration of the death of an anonymous child. Rather it
becomes an implicit reminder that, in the words of John Donne,
we all are "involved in mankind." [6] The death of a child is not
only a deprivation of the parents; it is an event which diminishes
all of us. And it poignantly reawakens our awareness of the brevity of human existence, an existence of which we are, as the child
once was, a part.

Another and somewhat more ambitious form of occasional
poem employed by Herrick is the elegy. Longer than the epitaph,
but associated like it by tradition with death, the elegy is meant in
theory at least to be sung as a part of the funeral ritual. Such a
poem is *"To the reverend shade of his religious* [venerable] *Father,"* in which Herrick brings his creative imagination, his concern for ritual, and his Classical learning to bear upon a circum-
stance of his life and transforms it into a moving poetic experience.
That the poem is addressed to his father's *"shade"* (implying a
spirit dwelling in Hades) suggests something of its "pagan" quality; but, at the same time, as Patrick notes, the title's emphasis upon
the venerability and piety of the poet's father may also indicate
that the poet believed that Nicholas Herrick's mysterious death
was due to an accident and not to the sin (in the Christian view)
of suicide.[7] The fact that the poem opens with an apology lends
some credence to this view:

> THAT for seven *Lusters* I did never come
> To doe the *Rites* to thy Religious Tombe:
> That neither haire was cut, or true teares shed
> By me, o'r thee, (*as justments to the dead*)
> Forgive, forgive me; since I did not know   5
> Whether thy bones had here their Rest, or no.

Assuming that Herrick is being historically accurate (and we can
only assume so), the elegy was written about 1627 ("luster" is a
Roman term for a five-year period), when the poet was thirty-six.
Owing to the suspicious circumstances of his father's death, which
might have required that the location of the grave be concealed, it
is quite possible that Herrick could have remained so long in

doubt as to "Whether thy bones had here their Rest, or no." But of
more concern here is the effect of these opening lines. The speaker
is seeking forgiveness because he has failed to do a son's duty to
his father by performing the appropriate funeral rites. That these
are dramatized as "pagan" rituals (cutting one's hair to commemorate the death of a loved one was a Greek custom) is less significant than the stress laid upon their necessity as *"justments* [due
ceremonies] *to the dead."* The rites are important because they
are formalizations and sanctifications of the powerful emotions inherent in the relationship of the persons involved and in the event
which has physically severed that relationship.

The concern for ceremony is a deep and abiding one in Herrick.
Modern man is accustomed to take particular pride in doing
things "without ceremony," not recognizing as Herrick clearly did
that the observance of countless ceremonies large and small is
part of and indeed vital to the conduct of civilized life. Thus it is
that in this poem he expresses relief at being able to perform rites
which he feels are long overdue:

> . . . Behold; behold, I bring
> Unto thy Ghost, th'Effused Offering:
> And look, what Smallage, Night-shade, Cypresse, Yew,
> Unto the shades have been, or now are due,   10
> Here I devote. . . .

The strange plants catalogued here, like the profusion of flowers
at modern funerals, have no intrinsic value, but are introduced for
their significance as commemorative symbols. But even these do
not adequately connote the speaker's feelings; he feels called upon
to produce something more:

> I come to pay a Debt of Birth I owe.
> Thou gav'st me life, (but Mortall;) For that one
> Favour, Ile make full satisfaction;
> For my life mortall, Rise from out thy Herse,   15
> And take a life immortall from my Verse.

Herrick recognizes that he has the one obligation (for the gift of
life) that all sons owe to their fathers and that never, under
normal circumstances, can be fully repaid. But at this point a sudden insight is gained; the pattern of the poem is reversed; and its
tone, which has been one of apology and regret, alters and rises to

a note of quiet triumph. His father's gift of life was, as it must be, only a temporary one; for human life must come eventually to an end. Herrick, however, as a poet can give his father the gift of eternal life. Immortalized in this poem, his father's name, and in a sense, his spirit, will be perpetuated as long as men shall read, which means as long as they shall endure. Thus the poem itself becomes not only a monument that will prevail over "*Times trans-shifting,*" but the means to a form of salvation. His father will have "life immortall" because he will live forever in the eternal world of the poem. This essentially religious faith in the immortal-izing power of poetry, which turns the tragedy of this poem into triumph, is, as Chapter 6 of this study will make clear, one of the major themes of Herrick's *Hesperides.*

II *The Fact of Death*

The occasion of the death of a child or of a father, of some human being whose life has in some way been involved with one's own, prompts even the dullest of mortals to contemplate, if only briefly, his own mortality. Poets, of course, with their height-ened sensibilities, are more prone to engage in such contempla-tions; and, like Herrick, they sometimes elect to embody them in their verses. What sets Herrick apart from most men and from many poets is the acuteness and frequency of his awareness of the irony that death is ever imminent in this life—that behind the rosy cheek lies the whitened skull, that the budding rose foreshadows the fall of its own petals. This irony is compounded in his poems about nature by Herrick's awareness that death in the natural world is demonstrably followed by regeneration, whereas no such demonstrations readily present themselves in the case of death in the human realm.

Such ironies are not, however, evident in the opening lines of "*The Argument*" about brooks and blossoms; and on the strength of these and of other such lines and of some of his poems on flowers Herrick has occasionally been regarded as something of a "nature poet." If, however, by this term is meant a poet who focuses con-siderable attention upon objects in the world of nature, who seeks to describe them vividly and in some detail, and who values them highly for their own sakes, Herrick is not a "nature poet" at all. First, though the natural realm provides a setting for a number of his poems, relatively few of them focus upon that realm to the exclusion of the human world. Second, while Herrick occasionally

writes poems about flowers or birds, for example, his images are
seldom realized with near-scientific precision—he is not a poet to
number the stripes of the tulip. Third, while a reading of his *Hesperides* is bound to give rise to the impression that Herrick the
man took pleasure in nature, generally speaking Herrick the poet
is less concerned with the intrinsic value of natural things than he
is with their utility as metaphors or symbols through which he can
comment on man's fate. For this poet the point is not that "a rose
is a rose is a rose," but that a rose is like a child or a beautiful
woman, a thing of beauty and a joy—not forever—but for all too
brief a span.

Like Sir Francis Bacon, Sir Thomas Browne, and most of the
other learned and devout men of his day, Herrick could view nature, with its infinite variety but apparent order and purpose, as a
great book in which a mysterious plan was made manifest and
which man could to some extent read and understand. And since
man, in "the great chain of being" which linked earth to heaven
and atoms to angels, was a part of nature, his destiny was charted
in that plan. It is for this reason—and because natural things, in
their beauty and familiarity are useful grist for his poetic mill, and
because nature, as transformed through the pastoral tradition,
provides a suitable framework for his book—that the world of
brooks, blossoms, birds, and bowers is so important to Herrick.

Death's omnipresence in this world is baldly stated by the poet
in an epigram with the singularly unromantic title of *"Putrefaction"*: "PUTREFACTION is the end / Of all that Nature doth entend."
Herrick's fondness for Latinisms stands him in good stead here,
enabling him to present his observation with all the succinctness
of a scientific fact: all things (for here "Nature" is employed as a
term for "life in general") eventually die and decompose—and this
is according to plan. Depending on one's point of view, the persona of this poem is either the cynical Herrick or the merely realistic Herrick; but however he is viewed, this is the persona of many
of the epigrams, one who simply purports to show "the way things
are." That this point of view is artistically presented, however,
should not be overlooked. The genre of the epigram is an ancient
and honorable one, and there is no reason to doubt that Herrick
labored as much over these poems as he did over his others, and
was likely as pleased with his successful epigrams as Ben Jonson
was with his. Both were doubtless aware that the epigram is a
highly limited poetic form, but also that, by its very limitations, it

presents a worthy challenge to the poet's powers of compression and to his ability to create an image or delineate a thought precisely, concisely, and poetically.

The theme of *"Putrefaction"* is expanded by Herrick in a poem entitled *"All things decay and die"*:

> ALL *things decay with Time:* The Forrest sees
> The growth, and down-fall of her aged trees:
> That Timber tall, which three-score *lusters* stood
> The proud *Dictator* of the State-like wood:
> I meane (the Soveraigne of all Plants) the Oke   5
> Droops, dies, and falls without the cleavers stroke.

The relevancy of the fate of trees to the human condition is implied in the opening maxim, for man obviously must be included in the category of "ALL *things.*" The remainder of the poem can then be read more as an allegory than as a mere description of a natural phenomenon. The forest becomes endowed with a kind of consciousness: it observes the growth and eventual decay of the individual trees which constitute it in much the same way that the state "observes" and endures the lives and deaths of the individuals who give it its being. The allegory becomes more overt with the words *"Dictator"* and "State-like": even the monarch—of the forest and the state—is subject to the natural cycle and it "Droops, dies, and falls." Nor is natural law the only threat; merely by his reference to "the cleavers stroke" Herrick raises the possibility that the oak could be laid low by a sudden coup d'état. His attitude here can only be described as realistic; he bemoans neither natural law nor the nature of *Realpolitik.* Not even the term *"Dictator"* is used in a necessarily pejorative sense; although it could be an oblique reference to Cromwell, the poem itself offers no evidence in support of the possibility. It is more likely that the reference is a general one consonant with the "Roman" quality (note the word *"lusters"*) of the poem. Thus the dictator would not necessarily be a tyrant but rather one who, according to Roman theory and practice, assumes responsibility for the conduct of the state during a period of emergency. He is, of course, "proud," but to Herrick pride was not necessarily a vice.[8]

There is a third and somewhat speculative level on which this poem might be read. *The Forrest* is the title of a collection of Ben Jonson's poems; a second collection is called *Underwoods,* and a compilation of his critical notes is entitled *Timber*. Could Jonson, whom Herrick regarded as his master and mentor, be the "proud *Dictator*" (Ben was not noted for his humility), the great "Oke" of the London literary forest? Herrick must have been aware of the decline from literary eminence that Jonson eventually underwent and could have regarded this unhappy event as an object-lesson in the vanity of literary ambition—but one which could only be covertly taught.

The analogy between the cycles of nature and the patterns of human life, which Herrick only hints at in the diction and personifications of "*All things decay and die*," is explicitly drawn in his poetic addresses, "*To Daffadills*" and "*To Blossoms.*" The first poem expresses regret for the transiency of natural beauty such as the daffodils exemplify, and observes, somewhat wistfully, the parallels between flowers and men:

> We have short time to stay, as you,   11
>   We have as short a Spring;
> As quick a growth to meet Decay,
>   As you, or any thing.

But the persona passes from this mood into one of pained but philosophical acceptance of the all-too-simple facts that "We die" and disappear, "Ne'r to be found againe." In this response he is in spirit obedient to the exhortation of the Athenian philosopher, Epicurus: "Accustom thyself to believe that death is nothing to us, for good and evil imply [consist in] sentience [sensation], and death is the privation of all sentience. . . ." [9]

The persona of "*To Blossoms*," however, is initially unable to confront the fact of transiency and its implications with such equanimity; on the contrary, while acknowledging the existence of transiency, he questions its rightness:

> 1. FAIRE pledges of a fruitfull Tree,
>   Why do yee fall so fast?
>   Your date is not so past;
>   But you may stay yet here a while,
>   To blush and gently smile;   5
>   And go at last.

Although the observer of the blossoms is at first unable to perceive it, his very phrasing of his question implies its own answer: the blossoms are the tree's "Faire pledges"—they promise fulfilment through fruition. Furthermore, that they have already partially fulfilled themselves is implied in the description of their pleasing coloration in terms of blushing and smiling: despite the brevity of their stay, they render the rare service of beauty to their beholders. This insight, however, is at this point of the poem still lost upon the persona, and his feelings are underscored by the meter: lines 2–3 are staccato, emphasizing the abruptness and swiftness of the blossoms' fall, whereas lines 4–6 are largo, their long vowels suggesting the extension of the blossoms' lives for which the persona hopes. And the manner in which this and the other stanzas taper off suggests the gradual fall of the blossoms to earth.

The irony, implicit in the first stanza, that the beautiful and the good are inevitably shortlived is made painfully explicit in the second:

> 2. What, were yee born to be
>   An houre or half's delight;
>   And so to bid goodnight?
>   T'was pitie Nature brought yee forth   10
>   Meerly to shew your worth,
>   And lose you quite.

The tyranny of transiency is emphasized as it is in *"To Daffadills"* by dramatic foreshortening: while blossoms in fact usually make the contribution of their beauty for longer periods of time than ninety minutes, Herrick's compression of the time sequence heightens the sense of irony and makes the persona's charge against nature of improvidence seem more justified.

But in the pause between the stanzas, as the first word of Stanza III suggests, the persona suddenly gains his insight:

> 3. But you are lovely Leaves, where we
>   May read how soon things have
>   Their end, though ne'r so brave: 15
>   And after they have shown their pride,
>   Like you a while: They glide
>   Into the Grave.

The initial conjunction throws the main emphasis of the first line upon the adjective "lovely," which suggests that persona has come to recognize that beauty, however fleeting, is its own justification and, furthermore, that the blossoms present him with a text out of nature's book from which he can read a necessary lesson—that nothing can alter the natural cycles. Thus, since neither the beauty and value of the blossoms nor human appeals can change the way things are, recriminations like those expressed in the first two stanzas are not only useless but improper. The blossoms are not "victims" of the natural cycle; their falling to earth is as necessary as their flourishing. Having gained this awareness, the persona becomes reconciled to the naturalness of death, to the fact that all things, men as well as blossoms, meet in the common grave of the earth. It is the verb "glide," connoting a quietly smooth and effortless act, that sets the tone of calm acceptance with which the poem ends. This then is less a poem about blossoms than it is about a state of mind and the changes that a particular insight can bring to that state. Essentially, the poem dramatizes a progression from naïve idealism to mature Neo-Stoicism; indeed the ultimate world view of the persona is one which agrees in all essential points with that of the Stoic philosopher-king, Marcus Aurelius:

Despise not death, but welcome it, for Nature wills it like all else. For dissolution is but one of the processes of Nature, associated with thy life's various seasons, such as to be young, to be old, to wax to our prime and to reach it, to grow teeth and beard and grey hairs, to beget, conceive and bring forth. A man then that has reasoned the matter out should not take up towards death the attitude of indifference, eagerness or scorn, but await it as one of the processes of Nature.[10]

In another poem in this Neo-Stoical vein, "A Meditation for his Mistresse," Herrick carries his contemplation of transiency and death two steps further by particularizing their implications for the lady he loves and for himself as well. But "A Meditation" is also a verse-compliment; in the manner of more conventional poems of this type, it takes the form of a catalogue-poem, with each of its seven triplet stanzas listing a different lovely object to which the lady is metaphorically compared. The metaphor of the first stanza and of all but one of the others are based upon Herrick's key analogy of the resemblances between plants and humans:

> 1. You are a *Tulip* seen to day,
>   But (Dearest) of so short a stay;
>   That where you grew, scarce man can say.

This stanza suggests the poem's theme, which in essence is that of "*To Blossoms*": the lady, like a flower is, despite her beauty, a transitory thing; consequently, there is an element of the unknown, the mysterious, about her. Stanzas II and III postulate phenomenal reasons to account for her transiency, but leave unanswered the pressing metaphysical question:

> 2. You are a lovely *July-flower*,
>   Yet one rude wind, or ruffling shower,   5
>   Will force you hence, (and in an houre.)
>
> 3. You are a sparkling *Rose* i'th'bud,
>   Yet lost, ere that chast flesh and blood
>   Can shew where you or grew, or stood.

In these stanzas two apparently separate elements of "*The Argument of his Book*" are brought together. The Herrick who sings of "*Birds*," "*Bowers*," and "*July*-Flowers" here dramatizes the fact that "*Times trans-shifting*" is no mere abstraction; it is an actual and powerful force. As manifested in the winds and rains of raw nature, it is a killing force against which the fragile beauty of flowers and the lady's mere flesh and blood are no match. Furthermore, transiency extends its tyranny not only over beauty, but over beauty's complement, love:

> 4. You are a full-spread faire-set Vine,   10
>   And can with Tendrils love intwine,
>   Yet dry'd ere you distill your Wine.

"*The Argument*" associates "*Youth*" with "cleanly-*Wantonnesse*" or love, but here youth is shown to be all too fleeting. Thus even though the lady still has the beauty and capacity for love with which youth is endowed, like a vine that withers before its wine-bearing grapes can be harvested, she is doomed never to experience fully love's fruition.

Herrick's next stanza to some extent mars his poem, for with it he temporarily abandons his already established pattern of plant metaphors:

> 5. You are like Balme inclosed (well)
>   In *Amber,* or some *Chrystall* shell,
>   Yet lost ere you can transfuse your smell.   15

Not only is a metaphor here replaced by a simile, but the ground of the comparisons is lost: balm, though a natural product, is an extraction and is thus once removed from the class of flowers and vines. Conceptually, however, the stanza is still another variation upon the poem's central theme: as perfume, no matter how carefully preserved, gradually loses its fragrance, so human life, regardless of how carefully it is nurtured, inevitably wastes away.

Another problem presents itself in Stanza VI. In it Herrick begins to distinguish between (but not to separate) the world of nature and the human world in order to prepare the way for the explicitly human and ultimately personal bearing of the final stanza:

> 6. You are a dainty *Violet,*
>   Yet wither'd, ere you can be set
>   Within the Virgins Coronet.

As real violets wither and die before they can fulfil their beauty by being woven into crowns of flowers, so will the lady to whom the poem is addressed. Herrick's metaphor advances the thematic development of the poem through its suggestion that his mistress, in addition to being denied physical fulfilment, will unhappily be bereft of the opportunity to achieve fulfilment in the social order. It is a convention of pastoral that rustic maids weave a crown of flowers for the shepherdess who rules over them; therefore, the lady, being a "dainty *Violet,*" will not endure long enough to serve her queen. Some consolation, however, is provided by Stanza VII. Though her flower-like beauty will never grace the court, his mistress is herself a queen, a paragon of the *"Sacred Grove":*

> 7. You are the *Queen* all flowers among,
>   But die you must (faire Maid) ere long,   20
>   As He, the maker of this Song.

True to the form of the preceding stanzas, the opening compliment of this triplet (and the consolation it affords) are to an extent dashed by the ironic confrontation of reality which follows. The lady is flattered as the possessor of a beauty and of a fragrance that are superior to those of all flowers, but the hyperbole of this tribute only increases the irony of her impending doom—her fall from eminence, which natural flux will precipitate, will be so much the greater.

The bitter truth of transiency, which the first six stanzas have hinted at, is at last plainly told in the matter-of-fact announcement, "die you must." The simplicity of the diction of lines 20–21 stands in contrast to the metaphorical language of the rest of the poem and it creates the impression that the speaker has been leading up to this point all along. He has been trying to prepare the lady to face the facts of life, of death, and, presumably, of love. The final line completes the chain of his inferences and to some extent cushions the shock of recognition—her lover must share her fate. And across the silence that comes after the poem, the reader perceives that he too must be cut down with the flowers, with the lady, and with "the maker of this Song."

In spite of the lapse in its metaphorical pattern, *"A Meditation"* is a successful poem. Its effect is sobering without being melancholic. Its very stress upon the brevity of life serves to emphasize life's values, such as glimpses of beauty, moments of love, and snatches of song. And herein lies a clue to the essential pattern of Herrick's thinking and feeling as they are expressed in his poems.

Thus far this study has shown that Herrick's contemplation of The Book of Nature gains him certain fundamental insights: that *"Times trans-shifting"* rules over Nature and, as a consequence, all things decay and die; that since man is a part of living Nature, it is inevitable that he share in this fate; and finally, that this fate prevents man, and to an extent, all living things, from achieving their complete fulfilment. But even though he perceives these insights and accepts them as valid, the large number of poems in *Hesperides* in which he treats them testifies to Herrick's unwillingness to let the matter die. He confronts it again and again. Why? A cynical answer would be that Herrick lacks invention, that he is too unoriginal to discover new subjects and new themes. Another answer might be that he is simply following the lead of his Classical masters, particularly Catullus, Propertius, and

Horace, in many of whose poems transiency and its implications provide a constant refrain. Still another answer might be that Herrick, like other sensitive men of his age, is truly obsessed with death.

There are elements of truth in all of these, but the answer which opens up the most fruitful line of inquiry for the reader of *Hesperides* is suggested in a comment by Douglas Bush: "The meditations on the brevity of life, so numerous and so rich throughout [English literature in the period between 1600 and 1660], are not the rhetorical funguses of an age of decay; they are the seventeenth-century version of the Dance of Death, and they tell rather of immense vitality contemplating its inevitable extinction." [11] In short, in much of the poetry of the earlier seventeenth century (and *Hesperides* is no exception) a crucial tension exists between extinction and existence, between a profound awareness of death and an equally profound sense of what Epicurus calls "the desirableness of life." [12] This tension is the result of knowing fully and of feeling intensely that of which all men are to some extent aware, but which most men, especially in certain ages, are prone to sublimate. And because they do sublimate their awareness that they must die, such men are not moved, as so many writers of the seventeenth century were moved, to ask consciously the crucial question: "How shall I respond while I live to the prospect of my inevitable death?" Of those who do ask this question, some respond by concentrating upon the life of the spirit or upon the vision of a life after death. Others respond by sinking into anxiety or by violent attempts to escape from or blot out that anxiety. Still others, and the Herrick of *Hesperides* is among them, respond by a decisive affirmation of life and its values. For Herrick, this affirmation takes the form of an exploration and exploitation of life as he knows it (or as he would wish it to be) in his verse. In this sense he is, like most poets, a critic of life as well as an artist of life.

Thus it is that in poem after poem he confronts extinction by affirming existence—by exulting in and exalting the values of food and drink, of kinship, friendship and love, of naturalness and virtue, of nature and art, and of the time-honored rituals that sanctify all of these. This is not to suggest that his *Hesperides* is, by any stretch of the imagination, a Neo-Epicurean philosophical tract; it is, as advertised, a collection of poems. Nor is it to suggest that Robert Herrick is, in essence, a humanistic philosopher; humanist he is, but first, last, and always he is a poet. Yet, like most perceptive men, Herrick's thoughts and feelings are, in the final analysis, reasonably coherent; and this coherence, as it is manifested in his individual poems, lends an underlying pattern of unity to the wide variety of his collection. Thus, to be aware of his fundamental concern—that death ultimately frustrates self-fulfilment, of his fundamental assumption—that life does, nevertheless, have value; and of his fundamental response to these—that, despite the fact that death dooms the enterprise to failure, self-fulfilment must at least be attempted through a deliberate effort to realize life's values—is to be better able to apprehend the individual poems of his *Hesperides* and to perceive some of their relevance to one another. To facilitate this process is the purpose of the chapters which follow.

CHAPTER 3

A Country Life *and* This Sacred Grove:
The Theme of the Good Life

ONE of the reasons sometimes advanced to explain the renewed interest of the twentieth century in the literature of
the seventeenth century is that both periods, more so than most
others, are ages of transition.[1] The transition that marked the seventeenth century, one which was eventually to transform the medieval world into the modern, did not take place, however, so
rapidly as the transition of the twentieth century nor did it entail
changes so sweeping and so sudden. Indeed, the England of the
earlier seventeenth century at least had so considerable a measure
of internal stability that for forty years she was able to weather
political, religious, and social storms of sufficient severity to have
destroyed lesser states. This internal stability was derived in large
part from a particular complex of spiritual and intellectual attitudes which was her inheritance from her own, relatively recent
past. This complex, as Douglas Bush has pointed out, also significantly affected her literature:

The working philosophy inherited by [English authors in the earlier
seventeenth century] was the Christian humanism which during the
Middle Ages and the Renaissance had fused Christian faith and pagan
reason into a stable framework of religious, ethical, political, economic
and cultural thought. That tradition, the main European tradition,
comes from Plato and Cicero down through Erasmus and others to
such men as Spenser, Hooker, Daniel, Chapman, and Jonson—and,
though less obviously, Shakespeare. Its central religious and philosophical doctrine is order, order in the individual soul, in society, and
in the cosmos.[2]

That this "working philosophy" and this doctrine of order are very
much Herrick's own is readily demonstrable.

I *The Sensuous Life*

Modern scholarship has shown that Herrick's *Hesperides,* so long thought to be a merely haphazard collection of miscellaneous poems, is in fact a text with considerably more than a semblance of order, both chronological and thematic.[3] One aspect of the book's thematic order, as Chapter 2 has indicated, is that it contains a series of significant poems in which the fact of death is resolutely confronted and ultimately accepted with equanimity. These, for purposes of classification, may be tagged as Herrick's "Neo-Stoic" verses. Another aspect of this same thematic order involves a particular series of poems which go one step further, which proceed from acceptance to activity. In a considerable number of secular poems of this latter type, Herrick's Neo-Stoicism is in a sense supplemented by his Neo-Epicureanism. Such a one is the epigram, *"To enjoy the Time":*

> WHILE Fate permits us, let's be merry;
> Passe all we must the fatall Ferry:
> And this our life too whirles away,
> With the Rotation of the Day.

The most striking difference between this epigram and the poems treated in the previous chapter is, of course, the speaker's positive and active response to his confrontation of death. Unlike the persona of *"To Blossoms,"* his recognition that death is as much a part of the order of things as "the Rotation of the Day" is not for him consolation enough. He turns, so to speak, from the grave to the *"Sacred Grove,"* to the best of all possible lives. The particular form that his affirmation of life takes is suggested by his exhortation, "let's be merry"; and it is one with which Herrick is frequently identified—with some justification. Herrick's best-known poem (to be discussed in more detail in Chapter 4) is, after all, the lyric that begins: "GATHER ye Rose-buds while ye may. . . ." The point of view implicit in both exhortations is succinctly summarized in Horace's phrase, *carpe diem,* whose literal translation—"seize the day," or "take advantage of the time"—is more meaningfully rendered in the title of Herrick's epigram as *"enjoy the Time."* If so universal a theme can be assigned a source, that source must be the poets of Rome's "Silver Age"— Horace, Tibullus, and Propertius. It is then no coincidence that

"Roman" elements are conspicuous by their presence in Herrick's poem: "WHILE Fate permits" acknowledges that human life is governed by forces unknown to man and over which he has no control; the only certainty is that eventually "Passe all we must the fatall Ferry"—we must be transported in death across the River Styx into the oblivion of Hades. And every rotation of the earth whirls us closer to this oblivion.

What is left then but "to be merry"? Readers only casually acquainted with Herrick are likely to reply that his answer probably would be, "Nothing"; but this response is another oversimplification since any number of his poems can be submitted as evidence that life for him has values *beyond* the merely sensuous. For the moment, however, it is necessary to consider a few more of those pieces that have advanced Herrick's wide reputation as a "Dionysian" or "pure" and simple sensualist. One such is *"Best to be merry:"*

> FOOLES are they, who never know
> How the times away doe goe:
> But for us, who wisely see
> Where the bounds of black Death be:
> Let's live merrily, and thus   5
> Gratifie the *Genius.*

Behind this short poem lies a phase of literary history (Herrick is borrowing from Simonides, Persius, and Horace)[4] and a philosophical tradition. In the first four lines the speaker, like a Stoic, unflinchingly confronts "black Death" with all of its impediments to fulfilment, and, like a satirist, scathingly exposes the folly of those who steadfastly ignore the fact that the dark curtain of death is deliberately being drawn around their existence.

Historically, it was not only the Stoics who held this view: both Epicurus, the Greek philosopher and his Roman disciple, Lucretius, stressed the omnipresence as well as the naturalness of death—and the folly therefore of fearing it. To the Epicurean, fear or pain of any kind, physical or mental, was inimical to the great purpose of life, the maximization of pleasure. And throughout intellectual history, Epicureanism has always been associated —though somewhat unjustly, as will be seen below—with the maximization of the kind of simple and sensuous pleasure that seems to be indicated in the last two lines of Herrick's poem. Living merrily, his speaker implies, is merely acquiescing to the natural order of things, to the very spirit or *"Genius"* of life here on earth. But there can be a great deal of difference between "living merrily" and "living well," and the latter phrase more accurately represents the philosophy of Epicurus than the former. *"Best to be merry"* therefore is an Epicurean poem only in the loose sense of the term. It indubitably shows Herrick as a lyrist of sensuousness, a singer of *carpe diem;* but, as has been suggested, other poems of his *Hesperides* reveal him to be this—and considerably more.

The slogan, "Eat, drink and be merry, for tomorrow we die," is a familiar modern version of *carpe diem;* but the self-conscious bravado so evident in this exhortation has been expressed in poetry at least since the time of Anacreon, the Greek lyrist of wine, women, and song. Herrick's imitations of Anacreon, such as *"On himselfe"* [III, VI], *"Anacreontike"* [I], and *"Anacrontick Verse,"* because they reproduce so accurately the spirit of their originals, bear the same stamp. As such they are representative, not of the essential spirit of Herrick's secular verse, as they are sometimes regarded, but of that Epicurean spirit carried to its Dionysian extreme. Indeed, the poet himself satirizes this extreme in the course of two of his more ambitious and less imitative poems, *"His fare-well to Sack"* and *"The Welcome to Sack."*

These two poems should be regarded as companion pieces, although they are separated in *Hesperides* by sixty-eight other poems. The purpose of the separation is dramatic: it suggests the lapse of time during which Herrick has abstained from drinking this popular white wine. *"His fare-well"* has been effectively analyzed elsewhere; [5] for the purposes of the ensuing discussion, it is sufficient to note that in its comic and satiric temper it is similar to *"The Welcome."* The latter begins with a series of humorously inflated comparisons, in the first of which Herrick sets up a sentimental analogy between the resumption of his "affair" with sack and certain reunions in nature:

> So soft streames meet, so springs with gladder smiles
> Meet after long divorcement by the Iles:
> When Love (the child of likenesse) urgeth on
> Their Christal natures to an union.

It is implied that the speaker's consumption of sack is as natural an act as the confluence of brooks. But Herrick is also recalling the myth of Altheus and Arethusa, who were metamorphosed into commingling streams for love. Such an allusion lends a kind of comic dignity to the subject, as does the allusion to the theory that love, such as Herrick's "love" for sack, arises out of the attraction between like qualities.

These references to love also serve to unite this poem with its companion piece, for in "*His fare-well*" Herrick depicts himself as sack's lover in a more than figurative but deliberately comic sense. This "amatory" motif establishes the grounds for the next two comparisons:

> So meet stolne kisses, when the Moonie nights   5
> Call forth fierce Lovers to their wisht Delights:
> So *Kings* & *Queens* meet, when Desire convinces
> All thoughts, but such as aime at getting Princes,
> As I meet thee.

Lines 5–6 inflate the poet's passion for sack even further, suggesting that it is not merely natural in the general sense, but natural in that it is comparable to instinctive and powerful human desires. The lovers described are "fierce," almost animalistic in the intensity of their passion; and their kisses are "stolne," obtained without the usual moral sanctions. Thus Herrick suggests that intensity (here exaggerated for comic effect), as well as naturalness, is a quality of this "emotion" he feels. This intensity is heightened still more in the third comparison. Kings and and queens are human beings, but they and their offspring can change the world. Hence their love is not only enhanced by the dignity of their persons but by its potentially historic significance. That Herrick's passion for sack is similarly momentous effectively brings the poem to the verge of the comedy of the absurd.

Herrick, the speaker in this poem, who now directly addresses sack as "Soule of my life, and fame," is depicted as being unaware of this absurdity (to which Herrick, the creator of this poem, has brought him). As persona, he is moved to claim that his love for sack, like the loftiest of passions, is spiritual as well as physical. It is both the quintessence of his being and the force that gives him his "fame"—his reputation as a poet (earlier, in "*His fare-well*," sack was glorified as the source of his poetic inspiration). Souls of course are eternal; thus it is fitting that sack next be addressed as "Eternall Lamp of Love." It is sack that makes his little world go round, in which respect the wine is also like the sun—except that it generates even more light and heat:

> Eternall Lamp of Love! whose radiant flame 10
> Out-glares the Heav'ns *Osiris;* and thy gleams
> Out-shine the splendour of his mid-day beams.
>
> * The Sun [Herrick's note]

At this point Herrick brings his vein of hyperbole to a halt before his comic bubble bursts from overinflation. The alteration is signaled by the relatively subdued tone of his next apostrophe: "Welcome, O welcome my illustrious Spouse." "Spouse" connotes love, and thus the intrinsic unity between this, the poem's second movement, and the first is maintained; but, even as it is modified here, "Spouse" is still a "domestic" rather than an "exotic" epithet and one which serves to bring the poem down to earth again. Indeed, it is a relatively earthy comparison that the lover of sack draws next; this wine, he says, is as welcome as the end of his abstinence:

> I! far more welcome then the happy soile, 15
> The Sea-scourg'd Merchant, after all his toile,
> Salutes with tears of joy; when fires betray
> The smoakie chimneys of his *Ithaca.*

The return of a traveller to hearth and home is always a sentimental experience, and it is just this sentimentality, as against the previous hyperbole, upon which Herrick as poet plays. He shows Herrick the speaker trying to wring some poignant moments out of his reunion with sack and he undermines them gleefully. The traveller is not a warrior or a sailor—he has been "Sea-scourg'd" for gain, not glory. As such, his return suffers somewhat by comparison with the famous home-coming to the original Ithaca of the valorous Ulysses.

In the question asked in lines 19–20, "Where hast thou been so long from my embraces, / Poor pittyed Exile," the persona plays Penelope to sack's Ulysses in an amusing but temporary reversal of genders. At this point too the literary and legendary context again begins to take on "amatory" overtones:

> Tell me, did thy Graces 20
> Flie discontented hence, and for a time
> Did rather choose to blesse another clime?
> Or went'st thou to this end, the more to move me,
> By thy short absence, to desire and love thee?

The long absence has become a short one, and the question, unanswered, suggests that sack is now the pouting mistress. To confirm this image, the wine is next specifically depicted as a cruel beauty who is worshipped to the point of idolatry by her "lover":

> Why frowns my Sweet? Why won't my saint confer   25
> Favours on me, her fierce Idolater?
> Why are Those Looks, Those Looks the which have been
> Time-past so fragrant, sickly now drawn in
> Like a dull Twi-light? Tell me; and the fault
> Ile expiate with Sulphur, Haire, and Salt.   30

Here the poet is not content to burlesque only love and his love for sack, but he also proceeds to burlesque a literary tradition which some Renaissance poets (and Herrick himself on occasion) were wont to take rather seriously—the tradition of "love's religion," with all its talk of saints and idolaters, confessions and expiations. The humor arises not only out of the exaggeration, but out of the incongruity in the speaker's use of stock devices of love poetry to sing the praises, not of women, but of wine.

This incongruity is heightened as Herrick the speaker, in the manner of all rejected swains, questions whether sack is rebuffing him because he has been too distant, because he has been too temperate in his "love," or because he is suspected of infidelity: "Have I divorc't thee onely to combine / In hot Adult'ry with another Wine?" This is dangerous ground, and so he is forced to cast about for a more acceptable rationale for his abstinence. Predictably, and thus humorously, he seizes upon the cliché about absence making for fonder hearts: "True, I confesse I left thee, and appeale / 'Twas done by me, more to confirm my zeale, / And double my affection on thee." Through such entertaining foolishness as this, the persona Herrick creates for himself begins to resemble that of Sir John Falstaff. Both are figures of fun because of their o'erweaning desire for strong drink but, at the same time, are admirable for their amiability and their eloquence.

It is still in the spirit of Falstaff that Herrick as persona turns songster by launching into a lyrical flight to describe the effects of sack upon him:

> Thou mak'st me ayrie, active to be born,
> Like *Iphyclus,* upon the tops of Corn.   50
> Thou mak'st me nimble, as the winged howers,

>   To dance and caper on the heads of flowers,
>   And ride the Sun-beams.

To give this particular contention the weight of a universal truth,
Herrick next assumes the role of a scholiast who pedantically cites
historical precedents for his authority. Wine's beneficent minis-
trations to man, he claims, are proven by the examples of "wise
Cato," the Roman Stoic philosopher who approved of wine, and
of the son of Jove himself, Hercules, who drank wine to maintain
his sexual prowess. On the strength of this last precedent Herrick
returns to his pseudo-amatory refrain; ready at last to put his lips
to the glass, he urges: "Come, come and kiss me; Love and lust
commends / Thee, and thy beauties. . . ." And still the pedant,
even in this moment of "high passion," he draws a historical
analogy:

>   . . . or come thou unto me,
>   As *Cleopatra* came to *Anthonie*;
>   When her high carriage did at once present   75
>   To the *Triumvir*, Love and Wonderment.

The comparison of the persona's amorousness toward sack to one
of the great love affairs of all time is, and is intended to be, farci-
cal; it compounds the absurdity of this comedy of the absurd.

There is nothing absurd, however, in Herrick's development of
his poem. His patterns of images in "*The Welcome*'s" final movement are organically related to those of earlier movements and
thus contribute measurably to the over-all unity of the poem. The
Antony-Cleopatra simile, for example, recalls "So *Kings* & *Queens*
meet" (line 7); the exhortation, "let my blood / Run through my
veines, like to a hasty flood," recalls the elaborate analogy initiated
by "SO soft streames meet" (line 1); and the persona's vow, "till I
turne Apostate to thy love, / Which here I vow to serve, doe not
remove / Thy Fiers from me," is a reprise of the earlier "religion
of love" motif. Even the theme of the mighty vow which climaxes
the poem—that wine is the source of the persona's poetic inspiration—has been alluded to in the reference to fame (line 9). As a
part of this vow, Herrick melodramatically calls down upon himself the curse of the god of poetry if he should ever again abstain
from the beverage that has made him a poet; in that unlikely
event, all manner of indignities, he vows—climaxing in the denial

of his claim to the honorable title of "Poet"—should be heaped
upon him:

> Call me *The sonne of Beere,* and then confine
> Me to the Tap, the Tost, the Turfe; Let Wine
> Ne'r shine upon me; May my Numbers all
> Run to a sudden Death, and Funerall.   90
> And last, when thee (deare Spouse) I disavow,
> Ne'r may Prophetique *Daphne* crown my Brow.

Beer, of course, is a plebian drink imbibed by the vulgar fre-
quenters of such taverns as "the Tap, the Tost, the Turfe." The
native English context that emerges here is new to the poem and
serves to counterpoint the Classical associations that have been
built up around wine: beer is the drink of the masses, wine the
beverage of Dionysius and poets; beer is imbibed in taverns, wine
in the "Sacred Grove." Implicit here is the schism between reality
and ideality which, in one of Herrick's basic esthetic assumptions, it is the function of art to bridge. Lacking wine then, the
poet would lack the "Prophetique" power to perform this function; cut off from the ideal and marooned in reality, his art would
decline and he would lose his right to wear the mark of his office,
the crown of laurel or "Daphne."

By means of these sly jibes at the favorite beverage of his native
land and the exaggerations of his vow and of its claim for wine,
Herrick sustains the comic spirit of his poem to the last. As a
comedy, "The Welcome" is on one level a burlesque of the Anacreontic poem and a satire upon the extremism of the Anacreontic
temper. On another level, it is a self-satire in which Herrick the
poet holds up to witty ridicule his own predeliction for alcohol.
But at the same time, no reader can be left in doubt that beneath
the self-satire lies a lusty regard not only for wine itself but, by
extension, for all such minimizers of pain and maximizers of
pleasure. Thus the ultimate effect of "The Welcome" may be to
strike a balance between unmitigated sensuousness and the near-
asceticism of classic Epicureanism, for in its comic way the poem
suggests how Herrick values, without overvaluing, what has been
called "the good life."

II *The Urban Life*

For the pastoral poet, the best things of life are mainly to be
realized in nature or at least in the country—of which most pas-

toralists have had an ideal vision but little actual experience. Robert Herrick, however, is an exception. Although born and bred a Londoner and, therefore, like many bucolic poets, an urban man, his years as a priest in rural Devonshire enabled him to experience firsthand the country life. The partial disenchantment which resulted from this experience and which is recorded in several poems specifically about Devonshire does not seem to have undermined appreciably his pastoral orientation. Rather, it seems to have heightened his awareness of the distance between the pastoral ideal and the rural actuality and to have impelled him to bridge this gap in his own bucolic verses. An example of this tendency is a poem that may have been written about 1647 when Herrick was removed from his position in Dean Prior because of his Royalist sympathies.[6] The poem's title, *"To* Dean-bourn, *a rude River in* Devon, *by which sometimes he lived,"* gives some hint as to its tone:

> DEAN-BOURN, farewell; I never look to see
> *Deane,* or thy warty incivility.
> Thy rockie bottome, that doth teare thy streams,
> And makes them frantick, ev'n to all extreames;
> To my content, I never sho'd behold,   5
> Were thy streames silver, or thy rocks all gold.

Implicit in Herrick's personification of the river is the analogy between man and nature which he employs in other poems to suggest insights into the transient beauty and worth of life; in this poem, however, the analogy is so focused as to expose life's primitive aspect. With its wild "extreames," the river stands for untamed nature; as such, it is the very antithesis of idyllic pastoral nature in which all streams are smooth and silvery. In the eighteenth century, a river like Dean-bourn, with its "rockie bottome," "frantick" currents, and air of "warty incivility," would have been regarded as "picturesque." For Herrick, however, "extreames" of any kind, whether natural or esthetic, threaten the order of existence. His images stress this point of view: Dean-bourn is physically ugly to the point of deformity (as warts mar the natural smoothness of the skin) and is by its "temper" odious (as crude behavior is repugnant because it mars the normal harmony of human relationships). Though he recognizes that the river is "real" and "natural," Herrick sees no reason to accept and admire it any more than he would admire the warts or uncouthness of an otherwise beautiful woman. In both cases, as shall be indicated below, he sees art as capable of ameliorating the given condition.

As he attributes human qualities to Dean-bourn to dramatize its deficiencies, so Herrick attributes subhuman qualities to the natives of Devonshire:

> Rockie thou art; and rockie we discover
> Thy men; and rockie are thy wayes all over.
> O men, O manners; Now, and ever knowne
> To be *A Rockie Generation!*   10
> A people currish; churlish as the seas;
> And rude (almost) as rudest Salvages.
> With whom I did, and may re-sojourne when
> Rockes turn to Rivers, Rivers turn to Men.

By treating the natives after he has described the river, Herrick creates the impression that the West-country environmnt has had a marked influence upon its human inhabitants—a view that contemporary sociology would, up to a point, support. Like Dean-bourn, these people exhibit little sense of order. Like the very rocks of the stream, they lack pliability and symmetry. Like savage dogs, they are wild and dangerous. Like the ocean itself, they are violent and ungovernable. In short, they are close to being savages, creatures at the very bottom of the human scale. But the Juvenalian satiric thrust of Herrick's lines is an indication that he does not feel called upon to accept such extremism in human nature and conduct simply because it is natural to a particular *"Generation."* Because he is a pastoral poet, which means that he is a type of idealist, it follows both that he is aware of the discrepancy between the real and his ideal and that he rejects whatever falls so far short of his vision. "Warty incivility" can only become acceptable when it is refined into "a wilde civility," that middle state in which nature and art have achieved a harmonious, ordered synthesis.[7] Herrick's version of pastoral, as it is expressed in *Hesperides*, can be seen to embody such a synthesis. Hence, though this poetic address is self-evidently an anti-Devonshire poem, it is not necessarily antipastoral.

The ode, *"His returne to London,"* is also an "anti-Devonshire" poem, but only incidentally. Panegyrical in mode, it hymns London as the poet's birthplace, spiritual home, and way of life:

> FROM the dull confines of the drooping West,
> To see the day spring from the pregnant East,
> Ravisht in spirit, I come, may more, I flie
> To thee, blest place of my Nativitie!
> Thus, thus with hallowed foot I touch the ground,   5
> With thousand blessings by thy Fortune crown'd.

The "drooping West" is, of course, "dull *Devon-shire*," which lies
to the southwest of the capital. Herrick plays upon the traditional
associations of west and east to sharpen his contrast: it is in the
"drooping West" that the sun goes down; in the East, the new day
is triumphantly born. The West suggests drab winter, which comes
in on the west wind, while spring comes from the East. The West
implies sterility; the East, fertility. Thus the highest compliment
that the poet can pay London is to compare it, first implicitly,
then explicitly, to the fabled city which lies to the east of Britain,
Rome:

> O fruitfull Genius! that bestowest here
> An everlasting plenty, yeere by yeere.
> O *Place!* O *People!* Manners! fram'd to please
> All *Nations, Customes, Kindreds, Languages!*   10

London, like Rome or any specific place, has its own "Genius," its
own spirit which gives character to a location and is solicitous of
its inhabitants. The contrast between the blest city and the cursed
country is dramatically underscored by Herrick's impassioned
paraphrase of Cicero's *O tempora O mores;* line nine also calls to
mind the bitter outcry, "O men, O manners," of "*To* Dean-bourn."
But the poem's main thrust is towards social criticism, not imitation; for, by his reference to "manners," Herrick is calling attention to the whole code or pattern of behavior which characterizes
a race and not merely to social niceties.

The manners which the poet admires are suggested in the second movement of the poem, in which both its Roman and autobiographical strains become more explicit:

> I am a free-born *Roman;* suffer then,
> That I amongst you live a Citizen.
> London my home is: though by hard fate sent
> Into a long and irksome banishment;
> Yet since cal'd back; henceforward let me be,   15

O native countrey, repossest by thee!
For, rather then I'le to the West return,
I'le beg of thee first here to have mine Urn.
Weak I am grown, and must in short time fall;
Give thou my sacred Reliques Buriall.   20

The metaphor of the speaker-as-Roman contributes more than
Classical overtones and imagistic unity to the poem; by recalling
the tradition that exile from Rome was to "a free-born *Roman*" the
supreme penalty, one worse than death itself, it communicates
dramatically the pull which London, the loadstone metropolis of
English life, could exert upon the imaginations of those separated
from her. Then too this metaphor also lends dramatic credibility
to the climactic prayer for death in preference to another banishment.

The poignancy inherent in *"His returne"* is complemented by
certain historical facts which, though external to the poem, may
yet be brought to a knowledgeable reading of it: in actuality Herrick did of course return to "the drooping West," eventually to die
and to be buried there, though no one indeed knows where his
"sacred Reliques" have their burial. But as the historical fact that
Herrick did return to Devonshire cannot be used to support the
hypothesis that he is essentially a pastoralist, so *"His returne,"*
which is only one poem in one mood, cannot invalidate the same
hypothesis. Devonshire and London are only geographical loca-
tions; his *Hesperides* is a world, one that is given its dominant
character by the vision of the good life which it contains.

III   *The Rural Life*

It has already been suggested that a careful reading of *Hesperides* reveals that Herrick has an unmistakable concern for establishing some kind of code by which to live. By this concern, it should
now be noted, he shows his kinship, both as a Neo-Stoic and as a
poet, with the Elizabethan writers of formal verse satire and with
their Roman forebears, Juvenal and Persius.[8] But, although all
satirists are social critics, the reverse is not necessarily true. Herrick, for example, shares with the Elizabethan satirists the basic
assumptions that the human mind is capable of being reformed
and that it is necessary to bring one's life "under the governance
of reason," [9] but his formal satire is largely confined to his epigrams. Had he been more of a philosopher-poet, he might have
written lengthy verse satires or extended philosophical poems in

which he explicitly defined his vision of the good life and his plan
for achieving it. But because he is essentially the lyrist, the maker
of short poems; because he has an affirming rather than a negating
temper; and because—unlike such satirists as Donne, John Mar-
ston, and Thomas Lodge—he regards Delight as being as much a
function of poetry as Instruction, Herrick tends to present his
vision and his plan informally and dramatically in such poems as
his series of verses on "the country life." One of his less familiar
poems in this genre is *The Wake.*

At first glance merely a charming verse description of a rural
holiday (specifically, an annual parish festival), *The Wake*
when read closely is both an appreciation of the simple pleasures
of rustic life and a gentle satire upon those happy primitives for
whom such a life suffices. The poem opens with the speaker ex-
tending an invitation to his lady, who presumably is, like him, not
herself a simple rustic:

> COME *Anthea* let us two
> Go to Feast, as others do.
> Tarts and Custards, Creams and Cakes,
> Are the Junketts still at Wakes:
> Unto which the Tribes resort,   5
> Where the businesse is the sport.

There is a slight note of condescension in the distinction the
speaker makes between "us two" and the "others," in his observation that the sweets catalogued (line 3) are "still" the delicacies
or "Junketts" served at country affairs—implying that more elegant
victuals would be featured at a more sophisticated function—and
in his epithet for the other revelers, "Tribes" (connoting a race of
primitives).

The speaker's air of condescension persists as he catalogues the
rustic dances, the pageants of Robin Hood, and the low-comedy
mimics; but he reserves his overt satire for some strangers:

> Players there will be, and those   11
> Base in action as in clothes:
> Yet with strutting they will please
> The incurious Villages.

The "Players" would, of course, be a troop of itinerant actors; the
fact that they were in this period regarded as mere riffraff might,

in addition to their lack of talent, explain the speaker's severity. The lack of discrimination on the part of the "incurious" villagers, however, causes them to stand in need of satiric correction as well. Just how low their tastes are is indicated by the kind of affair with which they climax their holiday:

> Neer the dying of the day,   15
> There will be a *Cudgell*-Play,
> Where a *Coxcomb* will be broke,
> Ere a good *word* can be spoke:
> But the anger ends all here,
> Drencht in Ale, or drown'd in Beere.   20

Herrick stresses the fact that, in this "drama," rough, knock-about action will take precedence over dialogue. In the course of the slapstick, someone inevitably will receive a cracked skull; but all will be forgiven in the general alcoholic haze. The speaker's appreciation of the pleasure the rustics take in their wake's inebriated grand finale paradoxically coexists with his critical awareness of the crudity of this pleasure. With this dual awareness he summarizes the whole experience of the wake with a reflective observation:

> Happy Rusticks, best content
> With the cheapest Merriment:
> And possesse no other feare,
> Then to want the Wake next Yeare.   24

The country folk are enviable in that they are quite satisfied with such simple pleasures. But, though he might wish it otherwise, they will not suffice for anyone who is as sophisticated (and perhaps as jaded) as the speaker. The irony of the situation becomes apparent in the final couplet: the ignorance of the rustics is their bliss, for their only worry is that they may "want" (be without) a holiday next year. The speaker cannot help but be aware that there are more and superior pleasures to be wrung from life than this, but he pays for his awareness: his sense of the multiplicity of life's values must inevitably compound his fears at the prospect of their loss.

While *"The Wake"* can legitimately be classified as a pastoral poem because it is a poem about country life, it is scarcely a conventional one. It is not set in some mythical Arcadia but in the

English countryside; its cast of characters includes no nymphs or satyrs but recognizably English peasants and no Pans or Floras but a sophisticated English gentleman and his lady. It affirms the good life to be had in the country, but resists overidealizing that life even while appreciating it. And it recognizes that the complexity as well as the value of life increases in direct proportion to the awareness of the individual who lives it. Though the bucolic world of *"The Wake"* is closer to the primitive actualities of English country life than it is to the Arcadian artifice of standard pastoral, the tendency it exhibits to sentimentalize, if only slightly, the happiness of the rustics makes the poem representative of Herrick's version and vision of pastoral. It is a pastoral, as has been suggested earlier, which accepts reality but tries to improve upon it through art, and which derives its being not simply from a convention but from an intelligence and sensibility that are capable of "living" and controlling that convention. Attempting thus to transform rocky Devonshire into a *"Sacred Grove"* is a familiar and fundamental process of Herrick's *Hesperides.* For example, its operation can also be observed in a poem called *"The Hock-cart, or Harvest home."*

The setting of *"The Hock-cart,"* like that of *"The Wake,"* is a rural holiday—in this instance, one which celebrates the completion of the annual harvest. The hock-cart—the wagon in which the last load from the fields is brought in—is the central symbol of the ritual. In addition to describing this ritual, Herrick's poem is itself a kind of ritual; for it is comprised of a series of poetic addresses to the country folk and to the lord of the manor. These addresses are not merely ceremonial; they are also didactic: they propagate certain economic and social principles. The latter are derived from two philosophical assumptions which serve as the main thematic strains of the poem; these assumptions—one having to do with the relationship between man and nature, and the other with relationships in the human hierarchy—are implicit in its opening couplet: "Come Sons of Summer, by whole toile, / We are the Lords of Wine and Oile." The epithet, "Sons of Summer," nicely elevates the simple farm laborers being addressed here; but, in the couplet as a whole, the distinction between them and the class represented by the speaker (the "We" of the poem) is preserved. And, by the poem's conclusion, the nature of this distinction and its implications are made abundantly clear.

"Sons of Summer" also suggests that the rustics are creatures of

the season, just as the land which they work is. This relationship,
however, is only partly harmonious, for it is they, these sons of
nature, "By whose tough labours, and rough hands, / We rip up
first, then reap our lands." The very sounds as well as the connotations of words like "tough," "rough," "rip," and "reap" evoke an
almost military image in which the rustics are the infantry (and
"We," the members of the higher class, are the generals). Happily, however, the warfare is ended every year in the symbolic
armistice of the harvest ceremony: "Crown'd with the eares of
corne, now come, / And, to the Pipe, sing Harvest home." The
ceremony both sanctifies the act of harvest (as well as those which
preceded it) and symbolically draws man and nature together:
the swains are crowned as victors, but they have literally and figuratively stooped to conquer—their crowns are made of the stalks
of grain they themselves have harvested.

In the next couplet the speaker turns to address Mildmay, the
Earl of Westmorland, to whom the poem is dedicated: "Come
forth, my Lord, and see the Cart / Drest up with all the Country
Art." Westmorland and the speaker, who functions dramatically
in the poem as a kind of chaplain to the earl, are, it is implied,
"the Lords of Wine and Oile" not only through their membership
in the ruling class, but by virtue of their more acute sensibilities:
they can perceive the difference between "Country" and more sophisticated "Art." This awareness of the speaker, which coexists
with his capacity to appreciate and enjoy "Country Art" and country activity, is apparent in the passage that follows, in which he
acts as the earl's guide to the festivities:

> See, here a *Maukin*, there a sheet,
> As spotless pure, as it is sweet: 10
> The Horses, Mares, and frisking Fillies,
> (Clad, all, in Linnen, white as Lillies.)
> The Harvest Swaines, and Wenches bound
> For joy, to see the *Hock-cart* crown'd.
> About the Cart, heare, how the Rout   15
> Of Rurall Younglings raise the shout;
> Pressing before, some coming after,
> Those with a shout, and these with laughter.

The speaker can savor the sight of a *"Maukin"* (scarecrow) being
paraded about and the spectacle of the excited, white-clad horses;
and he is very much in sympathy with the laughing boys and girls.

Yet he can at the same time be amused by these rustics' primitive pantheism:

> Some blesse the Cart; some kiss the sheaves;
> Some prank them up with Oaken leaves: 20
> Some crosse the Fill-horse; some with great
> Devotion, stroak the home-borne wheat.

These simple souls confuse symbols like the cart and the sheaves with that for which they stand, a benign and bountiful nature.[10] They mean well by their worship, but their lack of religious sophistication leads them into excesses.

The primitiveness of these peasants and their consequent excesses in social behavior are broadly satirized in a passage of slapstick comedy:

> While other Rusticks, lesse attent
> To Prayers, then to Merryment,
> Run after with their breeches rent.   25

The serious significance of the holiday is most likely to be lost upon such merry fellows as these. In an attempt to correct this deficiency, the speaker turns from addressing Westmorland and speaks directly to the celebrants. He first calls their attention to the custom which makes the day such a special one (and by so doing subtly emphasizes once again the class distinction between masters and servants)—that of making the earl's hearth and home theirs for the day:

> Well, on, brave boyes, to your Lords Hearth,
> Glitt'ring with fire; where, for your mirth,
> Ye shall see first the large and cheefe
> Foundation of your Feast, Fat Beefe:
> With Upper Stories, Mutton, Veale   30
> And Bacon, (which makes full the meale).

Though it is only sketched in, Herrick's metaphor creates a mouth-watering image of a veritable palace of roast meat, around which sweets, custards, pies, and puddings are tastefully arranged. And though the "brave boyes" may not be treated to the beverage of the gentry, "smirking Wine," they may have plenty of "that, which drowns all care, stout Beere." But, while beer may drown all care, it should not drown all concern; the proprieties must be maintained. Thus even beer-drinking must be conducted along ceremonial lines befitting the occasion; these lines are laid down by the speaker in a brief lecture on the order of priority to be observed in the offering of toasts:

> . . . freely drink to your Lords health,
> Then to the Plough, (the Common-wealth)
> Next to your Flailes, your Fanes, your Fatts;   40
> Then to the Maids with Wheaten Hats:
> To the rough Sickle, and the crookt Sythe,
> Drink frollick boyes, till all be blythe.

The lord comes first, not only because he has provided the feast, but presumably because he represents the social and political hierarchy to which the rustics owe their ultimate allegiance. The plow likewise is not only a tool but the very symbol of agriculture, as Herrick's pun indicates: it acts as the "Common-wealth" in the sense that it is the "domain" over which the peasant rules but also in the sense that it brings wealth of a kind to the peasant as well as to his lord. With this as a precedent, all of the farm equipment —the flails, the fans for winnowing the grain, and the vats for storing it—can be toasted as contributors to the harvest.

With this gentle reminder off his chest, the speaker is ready to pronounce a sterner one. In the process he reverts from his role of master of ceremonies back to that of chaplain. So that the significance of the holiday will not be lost upon the merry-makers, he draws for them from the day's rituals some pointed economic and social inferences:

> Feed, and grow fat; and as ye eat,
> Be mindfull, that the lab'ring Neat   45
> (As you) may have their fill of meat.
> And know, besides, ye must revoke
> The patient Oxe unto the Yoke,
> And all goe back unto the Plough
> And Harrow, (though they'r hang'd up now.)   50
> And, you must know, your Lords word's true,
> Feed him ye must, whose food fils you.
> And that this pleasure is like raine,
> Not sent ye for to drowne your paine,
> But for to make it spring againe.   55

The speaker displays his wit by intimating—in the broadest terms thus far in the poem—that his audience, the country folk, are so close to nature that they are in effect at the very bottom of the human scale. While literally he is merely urging them to enjoy themselves, by phrasing this exhortation in terms of "feeding" and "growing fat" he reduces them, so to speak, nearly to the level of domesticated animals. The superiority he feels to them and their primitiveness (his "civility" as opposed to their "wildenesse") is demonstrated by the very fact that he employs such diction—and the earl will see the humor even though the rustics do not. Since his subtlety will be lost upon the "Sons of Summer," lines 51–52 have the effect of a direct order, one whose rationale is given in the concluding triplet.

This rationale, however, is ambiguous; and the crux of the ambiguity lies in the word "paine." If "paine" is to be taken as referring to the rustic's capacity for labor (rather than to some injury), and if "spring" is to be taken as a verb, the triplet may be paraphrased thusly: "This holiday is celebrated—not to inhibit your capacity for labor—but to revitalize it." On the other hand, if "spring" is read as a noun, then "paine" would refer to the harvest season itself, thereby ringing in the concept of natural flux, of the death and rebirth of nature: "This holiday serves not to conclude the fruitful season so much as to signal its eventual transformation." In light of the double theme of the poem, both interpretations can obtain: the first suggesting the social and economic assumptions behind the holiday; the second, the real and symbolic relationships between man and nature that are crystallized in the holiday. Although these concepts may appear today to verge upon the feudal, in Herrick's time they must have been commonly accepted articles of the Royalist faith.

But for all its specific gravity, *"The Hock-cart"* is still a highly original, dramatic, and descriptive poem rather than a political polemic. In the context of *Hesperides* it is a pastoral which indirectly suggests how the good country life might be realized: although the man of sense and sensibility could not descend to the primitive level of rural existence that is all the "Sons of Summer" know, the country life as it is lived by the lord, or at least by the country squire or gentleman-farmer, is an attainable approximation of the pastoral vision come true. This indeed is the very assertion Herrick makes in a poem addressed to his friend, Mr. John Wicks.

The full title of this work, "*A Paranaeticall, or Advisive Verse, to his friend, M. John Wicks,*" promises that this is to be more of a philosophical than a descriptive poem. Herrick's role will be that of sage rather than priest; and, because he is speaking to one of his peers, he will advise rather than preach. The basic assumption behind his advice is the principle of moderation, as is apparent from the poem's opening lines:

> Is this a life, to break thy sleep?
> To rise as soon as day doth peep?
> To tire thy patient Oxe or Asse
> By noone, and let thy good dayes passe,
> Not knowing This, that *Jove* decrees   5
> Some mirth, t'adulce mans miseries?

Here the notion that work is a good, and its consequence, that to labor is to be virtuous, are abandoned in favor of the Old Testament view that work is a punishment for man's sinfulness (or of the practical view that work is a tiresome necessity). Whatever its sources, Herrick's attitude aligns him with the pastoral tradition in which the converse of that attitude—that it is leisure which has special value—is a prevailing assumption. In this, Herrick's "realistic" version of pastoral, it is implied that work is for creatures born to it, like the "patient Oxe or Asse," while man, in the divine plan, is born for something better—like life-affirming "mirth." Thus Herrick answers his own rhetorical questions, first, by denying that Wicks has been leading the good life, and then by suggesting that his exertions actually violate the principle of moderation by which nature herself operates:

> No; 'tis a life, to have thine oyle,
> Without extortion, from thy soyle:
> Thy faithfull fields to yeeld thee Graine,
> Although with some, yet little paine.   10

Behind this contention lies still another of pastoral's basic assumptions—that nature, being essentially benign and especially responsive to man, is in effect his "faithfull" servant, one dutifully supplying his wants and only requiring a minimum effort on his part.

Herrick continues his definition of the good life amid nature by showing that once labor has been put in proper perspective and subsistence has been attained, peace of mind follows; and it is

reinforced by the security and contentment afforded by the country life and by married love:

> To have thy mind, and nuptiall bed,
> With feares, and cares uncumbered:
> A Pleasing Wife, that by thy side
> Lies softly panting like a Bride.
> This is to live, and to endeere   15
> Those minutes, Time has lent us here.

The discrepancy between this "pastoral" response to the exhortation of *carpe diem* and the "orgiastic" response of Herrick's ex-
tremely Dionysian poems is an index of the flexibility of his temperament. But although the Dionysian response is more often
associated with his name, it is the "pastoral" one which receives
more extensive and more serious treatment throughout his *Hesperides.*

To live in accordance with the dictates of nature is for Herrick
to attain maximum freedom:

> Then, while Fates suffer, live thou free,
> (As is that ayre that circles thee)
> And crown thy temples too, and let
> Thy servant, not thy own self, sweat,   20
> To strut thy barnes with sheafs of Wheat.

Work inhibits freedom, and excessive work, such as Wicks has
been doing, inhibits freedom excessively. Not only does it run
counter to the "natural" principle of moderation but also to the
natural order in which some agents—men as well as beasts—function mainly as workers and others, like Wicks (and presumably
Herrick), are directed toward higher ends. But here, as in *"The
Wake,"* the poet makes it clear that the latter pay for their privi-
leges and their greater freedom by their awareness that

> No sound recalls the houres once fled,
> Or Roses, being withered: 25
> Nor us (my Friend) when we are lost,
> Like to a Deaw, or melted Frost.

Herrick's images underscore both the inevitability and the naturalness of death: time evaporates all, men as well as droplets and

flowers; and, once evaporated, all are beyond recall. Thus, after
having called into question the quality of Wicks' present life, defined the good life for him, and demonstrated the urgent need for
achieving it, Herrick is ready to advise his friend directly as to the
best means to this end:

> Then live we mirthfull, while we should,
> And turn the iron Age to Gold.
> Let's feast, and frolick, sing, and play,   30
> And thus lesse last, then live our Day.
> *Whose life with care is overcast,*
> *That man's not said to live, but last:*
> *Nor is't a life, seven yeares to tell,*
> *But for to live that half seven well:*   35
> And that wee'l do; as men, who know,
> Some few sands spent, we hence must go,
> Both to be blended in the Urn,
> From whence there's never a return.

The positive affirmation of life is not only a means to fulfil human
nature but to better it and even to improve the world and the age
itself. To live the good life is to reverse the degeneration of the
world that has been taking place since the Golden Age, that time
of human and natural perfection. The Golden Age was an age of
life, not mere existence; and, in envisioning it, Herrick again
shows philosophical and poetic affiliations with both Stoicism and
the pastoral tradition. While it is unlikely that he, any more than
those philosophers and poets, believed in the historical existence
of such an age, the feeling that there was a time when life was
measurably better is as strong in *Hesperides* as it is in the Stoic's
prose and in the poems of the Renaissance satirists.[11] The apparent
frivolousness of Herrick's prescription (lines 30–31) for recover-
ing that age is to an extent balanced off by the gnomic seriousness
of lines 32–35 and the philosophical detachment with which total
oblivion is confronted in the climactic couplets of the poem. Then
too, if Herrick's vision of the good life is frivolous, it should be
remarked that it differs little from traditional religious visions of
heaven or from the waking dreams of many men on earth.

Herrick's most detailed vision of rustic earthly bliss is developed
in "A *Country life: To his Brother,* M. Tho: Herrick." A striking
example of Herrick's eclecticism, this pastoral poem closely resembles Ben Jonson's poetic address, "*To Sir Robert Wroth,*" but

it also contains a number of echoes of contemporary writers ranging from Shakespeare to Robert Burton and of Classical authors
from Virgil to Horace.[12] That these diverse sources are unobtru-
sively blended into a unified pastoral is a considerable tribute to
the poet's craftsmanship. The world defined by this poem as the
one in which Thomas Herrick lives is described in conventionally
bucolic diction as a "Rurall Sanctuary" and an "*Elizium*," a paradise
of "Damaskt medowes," "peebly streames," and "Purling springs,
groves, birds, and well-weav'd Bowrs, / With fields enameled
with flowers" (lines 45–46). Yet at the same time, references to
such items as "Nettles, Colworts, Beets," the "singing Crickits by
[the] fire," "the brisk Mouse," and "the green-ey'd Kitling [kit-
ten]" lend a familiar English quality to this world.

   Although the poem is a versified tribute rather than an "advisive verse," Herrick once again adopts the role of the pastoral sage
who begins by commending his brother's judiciousness:

> THRICE, and above, blest (my soules halfe) art thou,
> In thy both Last, and Better Vow:
> Could'st leave the City, for exchange, to see
>   The Countries sweet simplicity:
> And it to know, and practice   5

The tension between the urban and the rural ways of life out of
which pastoral poetry is derived becomes in this poem the basis
upon which Herrick erects an ethical theory of some complexity.
It is well, he claims, that Thomas has determined to forsake the
city for the country because the good life is the natural one in
which we perceive and imitate the "sweet simplicity" inherent in
the natural order of things and by which we "grow the sooner
innocent." Innocence is not ignorance but rather that state of purity which prelapsarian Adam and Eve enjoyed in their "*Sacred
Grove*," a state in which the knowledge and the practice of virtue
were one. By electing the country life, Thomas draws nearer to
the condition of our original parents; he thus is able to live according to nature and reason, to live, as his brother notes,

> Led by thy conscience; to give
> Justice to soone-pleas'd nature; and to show,
>   Wisdome and she together goe,
> And keep one Centre   15

Free (in the country) to follow the dictates of his conscience, Thomas can easily satisfy the modest demands for food or shelter that his nature as a human being makes upon him. By so doing, he is wise in that he is simultaneously following nature—his physical self—and conscience—his moral self, both of which counsel moderation. The actual achievement of this coordination within the self is to Herrick vitally necessary; for—as he insists to his brother —both human nature and human wisdom ". . . teach Man to confine desires: / And know, that Riches have their proper stint [limit], / In the contented mind, not mint" (lines 16–18). By advocating these precepts, Herrick again reveals his kinship with the Stoics (for whom moderation is likewise a cardinal virtue) and with Epicurus (for whom moderation follows inevitably from prudence).[13] Like Epicurus, Herrick has reflected upon the psychology of human desire and has concluded with him that "some [desires] are natural, others are groundless; and [among] the natural some are necessary as well as natural and some [are] natural only."[14] Hence Herrick can commend his brother for being content "To keep cheap Nature even, and upright; / To coole, not cocker [enflame] Appetite" (lines 25–26).

Herrick also follows Epicurus in the specific example of the human desire for food. The latter's claim that "To habituate one's self . . . to simple and inexpensive diet supplies all that is needful for health . . ."[15] is versified by the English poet in two couplets:

> Thus thou canst tearcely live to satisfie
> The belly chiefly; not the eye:
> Keeping the barking stomach wisely quiet,
> Lesse with a neat, then needfull diet.   30

The same principle obtains with regard to the human sexual drive. Thus love—which in traditional pastoral poetry is sometimes mere sexuality, and which in some English pastoral is mere sentimentality—is here seen as, at its best, a golden mean between these two extremes, a state attainable through the sanctification of marriage:

> But that which most makes sweet thy country life,
> Is, the fruition of a wife:
> Whom (Stars consenting with thy Fate) thou hast
> Got, not so beautifull, as chast:

> By whose warme side thou dost securely sleep   35
>   (While Love the Centinell doth keep).

Herrick is not suggesting that his brother's wife lacks beauty but
that, however physically attractive she may be, her virtue is more
attractive. The virtue that they share, he goes on, keeps them secure; they enjoy the sleep of the just, their minds untroubled by
guilt or fear. Such virtue, complemented by their reverence (symbolized by the Roman ritual of offering up meal and salt to make
"peace with heav'n" [lines 58–60]), and sustained by some labor
(symbolized by the synechdoche of the farmer's "painfull [pains-
taking] Thumb" [line 61]), is rewarded by divine munificence:
"Jove for our labour all things sells us" (line 62).

With this aphorism Herrick concludes the first movement of his
philosophical, panegyrical tribute to Thomas and to the country
life; he then proceeds to draw some contrasts between the truly
good life and existence in the urban world. The commercial aspect of the city, for example, Herrick sees as entailing far more
pains than rewards:

> Nor are thy daily and devout affaires
>   Attended with those desp'rate cares,
> Th'industrious Merchant has; who for to find
>   Gold, runneth to the Western Inde,   65
> And back again, (tortur'd with fears) doth fly,
>   Untaught, to suffer Poverty.

Behind this image lies the centuries-old debate about the Active
Life versus the Contemplative Life which, since activity is associated with the city and contemplation with the solitude found in
the country, is related to the basic tension of the pastoral. As a
pastoralist, it is natural for Herrick to depict the Active Man, such
as the merchant, as a driven man who, in the words of the Epicurean Lucretius, "struggles to flee from himself," but finds only
frustration.[16] Escapist too, according to Herrick, is the yearning
for the glamor of the court, a glamor that Thomas himself knows
to be false:

> And when thou hear'st by that too-true-Report,
>   Vice rules the Most, or All at Court: 90
> Thy pious wishes are, (though thou not there)
>   Virtue had, and mov'd her Sphere.

Although these lines lapse into syntactic clumsiness, a fault of which Herrick is occasionally guilty in his longer poems, they show him once again to be true to the pastoral tradition in which the life of the court is generally regarded as the epitome of the Active Life and the perfect exemplar of that life's major vices.

The maxim of Epicurus, that "The greatest fruit of self-sufficiency is freedom," [17] is borne out in Thomas Herrick's life; because his needs are few and modest, he is free from want:

> . . . for thy desires are   105
> Confin'd to live with private *Larr:*
> Not curious whether Appetite be fed,
> Or with the first, or second bread.

This passage in part explains how Thomas can be free from fear: ". . . thou liv'st fearlesse; and thy face ne'r shewes / Fortune when she comes, or goes" (lines 93–94). Behind the entire passage in which these and similar assertions are made (lines 93–128) lies an essentially Stoic and Epicurean conception of freedom as the absence of restraints. Here, however, restraints are viewed as mainly self-imposed, for they consist of those things which the individual requires to satisfy his own desires. Hence, if man limits his desires in accordance with the principle of "nothing in excess," it follows that he will have fewer requirements and more freedom. This is true moderation, not miserliness:

> Nor art thou so close-handed, but can'st spend
> (Counsell concurring with the end)   130
> As well as spare: still conning o'r this Theame,
> To shun the first, and last extreame.

The moderate man is the contemplative man, whether his contemplation is about philosophy or his finances.

Throughout "*A Country life*" Herrick uses the circle, the perfect geometrical figure, as an emblem of the perfect life. In lines 13–15, for example, "nature" and "Wisdome" were described as comprising the common axis of this circle or sphere. And, in the lines quoted just above, Thomas is described as wishing that this sphere, with the benign influences that it contains, could be extended to encompass the sphere of court life. A variation upon this

figure is employed in a passage which contrasts the active merchant sailing the perilous seas and the contemplative Thomas doing his "sailing" via his maps and charts: the latter is able to enjoy
the pleasures of travel without enduring its pains because, as Herrick punningly puts it, he is guided by his "Compasse," which is at
one and the same time the instrument for navigation and the self-
imposed limitations of his life. Later, Thomas is urged to imitate
the Stoic and "Stand Center-like, unmov'd" (line 101). And, toward the end of the passage in which Herrick pays tribute to his
brother's Stoic and Epicurean qualities, an agricultural image is
employed to reiterate the point that self-limitation is essential.
Thomas keeps his fences mended, literally—"Ordaining that [his]
small stock find no breach"—and figuratively—by being careful
not "to exceed [his] Tether's reach" (lines 133–34). His self-
imposed tether keeps him within his own, well-defined sphere.

Herrick's final reiteration of his circle-motif comes in lines
135–36, where Thomas is shown to know how "to live round, and
close, and wisely true / To [his] owne selfe; and knowne to few."
The phrasing recalls Polonius' parting address to Laertes, but
both the speaker and the situation are different. Though Herrick
spouts nearly as many aphorisms as Polonius, the poet who dominates this poem is no ridiculous old man but a sage whose thinking is guided by major philosophical doctrines of the Stoics and
Epicureans and an artist who is able to embody these doctrines
within his own version of a great literary tradition, that of pastoral. Though this poem lacks the tight construction and dramatic
development of some of his other longer poems, "*A Country life*"
is significant as the most thoroughgoing philosophical poem of
Hesperides and as evidence that the doctrines this volume contains are both coherent and viable, and capable of being embodied in a vision of the good life that is considerably more than
an idyllic fancy.

As is appropriate to a poem on the good life which is also a Neo-
Epicurean poem, "*A Country life*" concludes with the speaker's
contemplation of a good death in the form of a blessing which he
extends to both Thomas and his wife:

> And as there is one Love, one Faith, one Troth,
>   Be so one Death, one Grave to both.
> Till when, in such assurance live, ye may   145
>   Nor feare, or wish your dying day.

Securely united by married love, Thomas Herrick and his wife can
hope to be united still in death, for they have lived so well that
they can say with Epicurus, "Death . . . is nothing to us. . . ."[18]

Ostensibly, Herrick's own practice of his Neo-Stoic, Neo-Epicurean preaching is depicted in a short poem called "*His content in the Country.*" The title recalls a gnomic line from "*A Country life*"—"*Content makes all Ambrosia*"—if one is satisfied with
what he has, what he has is luxury. Thus, though Herrick is in
actuality not one of "the Lords of Wine and Oile," he and Prew,
his maid, find contentment in mere sufficiency:

> HERE, here I live with what my Board,
> Can with the smallest cost afford.
> Though ne'r so mean the Viands be,
> They well content my *Prew* and me.
> Or Pea, or Bean, or Wort, or Beet,   5
> What ever comes, content makes sweet.

Herrick's catalogue of common, garden-variety vegetables and
herbs (like the "Wort") not only illustrates the Epicurean principle of simplicity announced in the opening couplet but places this
pastoral poem in an English setting. Both this principle and this
setting, the poet suggests, are conducive to freedom:

> Here we rejoyce, because no Rent
> We pay for our poore Tenement:
> Wherein we rest, and never feare
> The Landlord, or the Usurer.   10

Being a country parson, Herrick doubtless resides in the parish
house, which would be rent-free. Having this advantage, he does
not lose sleep over "The Quarter-day," the day the rent comes
due. Coupled with this freedom is that from want:

> We eate our owne, and batten more,
> Because we feed on no mans score:
> But pitie those, whose flanks grow great,   15
> Swel'd with the Lard of others meat.

Self-sufficiency has social ramifications, for one is able to thrive
("batten more"), but not at the expense of others (a "score" is an
account of debts owed). That this freedom and independence are

conducive to virtue is graphically portrayed in the contrast between the character of the speaker and the caricature of the profi-
teer who grows increasingly stout as he devours the products of
other people's labors.

It is, however, the private rather than the public benefits of the
country life that, for Herrick, give it pre-eminence:

> We blesse our Fortunes, when we see
> Our own beloved privacie:
> And like our living, where w'are known
> To very few, or else to none.   20

Here again Herrick is speaking very much as the pastoralist for
whom a public life is the equivalent of an active life, and an active
life the equivalent of the pastoralist's anathema—the urban life.
On the other hand, the opportunities for privacy afforded by the
country life make it well suited for contemplation and for the attainment of peace of mind, contemplation's goal. The desirability,
which the last couplet of "*His content*" stresses, of anonymity is
likewise a concomitant of the pastoral tradition; for both in this
tradition and in prevailing English Renaissance thought, ambition
—the fierce desire for power and glory—was viewed as the vice of
all vices. For, as ambition drove individuals to seek high places,
only to be toppled from them by others no less ambitious, it could
bring ruinous disorder down upon the state.

Herrick tactfully alludes to this thesis in a pastoral which he
dedicates to an individual who has already attained a high office,
"*The Country Life, to the honoured* M. End. Porter. . . ." After
an opening passage reminiscent of his pastoral to his brother, in
which he contrasts the freedom of the "SWEET Country life" to the
bondage of "serving Courts, and Cities," and decries the active
man who plows "the Oceans foame" to bring back "rough Pepper"
and "the scorched Clove," Herrick directly addresses Endymion
Porter by saying, "No, thy Ambition's Master-piece / Flies no
thought higher then a fleece" (lines 11–12). The couplet is, of
course, metaphorical: while courtier Porter is obviously no mere
shepherd, if his aims are as modest as those of a shepherd there
need be no doubt about the quality of his life or about the stability and order of the state over which he exercises his measure of
control.

The remaining seventy-three lines of this ostensibly unfinished

poem comprise an idealized description of and panegyric to the
country life as Porter knows it. This description is given form and
unity through Herrick's device of developing it within the framework of a familiar rural ritual—the lord-of-the-manor's tour about
his grounds. This passage also happens to comprise a tour of a
number of Herrick's poetic techniques: he juxtaposes passages of
poetic realism, of versified *sententiae,* and of pastoral idyllicism
without the least sign of strain:

> There at the Plough thou find'st thy Teame,   25
> With a Hind whistling there to them:
> And cheer'st them up, by singing how
> The Kingdoms portion *is the Plow.*
> This done, then to th'enameld Meads
> Thou go'st; and as thy foot there treads,   30
> Thou seest a present God-like Power
> Imprinted in each Herbe and Flower.

The image of the "Hind" or rustic whistling to his horses as they
move along the furrows comes straight from observation of the
English countryside, and line 28, like line 39 of *"The Hock-cart,"*
reads like a familiar and proverbial expression of the importance
of agriculture to the state. But, "th'enameld Meads" is a pastoral
cliché, and the pantheistic strain of lines 30–32 can be traced back
in the bucolic tradition at least as far as Virgil's *Georgics.* Added
to these and other juxtapositions are lushly vivid descriptions of
grazing livestock; a catalogue of country holidays whose idyllicism, in the manner of *"The Wake,"* is qualified by the lament that
the rural folk are unable to perceive that theirs is a "happy life";
and another allusion to ambition in which the poet makes the
point that Porter is interested in trapping the small game of the
fields, not the big game of the court. Although Herrick marks this
poem as unfinished, its beautifully painted portrait of rural existence at its best is complete enough. And when this portrait is set
alongside those of his other "country life" poems, the reader of
Hesperides is able to perceive a fully rendered poetic vision of the
good life and, what is more, to understand how this life can be
attained and maintained.

Falling as they do between his "anti-Devonshire" poems and
such thoroughly conventional if charming pastorals as *"A Beucolick, or discourse of Neatherds,"* Herrick's "country-life" poems
can be seen to describe a harmonious middle state between dis-

agreeable reality and impossible ideality, a state that can accommodate the desires of all individuals at all social levels—peasant, parson, or lord—for the good life. Out of the stuff of English life and the spirit of the pastoral tradition the poet has shaped a "*Sacred Grove*," a rural world that approaches perfection to the extent that his Art, which for Herrick includes a system of ethical as well as esthetic principles, is able to ameliorate Nature (by which is meant "life in general").

This process of the improvement of existence through poetry is in operation throughout Herrick's *Hesperides*. To understand it is to have a sense of the direction that so many of his poems take and thus to comprehend one significant aspect of their over-all unity. Indeed, this process can be seen to operate even in that largest and most perplexing class of his poems, the epigrams.

IV   *The Rules of Life*

One of Herrick's editors, A. C. Pollard, found some of the poet's epigrams to be so unpalatable that, out of deference to his gentle readers, he relegated them to an appendix. Other editors, in compiling selected editions, have chosen to omit the epigrams almost entirely. And yet, according to L. C. Martin, "Herrick's own explanation [for the presence of the "ugly" epigrams amid the "beauties" of his book] would probably have been on the lines of his epigram on love: 'Love's of it self, too sweet; the best of all / Is, when loves hony has a dash of gall—' and the apparent disorder of the poems in *Hesperides* may well have been calculated, so that each poem might be a foil to its immediate neighbours." [19]

This hypothesis has been supported and expanded by Richard J. Ross, for whom Herrick's epigrams are deliberate demonstrations of the poet's adherence to the principle of "Art above Nature." [20] The gross epigrams, in Ross's view, are illustrations of human nature in the raw—unimproved by Art. Art, in this case, includes the art of right living, an art achieved by imposing the principles of "manners," "civility," and "vertue" upon social behavior. [21] This thesis can be illustrated by a group of epigrams on an apparently unromantic subject which, nevertheless, frequently appeared in seventeenth-century poetic catalogues of ladies' physical charms—teeth. For example, in an epigram with the lengthy title of "*Upon one who said she was alwayes young*," Herrick treats this particular subject with brutal frankness: "You say y'are young; but when your Teeth are told / To be but three, Blackey'd, wee'l thinke y'are old." Distasteful though it may appear, this poem is not merely ugly, nor is it merely low comedy. Herrick's humor has a satiric point. Taking the title into account as an organic part of the poem (something it is frequently necessary to do in order to read Herrick's poems well), it is apparent the persona is exposing a type of lie—or to put it more kindly, a sham—that women traditionally are inclined to perpetrate. Furthermore, he holds this representative of a class up to ridicule: to "tell" someone's teeth is to count them, as one would do with a horse, to determine age. And the very ugliness of the image of the three remaining teeth, each decayed and black at the center, makes the ridicule more devastating.

In this and in other epigrams in a similar vein, Herrick again shows his kinship with the Elizabethan formal verse satirists. Like them, he is concerned with reforming human nature; like them, he attempts to do so by holding human deficiencies up to ridicule—even if it requires the plainest kind of speaking, even if it calls for introducing the most realistic (or naturalistic) kinds of images, and even if it demands that he devote his attention to subjects that are apparently trivial—for, as one scholar has observed, "to the Neo-Stoic moralist nothing reprehensible was trivial." [22] Furthermore, human beings are such that they sometimes respond more readily to the trivial than to the significant: the lady addressed in the epigram above must have been more wary from that point on about perpetrating her little sham than if she had been lectured in verse about the beauty of truth.

Beauty, however, also finds its way into Herrick's epigrams; "*Upon* Lucie" is one example: "Sound Teeth has *Lucie*, pure as Pearl, and small, / With mellow Lips, and luscious there withall." Part of Lucie's attractiveness is due to the nature of her teeth, their "soundness," as well as to their appearance. Since appearance mirrors reality, and since the result is esthetically pleasing, Art is unnecessary. But, when reality fails even to approximate the ideal, Art, according to Herrick, must be employed to improve upon Nature:

> Close keep your lips, if that you meane
> To be accounted inside cleane:
> For if you cleave them, we shall see
> There in your teeth much Leprosie.

The discrepancy between this epigram, which is entitled—with almost painful explicitness—"*To women, to hide their teeth, if they be rotten or rusty*," and the epigram upon the three-toothed lady is more apparent than actual. In the latter, the lady is satirized for claiming to be what she is not; in the former Herrick is merely advising women to consider appearances, which are after all important when it comes to preserving the amenities of life. His concern is essentially esthetic; as an artist could scarcely be called a hypocrite because he paints an object the way he would like it to be, so ladies should not be blamed for attempting to improve upon nature. Indeed, Herrick is quite explicit about this in another epigram, "*Painting sometimes permitted*": "IF Nature do deny / Colours, let Art supply." It may be worth noting that the twentieth century, in which "painting" or the applying of cosmetics begins before puberty and ends only upon interment, has increasingly lent support to Herrick's principle.

The charge that Herrick's more naturalistic epigrams lack the very art about which he is so concerned has been leveled by J. Press, for whom these poems are "pointless and dull as well as dirty." [23] Yet even Press acknowledges that Herrick may have printed the epigrams "to display his unruffled acceptance of life as he had found it among the rude and churlish savages of Devonshire." [24] In this view Press is moving in the direction at least of Ross for whom the significance and, to an extent, the justification of these epigrams reside in their demonstration of Herrick's "ambivalence toward nature, relishing its proper 'wildness' yet deprecating its 'incivility.'" [25] Ugliness, whether manifested in human nature or in life in general, is an aspect of "wildness" which Herrick, like many an artist before him, not only refuses to ignore but is able to recognize as further evidence of the vital multiplicity of existence.

While understanding this conception will not necessarily make his naturalistic epigrams more palatable, it can help put them in perspective as complements of certain other epigrams that depict the ugliness of nature as a whole. Because the latter are general rather than specific and philosophical rather than satirical, they tend less to involve matters of taste and hence are more readily "acceptable" than the former. Yet no less than the naturalistic epigrams, these philosophical epigrams attempt, either explicitly or implicitly, to work certain "reforms"—if they are only reforms in

the attitudes with which man views those ugly aspects of existence that obstruct his attainment of the good life. Such a poem,
for example, is "*Sorrowes succeed*": "WHEN one is past, another
care we have, / *Thus woe succeeds a woe; as wave a wave.*" The
alliteration and parallelism of the second line are effective in communicating a sense of an infinite succession of waves beating dully
against a shore and in evoking, as a response to this impression, a
feeling of weariness and futility. But at the same time, the very
brevity of the epigram form, the simplicity of its utterance, and
the simile of the waves itself help to suggest that the persistence
of woe is natural as well as inevitable and must be accepted.
Thus, although the melancholy of this poem's tone and the grim-
ness of its point of view are to a degree unusual in *Hesperides*, its
implicit Stoicism is of course not.

More representative of the major moods of *Hesperides* is "*To
live Freely*": "LET's live in hast; use pleasures while we may: /
Co'd life return, 'twod never lose a day." This abbreviated version
of the principle of *carpe diem*, which is reiterated in other epigrams like "*An end decreed,*" "*To Youth,*" and "*To be merry,*" and
in longer poems like those discussed earlier in this chapter, is of
course a popular reduction of Neo-Epicureanism to a blithe Dio-
nysianism. But regardless of the brevity and oversimplicity of
their message, these verses too are poems of "the good life"—ones
which adhere to the precept of Jonson that, in addition to providing us with "Delight," "Poemes" must offer us "a certain rule, and
Patterne of living well, and happily; disposing us to all Civill
offices of Society." [26] The very fact, however, that these epigrams,
unlike the "country-life" poems, do not "dispose" us to any of the
"Civill offices of Society" is some warrant for regarding them with
less than complete seriousness. While they do reflect an aspect of
the poet's temperament that is not unattractive, they do not with
finality set the intellectual and emotional mold of his book. Herrick is too much of a realist to assume that unbridled sensuousness
alone is sufficient to sustain human life, even in the "*Sacred
Grove.*"

And, in point of fact, as he implicitly qualifies his *carpe diem*
poems by confronting his reader with more artistically and intellectually ambitious works like the "country-life" poems (and thus
inviting contrasts), so Herrick provides an antidote to his Dionysian epigrams in the form of certain sententious epigrams. Such a

one is the poem entitled, *"Vertue"*: "EACH must, in vertue, strive for to excell; / *That man lives twice, that lives the first life well.*" That Herrick includes this poem in his collection for its artistic merit is unlikely in view of the stumbling gait of its initial line; that he includes it for the originality of its thought is even less likely, for the same idea appears in *"A Country life"* and *"A Paranaeticall,"* as noted above, as well as in *"A good death"* and *"On himself"* [XIII]. The main function of *"Vertue"* must, therefore, be to reinforce a "rule of living well" that the poet deems important.

Herrick analyzes the relationship between pleasure and virtue in an epigram entitled *"Pleasures Pernicious"*: "WHERE Pleasures rule a Kingdome, never there / Is sober virtue, seen to move her sphere." In its contention that living well does not consist in the maximization of pleasure, this poem appears to refute the Epicurean principle, as does another of Herrick's sententious epigrams, *"Choose for the best"*: "GIVE house-roome to the best; *'Tis never known / Vertue and pleasure, both to dwell in one.*" The conflict between these two poems and the generally Neo-Epicurean outlook of *Hesperides* is more apparent than real: it is less likely that Herrick is contradicting himself than that, in these epigrams, he is using the word "pleasure" to connote merely sensuous enjoyment.

This interpretation is to some extent confirmed in the epigram *"Excesse,"* in which the poet strongly implies that to abandon oneself to anything like the Dionysian mode of living could not be virtuous because it would violate the principle that is as important to himself as it is to Epicurus—that of moderation: "EXCESSE is sluttish: keepe the meane; for why? / Vertue's clean Conclave is sobriety." In spite of the cumbersomeness of the first line, Herrick is able to draw an effectively odious comparison between Excess, who is pictured as a low, unclean, and likely immoral woman, and Virtue, whom he depicts as a modest matron, or even—given the Roman Catholic associations of "Conclave"—as a pensive nun, the epitome of sober, good women. Sobriety is of course that quality of temperament which allows nothing in excess, which keeps to the mean or middle way in all things. Keeping to the mean does not, however, in Herrick's view (nor in the views of Epicurus or Aristotle) mean straddling ethical fences or settling for mediocrity; rather, it involves seeking out that which is most beneficial— but most beneficial relative to the general order of things. Because man lives in the order of society and amid the order of nature, whatever is best for himself can never be that which is worst for someone or something else.

Moderation then is the essence of order and the first cause, as Herrick proclaims in *"The Meane"* [I], of harmony, which is the visible effect of order: "IMPARITIE *doth ever discord bring: | The Mean the Musique makes in every thing."* Thus, moderation is that which maintains the balance of universal nature. When that balance is disturbed, discord interpenetrates all life from matter itself to the very music of the spheres; the good life is no longer attainable; chaos is come again. Although Robert Herrick's *Hesperides* has in the past been sometimes regarded as chaos incarnate, it has become increasingly evident that this "chaos" is only apparent. For, shaped by his Neo-Classical poetic temperament and his Neo-Epicurean intellectual bent, his poems constitute a world which has an order and a harmony that are no more blatantly obvious but no less effectually real than the order and the harmony of the actual universe.

CHAPTER 4

"Cleanly-Wantonnesse" *and* This Sacred Grove: *The Theme of Love*

FOR some readers Robert Herrick's name is synonymous with love poetry, with pleasingly light lyrics celebrating a score of pretty girls (or one girl under a score of names), with poems that are amorous without intensity, cynical without seriousness, or idealistic without elevation. Herrick has been portrayed as the very model of the "Cavalier Poet," one who courts love (rather than women) and dallies with it in his verse, who is attracted by but never really involved in amorous passion.

This picture is not entirely a distorted one. Some of his love poems are, as John Press charges, "faintly unpleasant because his sensuality is lukewarm and adulterated with a self-conscious roguishness." [1] But to hold that Herrick is merely "one of those who, in Meredith's phrase, 'fiddle harmonics on the strings of sensualism,'" is to misconstrue his highly individual conception of love and, as Press elsewhere acknowledges, to misread some of his finer poems.[2] To dismiss Herrick so lightly is also to be reprehensibly unresponsive to the implications of his paradoxical claim in *"The Argument of his Book"* that he sings as poet "of cleanly-Wantonnesse." For this phrase, as is indicated below, is in effect a capsule summary of his love-ethic, one which follows logically from his Neo-Epicureanism, from the principle of moderation that is central to that philosophy, and from his fundamental esthetic. The truth implicit in the paradox, as Herrick dramatizes it in so many of his amatory verses, is that ideally love must accommodate both Nature, man's physical being and the demands that it "wantonly" makes, and Art, that human capacity and compulsion to refine and ameliorate Nature, to make it "cleanly." Love of this kind hews to the mean; it is therefore conducive to the attainment of a maximum of pleasure with a minimum of pain. It is a "wilde civility" sanctioned by esthetic and philosophical traditions and by human psychology.

I *The Rituals of Love*

Herrick's awareness of the analogies between the natural and human worlds and of their grounding in the potential "wildness" and "civility" of both manifests itself in the metaphors of many of his amatory poems. In the case of one of the most widely known of Herrick's shorter pieces, "*Upon* Julia's *Clothes*," these analogies are drawn with such subtlety and wit that they frequently go unnoticed. As a consequence, far more critical ink has been spilled in controversies about the interpretation of this poem than Herrick could ever have used in composing it.[3] The most convincing analysis, however, and the one to which the study that follows is most indebted, is that of a critic sensitive to Herrick's diction and to his use of parallels, Louis H. Leiter. For Leiter has demonstrated that the peculiar effectiveness of this poem may well result from its "submerged metaphor," one which operates beneath the surface of the poem but which determines its structure and texture and indeed transforms the commonplace event of the poem—that of watching a pretty girl stroll by—into a memorable experience.[4] The manner of Herrick's presentation is, apparently, simplicity itself:

> WHEN as in silks my *Julia* goes,
> Then, then (me thinks) how sweetly flowes
> That liquefaction of her clothes.

In her silks and fine array, Julia is first associated with the urban and the urbane (country girls would be wearing cotton or wool); the verbs "goes" and "flowes" suggest the smoothness and grace, not only of her garment, but of her manner of walking, one which a sophisticated woman would take some pains to cultivate. However, as the sound and sense of "flowes" converge upon the key word of the stanza, "liquefaction," the world of nature is subtly drawn into the poem. The movements of Julia's dress seem to convert her otherwise substantial silks into rivulets of shimmering water. The eye of the beholder has been fooled into witnessing a kind of miracle: Julia, as she goes by, appears to be moving in water.

The fact that water is the natural habitat of fish—as silks, apparently, are the natural habitat of Julia—provides Herrick with the basis for the expansion of his metaphor in the second stanza:

> Next, when I cast mine eyes and see
> That brave Vibration each way free;
> O how that glittering taketh me!

Like a fisherman casting his line, Julia's admirer "casts" his eyes in the direction of the "brave Vibration"—the movement of the lady's silks (and presumably of the lady herself) as she passes by. Since "brave" can connote "wild" as well as "splendid," the impression is reinforced that Julia, for all her art, is a natural creature moving freely in her element. And implicit in the persona's glance is the hope that this lovely creature will rise to the bait of his open admiration. In the next moment, however, a surprising and comic reversal takes place: the "fisherman" is paradoxically hooked by his quarry; rather than landing Julia, Julia has landed him—the angler has been angled. The word "glittering" which literally completes the description of Julia in her silks and figuratively completes the vehicle of the submerged metaphor, ultimately stands for beauty, the beauty that can, as it does here, give love its initial impetus.

Herrick's model for this poem may have been John Donne's "The Baite," which employs a similar metaphor to describe a similar experience, but in "*Upon* Julia's *Clothes*" the younger poet surpasses the older and greater one in the wit and compression with which he dramatizes one of love's paradoxes. The comparison, however, can not be taken too far; for Herrick's poem is about the early stage of love whereas Donne's is a more conventional "invitation to love," a poetic attempt at persuading a lady to consummate an amorous affair. Like many another poet of his age, Herrick tried his hand at this genre; but his "*To* Phillis *to love, and live with him*" is an invitation-to-love poem which is somewhat more ambitious than most. Through its extensive elaboration of the pastoral context that is conventional in works of this type, it becomes an invitation to participate—not only in love—but in a bucolic vision, the "*Sacred Grove*" of nature refined by art.

The invitation of this poem's first couplet, "Live, live with me, and thou shalt see / The pleasures Ile prepare for thee," is followed by a catalogue of idealized pastoral delights that recalls the less elaborate one of Christopher Marlowe's famous "Come live with me and be my love":

> What sweets the Country can afford
> Shall blesse thy Bed, and blesse thy Board.

The soft sweet Mosse shall be thy bed,   5
With crawling Woodbine over-spread:
By which the silver-shedding streames
Shall gently melt thee into dreames.
Thy clothing next, shall be a Gowne
Made of the Fleeces purest Downe.   10
The tongues of Kids shall be thy meate;
Their Milke thy drinke; and thou shalt eate
The Paste of Filberts for thy bread
With Cream of Cowslips buttered.

The pleasures listed are seductive in themselves, and are made
more so by Herrick's skilful manipulation of long vowel sounds,
but the effects achieved are so far more sensuous than sensual.
And implicit in this catalogue is the argument that Phillis, by ac-
cepting the invitation, will only be doing what is natural—she will
literally and figuratively get closer to nature when she allows nature to feed, clothe, and shelter her. In this way love becomes a
means to the good life.

In the good life as Herrick views it nature becomes servant to
man:

Thy Feasting-Tables shall be Hills   15
With *Daisies* spread, and *Daffadils;*
Where thou shalt sit, and *Red-brest* by,
For meat, shall give thee melody.

Here the pathetic fallacy, which is based upon the assumption
that nature has human qualities and is thus responsive to man, is
carried to its logical conclusion: all nature serves Phillis. This is
also a subtle form of flattery, and it is extended by the vow of her
shepherd-lover:

Ile give thee Chaines and Carkanets
Of *Primroses* and *Violets.*   20
A Bag and Bottle thou shalt have;
That richly wrought, and This as brave;
So that either shall expresse
The Wearer's no meane Shepheardesse.

The gradual elevation of Phillis's stature that the flattery has suggested is here made explicit: her conventional flower necklaces
will be supplemented by emblems which signify that she is ex-

alted by nature as well as by her lover. Her actual rank in the pastoral hierarchy is defined in lines 25–32: she will be the *genius* of each holiday, crystallizing in her presence its prevailing spirit as a queen embodies the spirit of a nation. And it is as "*Queen of Roses*" that she is ultimately depicted, a queen to whom her subjects will dutifully bring offerings from nature's treasury:

> In Wicker-baskets Maids shal bring 35
> To thee, (my dearest Shephardling)
> The blushing Apple, bashfull Peare,
> And shame-fac't Plum, (all simp'ring there).

The personification of these lines, as an extension of the pathetic fallacy, serves to reinforce the image of Phillis's majesty that, it is promised, will awe both nature and her human subjects.

With this fanciful excursion into pastoral hyperbole the first movement of the poem reaches its climax. Its crescendo of flattery may appear to be excessive, but Herrick has effectively built up to it by following the principles of poetic structure and of the psychology of persuasion. In her own imagination at least, Phillis sees herself as a queen, and thus flattered is presumably more receptive to talk of love, a subject her admirer has not yet directly mentioned. Still playing the role of the conventional pastoral swain (to gloss over his intent), he suggests that he has carved her name in trees by the grove and that, as he kisses these trees which—being "straight, and smooth-skin"—resemble Phillis herself, he hopes to "twice kisse" her. This is his first overt advance, and to show that his intentions are honorable and motivated by love, he vows:

> To thee a Sheep-hook I will send,
> Be-pranckt with Ribbands, to this end,
> This, this alluring Hook might be 45
> Lesse to catch a sheep, then me.

Phillis's lover has moved a step beyond the admirer of Julia: he *wants* to be "caught" by his lady.

At this point, as the invitation to love becomes more overt, the "*Sacred Grove*" begins to fade into the background; the poem moves indoors, away from the innocent delights of the countryside. Although Phillis is still the queen, she will hold court near the hearth rather than on the hills and her pleasures will become more sophisticated:

Thou shalt have Possets, Wassails fine,
Not made of Ale, but spiced Wine;
To make thy Maids and selfe free mirth,
All sitting neer the glitt'ring Hearth.   50

Such beverages are conducive not only to merry living, but to
love, as are the gifts next promised—"Ribbands, Roses, Rings, /
Gloves, Garters, Stockings, Shooes, and Strings / Of winning Colours." These are far more fashionable items than gowns of "purest
Downe" and more intimate; they are obviously things that an
urbane lady might wear to attract admirers. This fact the persona
acknowledges when he claims that these notions "shall move /
Others to Lust, but me to Love." The very juxtaposition of Love
and Lust recalls the phrase, "cleanly-*Wantonnesse*"; and, though
the shepherd lover protests against Lust, the reader is probably
justified in suspecting that he protests too much, that he is at least
motivated by both emotions. That this is the case is further suggested by the just perceptible note of urgency that sounds in the
poem's concluding couplet: "These (nay) and more, thine own
shal be, / If thou wilt love, and live with me." Thus a poem which
initially appears to be a readily predictable, highly idealized vision of love ultimately can be seen to function on one level as a
dramatization of a lover's state of mind and the tensions which
characterize it. Thus though it remains a song of seduction, it exemplifies the mediation that Herrick's poetry achieves between
the convention and reality, between Art and Nature.

Although Herrick demonstrates—in a poem entitled "*The Eye*"
—that he is no stranger to the mode of metaphysical love poetry
and that he can, in the manner of John Donne, ingeniously explore and exploit a conceit, he fares best when he is true to his
Neo-Classical artistic temper: when, to effect his artistic ends, he
relies mainly upon "design," the deliberate structuring of a poem;
"decorum," the development of a poem's characters, subject, and
setting within pre-established limits; and upon "imitation," the
shaping of a poem in accordance with, but with original variations
upon, Classical models. These qualities are well represented in a
poem with the cumbersome title of "*Mrs.* Eliz. Wheeler, *under the
name of the lost Shepardesse*," in which Herrick is concerned with
a later and more serious stage of love than those dramatized in the
two poems just considered.

The explicitness of the poem's title and the fact that Mistress

Wheeler was Herrick's married cousin suggest that the work is intended as a verse compliment, yet it effectively re-creates the emotions attendant upon a doomed love. Its opening, however, is conventional in its imitation of the traditional pastoral love complaint. The persona, apparently a forsaken shepherd, is engaged in a colloquy with the god of love, who in this case is the personification of the lover's own worst fears:

> AMONG the *Mirtles*, as I walkt,
> Love and my sighs thus intertalkt:
> Tell me, said I, in deep distresse,
> Where I may find my Shepardesse.

In the tradition of English pastoral poetry, love is usually depicted as an intrusive force since it tends to upset the idyllic equilibrium. By its very nature, love is the catalyst of extreme forms of behavior; and, since moderation, as noted in Chapter 3, is essential to order, such behavior imperils the integrity of the "*Sacred Grove*." Hence it is appropriate that love be depicted, as he is here, as a cruel deity; his speech to the persona is peremptory in tone and ominous in its implications:

> Thou foole, said Love, know'st thou not this?   5
> In every thing that's sweet, she is.
> In yond' *Carnation* goe and seek,
> There thou shalt find her lip and cheek:
> In that ennamel'd *Pansie* by,
> There thou shalt have her curious eye: 10
> In bloome of *Peach*, and *Roses* bud,
> There waves the Streamer of her blood.

On the surface, Love's speech is simply a catalogue of the lost shepherdess' beauties in floral terms; that an aim of these analogies is to call attention to her impermanence, as well as to her beauty, is pointed up only with the flickering image of "the Streamer of her blood."

The theme of human mortality and its frustrating and melancholic consequences for love is dramatized in the impulsive reaction of the shepherd-persona to the insight that Love has given him. Seeking to perpetuate Elizabeth's image, he plucks the flowers with the intention of making them into a wreath:

'Tis true, said I, and thereupon
I went to pluck them one by one,
To make of parts an union;   15
But on a sudden all were gone.
At which I stopt. . . .

In attempting to hold beauty fast, he has ironically lost it. In the withering of the flowers can be seen the way of this transient world: the blight of time is an irresistible force. As implacable as ever, the persona's realistic alter ego, personified as Love, explicates the lesson of this experience:

. . . Said Love, these be
The true resemblances of thee;
For as these flowers, thy joyes must die,
And in the turning of an eye;   20
And all thy hopes of her must wither,
Like those short sweets ere knit together.

The analogy of the flowers applies to the lover as well: his amorous hopes will be frustrated and he and his lady will never be "knit together." Although pastoral love complaints customarily end upon such a note, Herrick broadens and deepens the effects of this one by ringing in the theme of transiency through his metaphors; thus he links the form of the conventional love complaint with that of the traditional poetic complaint upon the brevity of human existence. The poem also suggests that, in Herrick's view, love, for all its powers, does not enable man, a creature of nature, to transcend nature's laws. Appearing and reappearing as a motif throughout *Hesperides*, this view lends a certain depth and seriousness to Herrick's amatory strain; for it serves to balance off to an extent the undoubtedly pleasant but lighter elements of that strain.

II *The Implications of Love*

Something of the rich variety of the amatory verse of *Hesperides* is indicated by the fact that in merely two pages of Herrick's book are juxtaposed a serious love poem, "*The Changes* to Corinna"; a fanciful lyric about an unhappy lover, "*Upon* Cupid" [III]; a highly sensual but at the same time humorously pedantic epigram, "*Upon* Julia's *breasts*"; a scurrilous epigram, "*No Lock against Letcherie*"; an epigram about physical beauty, "*Neglect*";

and a short poem on bachelorhood, "*Upon himselfe*" [I]. As this sampling suggests, Herrick's lighter verses on love, through the sheer weight of their numbers, can deflect attention from his more serious amatory poems. Yet the latter are usually the more ambitious efforts and frequently excel in poetic quality those casual, sensual verses with which Herrick's name is most frequently associated.

"*The Changes* to Corinna," for example, is so unrelievedly grim as hardly to pass for a love poem at all; but it is a perfectly structured, powerfully developed poem in the genre of admonitions to disdainful women. It is addressed to Corinna, who, it is suggested, in her pride has rejected the love of the speaker: "BE not proud, but now encline / Your soft eare to Discipline." "Discipline" is here to be understood as "instruction," for the speaker addresses Corinna in order to woo her by reminding her of her mortality. For the first stage of his instruction he has recourse to basic physics, drawing an implicit comparison between the flux of the four elements which compound her mortal body and the changes which occur in her mortal existence: "You have changes in your life, / Sometimes peace, and sometimes strife." The type of precarious and shifting balance that exists among earth, air, fire, and water characterizes her life, as it does the lives of all human beings. And this flux is reflected in her physical appearance, which changes with her health as tides change with the moon: "You have ebbes of face and flowes, / As your health or comes, or goes." Even Corinna's mental state has its cycles, for she experiences all the psychological highs and lows to which human minds and hearts are heirs: "You have hopes, and doubts and feares / Numberlesse, as are your haires." Finally, the very forces which animate her, the rhythm of her heart and her feelings—whose source the heart is—render her existence inevitably restless: "You have Pulses that doe beat / High, and passions lesse of heat."

That the "Discipline" which Corinna has been receiving has more than personal relevance is made clear in the second and final movement of the poem in which the speaker largely abandons figurative language in favor of directly addressing, first Corinna, then himself, and, finally, by implication, the reader:

> You are young, but must be old,
> And, to these, ye must be told,
> Time, ere long, will come and plow

> Loathed Furrowes in your brow:
> And the dimnesse of your eye   15
> Will no other thing imply,
> But you must die
> As well as I.

That the transiency of human existence is a hard but universal truth can be inferred from the statement of the final couplet, and that the speaker accepts it as such can be inferred from the very brevity and simplicity of that couplet's diction. The conclusion to be deduced from this truth—that love must be enjoyed while the opportunity and the means present themselves—is left unspoken, for it is given sufficiently eloquent if indirect expression in the image of the ugly, wrinkled brow and lacklustre eye which signal the end of youth, beauty, and love.

Basic to the invitation-to-love genre, of which *"The Changes to Corinna"* is a variation, is the principle of *carpe diem;* and basic to this principle is the assumption that love is a pleasurable means by which man can achieve fulfilment in his all-too-brief existence. Herrick accepts this assumption; and, even while he recognizes that love can maximize pain as well as pleasure, the dominant impression that his amatory poems evoke is that "cleanly-*Wantonnesse*" is life-affirming. This view is dramatized in highly Dionysian and sensual terms in a number of short poems like the following, *"To* Sappho":

> LET us now take time, and play,
> Love, and live here while we may;
> Drink rich wine; and make good cheer,
> While we have our being here:
> For, once dead, and laid i'th grave,   5
> No return from thence we have.

This poem, of course, is Herrick in his familiar Anacreontic vein; but, in spite of the frivolousness of the poem's first three lines, its last three have something of the irony and essential seriousness (if not the wit) of Andrew Marvell's "The Grave's a fine and private place, / But none, I think, do there embrace."

While it is only in his *"Corinna's going a Maying"* that Herrick equals Marvell's *"To his Coy Mistress,"* one of his more memorable variations upon the same theme is *"To the Virgins, to make much of Time."* Scholarly investigation has revealed that Herrick

is heavily indebted for this poem to a variety of sources, some
Classical, some English;[5] but his synthesizing is so artful that it
bears no marks of being a poetic pastiche. Not at all pedantic, this
lyric has been so popular that its opening line has become proverbial:

> 1. GATHER ye Rose-buds while ye may,
>   Old Time is still a flying:
>   And this same flower that smiles to day,
>   To morrow will be dying.

Neither the exhortation of the title nor the images of the first two
lines of this stanza have the effect of communicating an urgent
warning. Rose-buds are still beautiful, even if short-lived; and the
epithet, "Old Time," suggests a genial greybeard rather than a
grim reaper. Even the fact that this ancient is "a flying" makes
him more amusing than ominous. But the image of the flower
smiling and then dying begins to darken the mood with irony.
The second stanza of the poem intensifies this mood with an
image which suggests that transiency is inherent in the cosmos as
well as in nature:

> 2. The glorious Lamp of Heaven, the Sun,   5
>   The higher he's a getting;
>   The sooner will his Race be run,
>   And neerer he's to Setting.

The somewhat pompous poetic diction of line 5 serves to inflate
the seeming importance and power of the sun, but the deflation
(lines 7–8) is as rapid as his own descent. There is more irony if
less pathos in his fate than in that of the rose-buds: even as he
ascends in height and brilliance to his zenith, he draws ever closer
to the moment of his eventual decline.

The object lesson to be drawn for the virgins from these natural
phenomena is outlined in argumentative fashion in the two remaining stanzas. First, they are presented with a two-pronged
proposition:

> 3. That Age is best, which is the first,
>   When Youth and Blood are warmer;   10
>   But being spent, the worse, and worst
>   Times, still succeed the former.

Since human beings are subject to the natural law which declares that *"All things decay and die,"* youth, when by definition growth is still occurring and decay is minimal or nonexistent, must be the optimum time of life; and, since love is a function of life, it must also be the optimum time for love. The conclusion is self-evident:

> 4. Then be not coy, but use your time;
>   And while ye may, goe marry:
>   For having lost but once your prime,   15
>   You may for ever tarry.

Stanza III makes it clear enough that young girls are coy by custom rather than by inclination. Thus Herrick calls for revolt, pointing out that by their delaying tactics they lose their two most precious commodities, time and youth. Procrastination then is not only the thief of time but of life and love. Without the latter, the former can not be fulfilled.

Herrick reiterates these themes and more in a work which is fully as derivative as *"To the Virgins,"* but which is also generally regarded as his greatest poem, *"Corinna's going a Maying."* This poem has received more attention (and more acclaim) than anything else Robert Herrick ever wrote. The most comprehensive and perceptive critical study, and the one to which the re-examination which follows is considerably indebted, is still that of Cleanth Brooks in his essay, "What Does Poetry Communicate?" [6] As Brooks points out, "Corinna" is a "traditional" poem in the sense that its form and much of its content can readily be seen to have various precedents in poetry of the past. Indeed, so heavily informed by tradition is this work that it appears to be several poems in one: it is, for example, a love poem—in particular, a variation upon the "invitation-to-love"; furthermore, as is often the case with regard to this genre, it is also a pastoral poem, one which is predicated upon the existence of a certain sympathy between man and nature, which is informed by a certain tension between rural and urban life, and which is set against an idealized rustic background.

"Corinna" is also a "ceremonial" poem, for it not only celebrates the traditional holiday of May Day and the rites that appertain to it, but is also itself in some sense an actual part of those rites. And finally, Herrick's masterpiece is in some ways a "metaphysical" poem, a seriously witty, argumentative, dramatic, and ingenious

work characterized by a powerfully emotional and intellectual apprehension of the realities of life, love, and death. Unlike the
usual run of metaphysical poems, however, Herrick's work is carefully and formally structured. Its metrical scheme, for example, is
one of classic symmetry: each of its five fourteen-line stanzas
consists of seven couplets—the first, fourth, and seventh of which
are normally in iambic pentameter, with the second, third, fifth,
and sixth in iambic tetrameter. This distinctly formal and relatively complex pattern serves to contain and control the onrushing
tempo of the poem and the welling of its emotion (and in so
doing, to exemplify the intellectual and artistic "poise" that is so
characteristic of the majority of poems in *Hesperides*).

The deliberately dramatic quality of its texture is apparent in
"Corinna's *going a-Maying*" from the very start. The poem begins
with an exuberant and colloquial exhortation that is reminiscent
of the openings of such metaphysical love poems as Donne's "*The
Sunne Rising*" and "*The Canonization*":

> GET up, get up for shame, the Blooming Morne
> Upon her wings presents the god unshorne.
>> See how *Aurora* throwes her faire
>> Fresh-quilted colours through the aire:
>> Get up, sweet-Slug-a-bed, and see   5
>> The Dew-bespangling Herbe and Tree.
> Each Flower has wept, and bow'd toward the East,
> Above an houre since; yet you not drest,
>> Nay! not so much as out of bed?
>> When all the Birds have Mattens seyd,   10
>> And sung their thankfull Hymnes: 'tis sin,
>> Nay, profanation to keep in,
> When as a thousand Virgins on this day,
> Spring, sooner then the Lark, to fetch in May.

The originality of this stanza, like the originality of the entire
poem, resides in Herrick's unique blending of traditional elements. Juxtaposed, for example, with the dramatic realism of
"GET up, get up for shame," are the delicately idealized personification, "the Blooming Morne," and the mythic identification of
the sun with Apollo—the young god of the golden hair—whose
arrival the goddess-like morning announces by the spreading of
her wings. Here Herrick has done more than merely set the scene:
he has given an ordinary event, the advent of the day, a visionary

quality and endowed it with a beauty and vitality which make the event seem not only special but of almost transcendent importance. The world has a unique radiance, taking its color from the dawn's cosmic quilting and its glitter from dew-bejeweled nature.

Following the usual pattern of the invitation-to-love, Herrick, at this early stage in his poem's development, deliberately subdues its amatory strain. Nevertheless, hints of its existence are discernable in the easy familiarity and even intimacy with which the persona addresses Corinna and in the fact that the holiday which he is so urgently requiring her to celebrate is, with its origin in ancient fertility rites, one long associated with unbridled sensuality on the part of its celebrants. This association, however, Herrick to some extent qualifies by couching his images in nuptial terms. Nature, for example, is described as if she were Apollo's bride, bedecked with jewels but tremulous in anticipation. The very context of the poem then is conducive to love, but to love which, though natural, is neither licentiously immoral nor amoral; rather it is a love which, by implication, will be sanctified by ceremony. In addition to its other aspects then, Herrick's poem is a type of prothalamion, a poetic ritual that precedes Nature's "wedding" and, in a sense, Corinna's.

Thus, because she could be a key participant and because a wedding is, among other things, a religious event, Corinna has an obligation to attend. By staying in bed, she is guilty of a "sin," not so much against religion in the usual sense but against the "religion" of nature and thus against human nature. The sympathy between the natural and human worlds upon which this concept depends is illustrated in the actions of the birds, who have performed the human ritual of singing the morning hymn, and in the actions of the other maids, who have taken over the function of the larks as the harbingers of the day. Corinna then is being subtly and whimsically argued into arising on the grounds that she is being negligent in the performance of her proper duties. And though the tone which the persona takes with her is as yet far from solemn, words like "sin" and "profanation" carry with them intimations at least of the more serious overtones of the poem that emerge in its final stanza.

But in the first stanza and in the second, the persona's tone is predominantly playful. In order to spur Corinna into action, he promises her that her appearance will be rewarded:

Rise; and put on your Foliage, and be seene   15
To come forth, like the Spring-time, fresh and greene;
 And sweet as *Flora*. Take no care
 For Jewels for your Gowne, or Haire:
 Feare not; the leaves will strew
 Gemms in abundance upon you: 20
Besides, the childhood of the Day has kept
Against you come, some *Orient Pearls* unwept:
 Come, and receive them while the light
 Hangs on the Dew-locks of the night:
 And *Titan* on the Eastern hill   25
 Retires himselfe, or else stands still
Till you come forth. Wash, dresse, be briefe in praying:
Few Beads are best, when once we goe a Maying.

The sympathy between nature and human nature, at which the first stanza hints, is here dramatically exemplified by the persona in his portrait of Corinna herself: she is pictured not only as a creature of nature but as a living symbol of it. She is to be like Flora herself, a goddess of the spring, tricked out in the "Foliage" of her dress and in her brilliant pearls of the morning's dew. The images the persona weaves for Corinna are complimentary as well as vivid; and they culminate, in the concluding lines of the stanza, with the suggestion that she will be goddess-like in her beauty, a fit paramour for Apollo himself, who now waits as impatiently for her appearance as Nature waited for him.

The tension between orthodox religion and the religion of nature which has its covert beginnings in the first stanza and which is one of the continuing motifs of the poem emerges more clearly in the final couplet of Stanza II. Corinna is urged to get the everyday religious formalities over and done with in order that she may participate the sooner in a ritual which, it is openly suggested, is of greater pith and moment. On this day, her lover openly declares, the beads of nature's dew take precedence over the beads of the rosary, just as the morning hymns to God are eclipsed by the worship of the reigning gods of nature and the cosmos. Yet, as the third stanza indicates, orthodoxy is assimilated rather than discarded:

 Come, my *Corinna,* come; and comming, marke
 How each field turns a street; each street a Parke   30
  Made green, and trimm'd with trees: see how
  Devotion gives each House a Bough,

> Or Branch: Each Porch, each doore, ere this,
>   An Arke a Tabernacle is
> Made up of white-thorn neatly enterwove;   35
> As if here were those cooler shades of love.
>   Can such delights be in the street,
>   And open fields, and we not see't?
>   Come, we'll abroad; and let's obay
>   The Proclamation made for May: 40
> And sin no more, as we have done, by staying;
> But my *Corinna*, come, let's goe a Maying.

The metamorphosis of Corinna into Flora has become general: village and countryside both have undergone transformations; they have achieved, in effect, a synthesis in which, among other things, their respective patterns of religion have been blended. The countryside, as Brooks points out, has become a kind of church and the "village itself has become a grove, subject to the laws of nature." [7] Corinna then "is actually being reproached for being late to church—the church of nature." [8] By decorating the village with woodland greenery, the May Day celebrants have, on the surface at least, eliminated the distinctions between the natural and the human worlds and have symbolically effected a resolution of the tension between town and country. As befits a pastoral poem, this unique if temporary resolution is primarily but not wholly in favor of the country.

The May Day ritual, however, is only the means by which this end is achieved; it is love—or to put it in terms of the persona's argument, the acceptance of the dictates of nature—that is or should be the prime mover of all this activity. Even the village, having transcended its everyday mores, seems to extend an invitation to love; for each house, decorated as it is with boughs and flowers, resembles nature's own tabernacles—those cool arbors of the "*Sacred Grove*" where lovers can conveniently meet. To decline this invitation, the persona argues, is to violate that which the season, human nature and custom all proclaim.[9] And, since the fulfilment of love is sanctified by the season, by human nature, and by custom, to reject it is to commit a "sin."

With Stanza IV Corinna's lover returns to argument by analogy, but here the terms of the analogy are different from those employed in Stanza I; the rest of the human world, he points out, has joined with that of nature to celebrate the holiday:

> There's not a budding Boy, or Girle, this day,
> But is got up, and gone to bring in May.
> A deale of Youth, ere this, is come   45
> Back, and with *White-thorn* laden home.
> Some have dispatcht their Cakes and Creame,
> Before that we have left to dreame.

Like Corinna in her "Foliage," the young people too are creatures of nature—they are "budding" boys and girls. But, unlike her, they have been obedient to the dictates of the season, of their own natures, and of custom by bringing nature, in the form of buds and branches, into the village; more importantly, they have been performing love's preliminary rituals: "And some have wept, and woo'd, and plighted Troth / And chose their Priest, ere we can cast off sloth." Although the compression of this couplet creates an impression that these rituals are performed rather hastily and even perfunctorily, the very fact that the celebrants find it necessary to perform them suggests an awareness that love, however natural and thus rightful an impulse it may be, is merely "wanton" until it is "cleansed"—given order, meaning, and final sanctification—through ceremony.

The rituals of formal courtship have been preceded by amorous games so typical in all respects that, as viewed through the amused eyes of the persona, they too take on the aspects of rituals:

> Many a green-gown has been given;
> Many a kisse, both odde and even:
> Many a glance too has been sent
> From out the eye, Loves Firmament:
> Many a jest told of the Keyes betraying   55
> This night, and Locks pickt, yet w'are not a Maying.

Here Herrick has catalogued the whole range of dalliance, from rumors of physical consummation in the jests bandied about the company to circumstantial evidence of it in the grass-stained gowns of some of the girls. Yet the speaker's tone makes even the latter seem as innocent—as "cleanly-wanton"—as the flirtatious glancing and kissing. At the same time, however, as he becomes more explicit about his intentions, the note of urgency in the poem continues to rise to its culmination in the moving and dramatic final stanza:

> Come, let us goe, while we are in our prime;
> And take the harmlesse follie of the time.
>   We shall grow old apace, and die
>   Before we know our liberty.   60
>   Our life is short; and our dayes run
>   As fast away as do's the Sunne:
> And as a vapour, or a drop of raine
> Once lost, can ne'r be found againe:
>   So when or you or I are made   65
>   A fable, song, or fleeting shade;
>   All love, all liking, all delight
>   Lies drown'd with us in endlesse night.
> Then while time serves, and we are but decaying;
> Come, my *Corinna,* come, let's goe a Maying.   70

Structurally parodying the behavior of procrastinating Corinna, Herrick has skilfully delayed announcing his major theme until the climactic moment. By so doing he insures that the urgency and irony of *carpe diem* will be felt with maximum effect. But, even though the potential seriousness of the poem is here fully and finally realized, its vein of playfulness has not been entirely displaced. The seduction is still a kind of game, and the argument from *carpe diem* is a familiar gambit in such a game. They are part of the age-old ritual of love. Still, the very fact that the ritual is a time-honored one indicates its continuing relevance: because youth *is* fleeting and because the "liberty" of the body, mind, and sensibilities it affords is gradually impinged upon by age—love, which seems of such paramount importance is, in the long view, the philosophical view, a "harmless follie," something less perhaps than even "cleanly-*Wantonnesse*." It is natural, but what is natural is inevitably "lost" because it is subservient to nature's immutable laws, whose sentence is death. For some few lovers there is a kind of reprieve from this sentence if they are remembered in an enduring tale, a "fable"; for others, there is the still more transitory fame of a "song"; but most will only know an existence as "fleeting shade[s]" who, being denied all pleasure, all fulfilment, know only oblivion. The logic of the ritual leads inevitably to the conclusion that it does behoove youth to seize and master the day "while time serves"—before the inevitable reversal takes place and youth must begin to "serve" Time.

Taken out of context, Stanza V would appear to be grimly melancholic in tone, and its speaker would seem to be a bitter, beaten man. In context, however, this stanza has an undeniable vitality that is given depth and direction by its ironic cast. This irony, furthermore, serves to balance off the general exuberance of the poem and thus to make it abundantly clear that—while love is pleasurable and life-affirming, and as a consequence, important—it is not of transcendent importance because it offers no transcendence of time, death, or even pain. "Corinna's *going a Maying*" thus is still another poetic exemplar of the recurring *Hesperidean* motif that love is a means of easing, not resolving, the tension between existence and extinction.

III   *The Varieties of Love*

The poems analyzed thus far in this chapter may tend to create the impression that Herrick's amatory verse is concerned almost exclusively with love as a physical experience, as a means of affirming the sensuous values of life as they are realized and refined in accordance with certain forms of behavior. Yet Herrick's apprehension of love, or at the very least, his awareness of the several traditions of love poetry, enables him to range widely over the various aspects of the amatory experience beyond the merely physical. He can, for example, write in the spirit and manner of the Elizabethan versifiers who attempted to recapture in English the bittersweet apprehension of love that was Petrarch's. To their stock situations, images, and epithets, however, he brings his unique skill, which is capable of restoring dramatic and emotional intensity to such clichés as the disdainful fair and the doting lover. Such is the case with his lyric, "*The Teare sent to her* [Mrs. Dorothy Keneday] *from* Stanes." This poem is the second of a pair of love complaints, the first of which ("*His parting. . . .*") dramatizes the lover's bewilderment at the lady's coolness on the occasion of their recent parting. In "*The Teare*" he has come to recognize that he has been rejected, but the wit, the dialectic, and the emotional development of the poem transform what might otherwise be a conventional complaint into one that possesses the virtues of both the Neo-Petrarchan and the metaphysical amatory modes.

The poem takes the form of an apostrophe, with the speaker addressing, presumably, the Thames (on whose bank Stanes is situated):

1. GLIDE gentle streams, and beare
   Along with you my teare
   To that coy Girle;
   Who smiles, yet slayes
   Me with delayes;   5
   And strings my tears as Pearle.

The situation is ripe for sentimentality: the lover weeps, a tear falls into the stream, and he begs the current to carry it to his beloved. Herrick's wit, however, expressed in the image of the lady treasuring the tears as if they were pearls and going so far as to make a necklace of them, enables him effectively to skirt mere sentimentality. On the contrary, the lady is tersely anatomized as a cruel tease who takes pleasure in his suffering and egoistically regards it as evidence of her amorous power. She wears his sorrow like a necklace whose beauty enhances her own.

The next stanza points her out: she is nearby making another "Carkanet" or necklace, this time of "Maiden-flowers"—an ironic touch, since she shows none of the modesty and kindness generally associated with young maids. Her lover once again requests the stream to bear his tear, "This Orient, / and Pendant Pearle," to her, with, in Stanza III, this further instruction:

3. Then say, I've sent one more
   Jem to enrich her store;
   And that is all   15
   Which I can send,
   Or vainly spend,
   For tears no more will fall.

Herrick's use of such terms as "enrich," "store," and "spend" follows from the simile of tears as pearls, but it also serves to impute a kind of amatory mercantilism to the lady. Like a ruthless merchant, she has driven her lover into emotional bankruptcy; he has no more of the currency of sorrow to send to her. This submerged metaphor provides the imagistic base for the remainder of the poem: in Stanza IV the lover refuses to seek out a new "supply" of tears, for now he can only attempt to save their sources, his eyes. And if, he continues in Stanza V, she should demand that he "surrender" these, if she should require him still to concentrate only upon her,

> . . . my part
> Must be to weep
> Out them, to keep
> A poore, yet loving heart.   30

He must weep himself blind in order to preserve his heart; for, if he were to "give" her his eyes (through which beauty, the catalyst and continuing impulse of love, is perceived), his heart and thus his life would go with them.

But at this climactic moment, the lover suddenly reverses his decision:

> 6. Say too, She wo'd have this;
>   She shall: Then my hope is,
>   That when I'm poore
>   And nothing have
>   To send, or save;   35
>   I'm sure she'll ask no more.

If he lets her have eyes, heart, all, he will be completely bankrupt; she will be able to make no more demands upon him. The irony of this hypothesis reflects the lover's increasing bitterness and gives an even sharper edge to his implicit rebuke of the lady herself. The "coy Girle" of Stanza I has become a callous trader in human misery; as a result, her onetime lover has been transformed into a hollow man, bereft almost entirely of the emotions which earlier had animated him. Such development of emotion, character, and situation is only infrequently encountered in the tradition of the love complaint; but Herrick is able to invest the form with an aura of the dramatic that is often conspicuously absent in the amatory verses of the Neo-Petrarchans.

Herrick's special skill at revivifying—and occasionally even re-shaping—familiar poetic genres is much in evidence when he elects to play the role of the "Cavalier Poet"—one of those Royal-ist gentlemen of the earlier seventeenth century like Suckling, Carew, or Lovelace who wrote with ease and sometimes with cyn-icism about love and women. Because of Herrick's artistic kinship with such poets, who were, like himself, "Sons of Ben," and be-cause he shares their tendency to write amatory poems in the tra-dition of Ovid, Catullus, and Propertius, Herrick is sometimes re-garded as purely and simply a "Cavalier Poet." But, like most of Herrick's other popular tags, this one errs on the side of oversim-

plification. By his very range, his not infrequent complexity and
seriousness, and his extraordinary craftsmanship he is set apart
from and above Jonson's other poetic "sons." Yet when he chooses
to do so, Herrick can write verse that is as cynical as Suckling's
(see, for example, *"Upon some women"* and *"No fault in
women"*), as sensual as Carew's (see *"Upon* Julia's *unlacing her
self"*), or as romantic as Lovelace's. Lovelace's lyric *"To Amarantha, that she would dishevel her Hair,"* for example, has its
parallel in Herrick's *"Upon* Julia's *haire, bundled up in a golden
net."* The poem itself depicts the persona's reaction to the subject
imaged in the title; his response takes the form of a playful argument addressed to Julia that is one part the rhetoric, and one part
the esthetics, of love. Thus the accusation with which the poem
opens is also a compliment:

> TELL me, what needs those rich deceits,
> These golden Toyles, and Trammel-nets,
> To take thine haires when they are knowne
> Already tame, and all thine owne?

That the lady does not require a wig is a left-handed but deliberately humorous compliment. In the same vein is the implied accusation that she is guilty of excess: the golden net is not needed to
keep her coiffure in place because her hair is beautifully trained.
In addition to setting the poem's tone, these lines, in their implied
opposition of the natural and the artificial, the wild and the tame,
and the free and the enslaved, and in their submerged metaphor
of the hunter and the hunted, provide the bases for the wit and
the tension of the rest of the poem.

By way of answering his own question, the persona claims:
" 'Tis I am wild, and more then haires / Deserve these Mashes and
those snares." "Wild" can suggest the extent of his passion for
Julia, but it also implies "free," "not entrapped." Deliberately ambiguous too is "Deserve," which permits the clause to be interpreted in two ways: either the persona is a wild creature (note
the pun on "haires") who should be caught up in Julia's net and
thus tamed, or he is a free spirit who actually desires to be thus
entrapped and enslaved. These interpretations are not incompati-
ble: the persona recognizes that he should succumb to Julia's
charms and, furthermore, that he wants to. This being the case,

the conclusion of the argument is foregone: Julia should liberate
her hair and incarcerate her admirer:

> Set free thy Tresses, let them flow
> As aires doe breathe, or winds doe blow:
> And let such curious Net-works be
> Lesse set for them, then spred for me.   10

In esthetic terms this is a plea for naturalness, but a naturalness
that is qualified by art—Julia's hair, it should be remembered, has
already been trained. In amatory terms the plea implies that love
has at least one of its sources in esthetics: in this case, the beauty
of Julia.

Though neither Herrick's poem nor Lovelace's is at all original
in its subject, images, or central idea, Herrick's is considerably
more witty, far more compressed, and clearly more artfully structured. *"To Amarantha"* is a pleasant, typically Cavalier work; but
"Upon Julia's *haire"* is Cavalier verging upon the metaphysical—
in its ingenuity, if not in its profundity. As the latter poem is implicitly expressive of the esthetics of "cleanly-*Wantonnesse*," so an
equally ingenious and even more successful amatory piece, "Julia's
Petticoat," dramatizes Herrick's paradox in humorously semireligious terms. While the object identified in the poem's title is in
itself Cavalierly trivial, it is to be the central image of the entire
work and one that is elevated to a conceit and ultimately to a
symbol through the play of Herrick's wit and imagination. This
process begins almost at once, as the persona, addressing Julia,
launches into a heightened description of her petticoat:

> THY Azure Robe, I did behold,
> As ayrie as the leaves of gold;
> Which erring here, and wandring there,
> Pleas'd with transgression ev'ry where.

The image under development here is one of Herrick's most vivid:
Julia's blue and gold petticoat resembles an autumn sky seen
through a shower of autumn leaves and it drifts with the lightness
of leaves and sky. Its texture is suggested by the alliteration of
"Azure," "ayrie," and "erring." Herrick also plays upon the similar-
ity in the sounds of "ayrie" and "erring" to suggest the garment's
graceful motions as Julia walks and, at the same time, to imply

that this display of her petticoat is rather daring. Both of these implications are embodied in the noun "transgression," which denotes in its Latin sense, movement, and in its English sense, a violation. Here, since the transgression is "pleasing," sin is not imputed; but a sensuality that just borders on the sinful is. This sensuality in fact receives the emphasis in the succeeding four lines:

> Sometimes 'two'd pant, and sigh, and heave,   5
> As if to stir it scarce had leave:
> But having got it; thereupon,
> 'Two'd make a brave expansion.

On the literal level Herrick is merely describing the billowings and contractions of the petticoat as it stirs in the breeze, yet his choice of verbs serves as a reminder that lovers also are wont to "pant, and sigh, and heave" while in the grips of their emotions. And if lovers are allowed to have their way (given "leave"—which is also a play upon "leaves" of line 2), their passion can swell to a climax, "make a brave [wild, beautiful] expansion."

Herrick prevents his poem from rising, at this point, to a climax of sexuality by shifting the level of his imagery in lines 9–10: "And pounc't with Stars, it shew'd to me / Like a *Celestiall Canopie*." Here the poet reverts to the celestial image of the poem's opening lines—with this difference: the petticoat, with its gold on blue, is now compared to the sky at night. Night is, of course, the time for lovers, so the amatory vein remains intact; but the petticoat now appears to be *"Celestiall,"* which bears heavenly and spiritual rather than earthly and sensual connotations.

To complement the simile of the night sky and the submerged metaphor of the lovers' emotions, Herrick inserts still another simile:

> Sometimes 'two'd blaze, and then abate,
> Like to a flame growne moderate:
> Sometimes away t'wo'd wildly fling;
> Then to thy thighs so closely cling,
> That some conceit did melt me downe,   15
> As Lovers fall into a swoone.

As it is alternately revealed and concealed by her movements, Julia's petticoat resembles the stars in their flickerings as well as in their luminosity. And, as light is also associated with heat, her garment resembles a flickering flame—which in turn suggests the cyclical emotions of the typical lover. Julia's admirer, with the hyperbole common to such a lover, swears that the heat of her inflammatory petticoat, combined with its light, which both reveals and conceals her body, and with his feverish and over-wrought imagination ("some conceit"), is enough to overpower him. And, since he has reached the point where the sight has become too much for him to stand, he falls. But his "swoone" is brought on as much by sensuality as by sentiment: "And all confus'd, I there did lie / Drown'd in Delights; but co'd not die." Though Julia's lover is prostate with love, he is not prone to die—in the literal sense, at least. For here again Herrick is making a play on words, using "die" to mean both "expire" and "achieve a sexual climax."

The effect of the poet's wordplay, however, is, as it was earlier, to keep the poem's vein of sexuality submerged; thus his return, in the work's final movement, to his pattern of "celestial" imagery (with its more elevated connotations) is accomplished with no sense of strain:

> That Leading Cloud, I follow'd still,
> Hoping t'ave seene of it my fill;   20
> But ah! I co'd not: sho'd it move
> To Life Eternal, I co'd love.

"That Leading Cloud" is still, on the literal level, Julia's petticoat, which Julia's admirer continues to follow and eye; but it has also become identified with the "pillar of a cloud" in which the Lord led the Israelites out of Egypt (Exodus xiii.21). This identification of the sensual with the awesomely spiritual is shocking, outrageous, comic, and significant; and it is complemented by a parallel identification in the final couplet in which the persona becomes a second Moses. In this role, the incongruities of which lend further comedy to the climax, he maintains that even if Julia's petticoat—which by now has come to symbolize the divine Julia herself—should be the death of him ("move / To Life Eternal") before he reaches the Promised Land of her love (as Moses died before attaining Gilead), his passion will neither alter nor abate. His love is like that of all lovers, "undying." All of Herrick's art, however, has been mustered to point up the possibilities for discrepancies between such ideals and the reality, between amatory posturings

and actualities, and between lofty affirmations and more fundamental motivations—like simple lust. But though the reader may
be disinclined to take very seriously the ideal aspect of the persona's love, Herrick's very juxtaposition of the sensual and the
spiritual, even in a poem that is far from solemn, suggests his
awareness of the demands which both impose—and which can be
satisfied by adherence to the principle of "cleanly-*Wantonnesse.*"

Specific applications of this principle to human behavior are
made most directly in certain didactic epigrams. What also
emerges from these poems is that, for Herrick, the assumption
that dictates this principle is his fundamental one of the need for
achieving a mean in all aspects of life. From both assumption and
principle, it follows that merely physical love, the kind celebrated
in so much Cavalier verse, and strictly spiritual love, as hymned
by so many of the Neo-Petrarchan poets, are both, in their respective ways, excessive and incomplete. The *via media* then is the
only way in love as well as in life, as the proverbial *"Love me
little, love me long"* makes plain:

> You say, to me-wards your affection's strong;
> Pray love me little, so you love me long.
> Slowly goes farre: The meane is best: Desire
> Grown violent, do's either die, or tire.

Though it is stated here rather gracelessly (but not without
humor), this thesis—as the epigram, *"Moderation"* [II], proclaims—is grounded in fundamental if simplistic human psychology: "Let moderation on thy passions waite / Who loves too
much, too much the lov'd will hate." The best short summary of
Herrick's amatory Neo-Epicureanism is contained in a sententious
passage from a poem called "Connubii Flores," in which a chorus
of old men give a bridal couple some sage advice:

> Love is a thing most nice; and must be fed   20
> To such a height; but never surfeited.
> What is beyond the mean is ever ill:
> *'Tis best to feed Love; but not over-fill:*
> Go then discreetly to the Bed of pleasure;
> And this remember, *Vertue keepes the measure.*

Polonius can easily be imagined giving out the same sort of advice. But Polonius is not a complete fool nor is Robert Herrick.

Both are, in many ways, realists; and Herrick, although he is sometimes regarded as a libertine poet, is realist enough to recognize that it is married love that offers the most favorable opportunities for maximizing the pleasure while minimizing the pain of love. Thus it is no coincidence that the theme expressed in the lines quoted above strikes its dominant note in a marriage-poem. Variations upon it reappear in Herrick's epithalamia or post-nuptial poems. These are works which, by virtue of their scope and art, lend a special emphasis to the amatory vein of his *Hesperides*.

IV   *The Ideal of Love*

One memorable passage of John Milton's *Paradise Lost* (IV.750–52) begins:

> Hail wedded Love, mysterious Law, true source
> Of human offspring, sole propriety
> In Paradise of all things common else.

Almost twenty years before these lines were printed, Robert Herrick had anticipated them in *"An Epithalamie to Sir* Thomas Southwell *and his Ladie"* and in *"A Nuptiall Song, or Epithalamie, on Sir* Clipseby Crew *and his Lady."* These two poems can with some justice be regarded as qualifying and, in a sense, as culminating the hundreds of love poems of his collection. They are that collection's longest and, in some ways, its most ambitious works, even though both are occasional poems written to celebrate actual weddings. Still, like the majority of Herrick's other love poems, they are grounded in the principle of "cleanly-*Wantonnesse*."

As is the case with most of the poetic forms with which Herrick chooses to work, the epithalamium has a long literary history. *"The Song of Solomon"* is one of the earliest and best-known examples of the form; another is *Carmina* LXI of Catullus, *"The Nuptials of Julia and Manlius."* There can be little doubt that Herrick was aware of both poems, and that he had also read Edmund Spenser's *"Epithalamium"* and *"Prothalamium,"* as well as Ben Jonson's masque, *Hymenaei*, which includes an epithalamium. Like most epithalamia, Herrick's are lyric sequences composed of semidependent stanzas. In *"A Nuptiall Song"* the form of the stanzas themselves is unusual: each consists of a heroic couplet, a tetrameter couplet, and then a single dimeter line rhyming with a single

pentameter line; here a full stop usually halts the stanza before it
moves on into a pattern consisting of a single tetrameter line
rhymed with a single pentameter line, and finally, a single trime-
ter line rhyming with a single tetrameter line. The apparent irreg-
ularity in the meters of the paired lines lends a sense of nervousness, spontaneity, and excitement to the poem; but this air of agi-
tation is tempered and controlled by the linking rhymes and by
the very repetition of this consistently irregular pattern in every
stanza of the poem. Thus, on the grounds of prosody alone "A
Nuptiall Song" strikingly exhibits the unity in variety, the "orderly
disorder," for which Herrick continually strives in his art.

To a somewhat lesser degree "An Epithalamie" possesses the
same quality, but in neither poem is it realized through prosody
alone; for both also exhibit a fundamental unity of structure that
is based upon the very event they dramatize—the post-nuptial
rites in all of their stages. Herrick further unifies his poems by
centering these rites upon the actions and reactions of the bride
and by filtering his description through a persona who is both an
observer of and a participant in the ceremonies. Finally, the poet
carefully integrates his images and symbols to create patterns
which lend a high degree of consistency to the textures of both
poems. Although these qualities are, as suggested, characteristic
of both epithalamia, limitations of space make it necessary to
demonstrate their presence in "A Nuptiall Song" only, which is by
a small margin the finer of these two magnificent poems.

The epithalamium opens as the persona, peering off into the
distance, sights the approaching bride. But, he asks, is this truly
the bride or are we being blessed with a vision?

1. WHAT'S that we see from far? the spring of Day
Bloom'd from the East, or faire Injewel'd May
　　　Blowne out of April; or some New—
　　　Star fill'd with glory to our view,
　　　　　　　Reaching at heaven,　　　　　　　5
To adde a nobler Planet to the seven?
　　　Say, or doe we not descrie
Some Goddesse, in a cloud of Tiffanie
　　　　　　To move, or rather the
　　　Emergent *Venus* from the Sea?　　　　　10

In reply to his own question, the persona has posited a whole
series of alternative answers which are also compliments to the

bride and which are advanced in order of increasing importance: she is implicitly likened to the fresh dawn of a new day; to the springtime month of May, the harbinger of a new season; to a heavenly body adding new luster to the cosmos; and, since the planets are named after the gods and this is a love-ritual, to Venus herself, the goddess of love and beauty.

The second stanza answers the first. The bride is closer now, so the persona is able to affirm:

> 2. 'Tis she! 'tis she! or else some more Divine
> Enlightened substance; mark how from the Shrine
> Of holy Saints she paces on,
> Treading upon *Vermilion*
> And *Amber;* Spice-   15
> ing the Chafte Aire with fumes of Paradise.
> Then come on, come on, and yeeld
> A savour like unto a blessed field,
> When the bedabled Morne
> Washes the golden eares of corne.   20

Coming as she does from the temple, the bride looks all the more like a goddess; but her divine aura is evoked more with olfactory than with visual images. Her approach is heralded by a rich fragrance wafted in by the breeze; and, as if to suggest both her divine and human qualities, this scent is a combination of the exotic aromas of rare and precious spices and of the more familiar but no less pleasing aromas of a field of waving grain. The sensuousness of these images serves to create the proper mood for the modulation of the poem into the sensuality of the third stanza:

> 3. See where she comes; and smell how all the street
> Breathes Vine-yards and Pomgranats: O how sweet!
> As a fir'd Altar, is each stone,
> Perspiring pounded Cynamon.
> The Phenix nest,   25
> Built up of odours, burneth in her breast.
> Who therein wo'd not consume
> His soule to Ash-heaps in that rich perfume?
> Bestroaking Fate the while
> He burnes to Embers on the Pile.   30

The bridal procession has now reached the city proper; as the bride treads the street, each paving block becomes an altar from

which the warm incense of her fragrance rises. This, of course, is
sheer hyperbole, but so carefully has Herrick built his mood up to
this pitch that the exaggeration does not appear comic. Exaggerated too is the development of the conceit of the Phoenix in lines
25–30, but Herrick's exaggeration is accomplished with the kind
of wit that Donne exhibits in his reference to this mythical bird in
"*The Canonization.*" The bride is enveloped in fragrance because
the nest of the Phoenix, which is regenerated periodically on the
pyre of that nest, "burneth in her breast." The nest is "built up of
odours" arising from the sweetness of her presence, and these
vapors are ignited like incense by the warmth of her emotions.
She is her own altar to which any flesh-and-blood man would
bring himself as a sacrifice and consider himself blessed as he is
wholly consumed.

Although Herrick has by this point gradually intensified the
mood of his poem from sensuousness to something akin to pure
"*Wantonnesse,*" no hint of immorality is present; indeed, the persona, who is about to combine his role of observer with that of
priest, calls upon the god of marriage to sanctify the occasion by
his presence:

> 4. *Himen, O Himen!* Tread the sacred ground;
> Shew thy white feet, and head with Marjoram crown'd:
> Mount up thy flames, and let thy Torch
> Display the Bridegroom in the porch,
> In his desires   35
> More towring, more disparkling then thy fires:
> Shew her how his eyes do turne
> And roule about, and in their motions burne
> Their balls to Cindars: haste,
> Or else to ashes he will waste.   40

Here again a pattern of imagery developed in one stanza provides
continuity with another: Hymen is emblematically represented as
bearing a torch which might well have been ignited by the flames
of passion that play about the third stanza. Since it lends both
light and heat, the torch fittingly serves to symbolize the act of
marriage while literally it illuminates the anxious bridegroom,
who—as the persona, with lurid humor, suggests—is himself a
torch, consumed by the heat of his desire.

Speaking directly to the bride (she is now, presumably, within
hailing distance), the persona-priest jokingly urges her to hurry

before her groom, whose heat matches hers, burns to ashes. The joking has the effect of lowering the temperature of the mood, a deliberate move on Herrick's part, for he is at this point far from ready to bring the poem to its climax. The bride has just drawn nigh her future home, so the poet turns the attention back to her and to the crowd that has gathered to observe her. To describe her progress he reverts again to nature imagery: passing through the crowd she is like a gentle stream, gliding through "banks" of young girls who line her path and strew it with "Shewers of Roses" and four-leaf clovers, while up above—presumably on a balcony—a chorus of children, looking like a cloud in their white vestments, sings the exultant nuptial songs (lines 41–44). The older members of the crowd praise and bless the bride and call out homilies like *"Blest is the Bride, on whom the Sun doth shine."* Others, in an amusing if somewhat unromantic extension of the stream metaphor, "wish / You multiply, as doth a Fish" (lines 49–50). Though this simile is laughable in its crudity, it embodies a significant truth to which Herrick obliquely alludes in the next stanza and which he ultimately makes the climactic theme of the epithalamium.

In his role as Love's priest, the persona next reminds the lady that, while it is customary for brides to blush, to be hesitant about taking the step that confronts them, such delaying tactics can be overdone:

> What now you seem, be not the same indeed,
>   And turne *Apostate*: Love will
> Part of the way be met; or sit stone-still.   58

Her show of reluctance must not become an actuality; for, if it should, she would become a defector from the religion of love. If the homily of the fish in the previous stanza is recalled, the consequences of such a defection can be seen to be potentially serious.

But at this point in the poem, as the bride actually crosses the threshold of her new home, Herrick contrives to alter the mood once more. He has his persona-priest cease his half-serious, half-comic exhortations and try to put the bride at ease by humorously pointing out the actions and expressions of the collected servants: the "Codled" or parboiled cook has run from his steaming kitchen, his *"Torrid Zone,"* to witness the great event; the older servants, who perhaps have been with the family for generations have

come to view their latest mistress; and "the smirk Butler," that
imposing functionary, condescends to make some witticisms.
Each of them, by his expressions and gestures, seeks to catch his
new mistress's eye.

But the bride doubtless has eyes only for her groom, with whom
she has at last been reunited. Now the persona addresses both of
them:

> 8. To bed, to bed, kind Turtles, now, and write
> This the short'st day, and this the longest night;
> But yet too short for you: 'tis we,
> Who count this night as long as three,
> Lying alone,   75
> Telling the Clock strike Ten, Eleven, Twelve, One.
> Quickly, quickly, then prepare
> And let the Young-men and the Bride-maids share
> Your Garters; and their joynts
> Encircle with the Bride-grooms Points.   80

Although he plays wittily upon the paradox of the relativity of
time, which can seem short on some occasions and long on others,
a note of poignancy creeps into the persona's speech as he contrasts the night to be enjoyed by the newlyweds with that which
he and other solitary souls will spend—"Lying alone," wearily and
sleeplessly hearing the chimes mark the passage of time. But he
soon recovers from his momentary attack of melancholy to urge
the pair to complete the public aspect of the ceremony by distrib-
uting small items of their wedding costumes such as garters and
"Points" (laces) for souvenirs. Furthermore, he warns them, in
Stanza IX, to allow no animosity to creep into the scramble for
these prizes lest conflicts between the bride's friends and the
groom's divide the just-united pair.

In Stanza X the next stage of the ritual, the preparation of the
bride for bed, is under way. And once more Herrick reverts to
nature imagery to lend vividness and meaning to the moment;
addressing the bride's attendants, the persona says:

> 10. Strip her of Spring-time, tender-whimpring-maids,
> Now *Autumne's* come, when all those flowrie aids
> Of her Delayes must end; Dispose
> That *Lady-smock,* that *Pansie,* and that *Rose*
> Neatly apart;   95

> But for *Prick-madam,* and for *Gentle-heart;*
> And soft-*Maidens-blush,* the Bride
> Makes holy these, all others lay aside:
> Then strip her, or unto her
> Let him come, who dares undo her.   100

Bedecked in all her flowers the bride (like Corinna) resembles Flora, the goddess of the spring. But spring is the time of raw youth and the bride, being newly married, must take on a new maturity, as is suggested in the phrase, "Now *Autumne's* come." Her "green season" must now give way to her gold.

In Stanza XI the romance of this moment is heightened with the introduction of background music—music that is imagined as coming from the spheres (a sign of the bride's innocence and goodness, for only such persons could hear the cosmic notes), and from a heavenly chorus (which suggests the sanctity of the occasion). Music, of course, can both soothe and heighten the emotions. That this music, which helps sanctify the event, also generates warmth is suggested by the second verb of lines 105–6: "O marke yee how / The soule of Nature melts in numbers [notes] . . . ." The aura of romance and the sense of increasing passion are summarized in the conceit that closes the stanza, one which takes its cue from the images of light and heat of the earlier stanzas:

> See, a thousand *Cupids* flye,
> To light their Tapers at the Brides bright eye.
> To bed; or her they'l tire,
> Were she an Element of fire.   110

Symbolizing the natural course of human affection, the gods of love become gods of marriage, each bearing a hymeneal torch kindled by the passions of the bride as they are revealed in the brightness of her eyes.

By way of leading up to the sensual and romantic climax of his poem, Herrick next focuses attention upon the marriage bed, which is described in images that closely parallel the nature images of Stanza V: it is compared to a cloud, to a swan, and to the stream in which a swan might swim. Good-humoredly, the persona urges the pair to throw themselves into this "mighty overflow" and thereby drown themselves in pleasure. In the next stanza this vein of humor becomes more pointed and more "wan-

ton," as the bed is described as a maze at whose end lies the mystery of consummated love. As a mystery must be studied and un-
raveled to be understood, so must love. A lover must know "each
wile, / Each hieroglyphick of a kisse or smile" (lines 125–26). And
once he apprehends the nature of the mystery, he must impose
esthetics upon it; "reach," says the persona,

> High in your own conceipt, and some way teach
> Nature and Art, one more
> Play, then they ever knew before.   130

The mind, in its inventiveness ("conceipt"), can extend the limits
of Nature (of the flesh) and of Art. And being natural, love too
requires refinement. By indicating that this can be accomplished,
that the application of human sense and sensibilities to human
desires can maximize love's pleasure, Herrick again demonstrates
the relevance and consistency of his esthetic and his philosophy.

Since the time for the bridal pair to put all of the persona's
advice into practice is rapidly drawing near, the ceremonies, like
Corinna's beads, must be quickly dispensed with: "If needs we
must for Ceremonies-sake, / Blesse a *Sack-posset;* Luck go with
it; take / The Night-Charm quickly . . ." (lines 131–33). Such
superstitions as the warm bed-time drink and the spell against
night's harms, the persona acknowledges, have their place; love is
still the ultimate spell, the most powerful of "magicks." But, since
spells and magic are associated with the devil and the devil with
hell, he cannot resist another attempt at humor: the lovers, he
asserts, will have to pass through the "hell" of physical love before
they can arrive at love's mystery, but it is so pleasant a hell that
anyone would be glad to endure it forever (lines 134–37). This
image in the final lines of the stanza is wittily linked to the conceit of the phoenix of Stanza III, as the persona gives the newlyweds the following charge:

> . . . Frie
> And consume, and grow again to die,
> And live, and in that case,
> Love the confusion of the place.   140

They will burn in their passion, be consumed by it, and die (in the
sexual sense of the term); but they will miraculously rise again
in triumph from the nest of their bed and renew their lives. Such a

state might well be one of "confusion," but the lovers would love it because, in the Latinate sense of the term, it proceeds from the "pouring together" of their nuptial union.

From such verbal jokes the persona turns his attention to a practical one—that of sewing the bride up in a sheet so as to provide still another obstacle to the eager groom. Yet, as the persona acknowledges, the young man will be no more deterred by this than if she were imprisoned with rocks, with "walles of Brasse," or within a tower like Danae, the human maid seduced by Jove. For as the bride, at the beginning of the poem, appeared like a goddess, so now the bridegroom himself appears godlike:

> . . . like a
> Bold bolt of thunder he will make his way,
> And rend the cloud, and throw
> The sheet about, like flakes of snow. 150

The tempestuous mood that concludes Stanza XV is displaced at the very beginning of the final stanza with the line, "All now is husht in silence. . . ." The last wedding guests have departed, and the young couple is left alone with the persona-priest to receive at last his final benediction. Only the *"Midwife-moone"* and her *"Owle-ey'd"* issue," the moon-beams, are in attendance; they are outside, waiting for the shutters of the bedroom windows to be thrown open. In this image Herrick departs from the tradition that Artemis, the moon-deity, is a virgin goddess; rather, in order to prefigure his concluding theme, he emphasizes her function as the deity who presides over childbirth. To the blessing of this goddess he adds his own, praying that the influence which the heavenly bodies exert over the affairs of men may be propitious with regard to this marriage:

> . . . so commence
> All faire *Constellations*
> Looking upon yee, that Two Nations
> Springing from two such Fires,
> May blaze the vertue of their Sires. 160

If the stars are favorable, the blessings of this union will literally be manifold: the couple will have children, both male and female; from each of these two familial lines will come a "Nation" that will by its own virtue make manifest the virtues of Sir Clipseby and Lady Crewe.

The epithalamium thus ends as it began, with a vision. But whereas the opening vision, with its elevation of the bride to divine status, was narrow in scope, the poem's ultimate vision is vast. In the course of this development the occasion itself has been transcended by the sweep of futurity, and sensuality and sexuality have been translated—through ceremony and sensitivity—into nuptial virtue. Within the framework of marriage, "cleanly-*Wantonnesse*" has become a key to pleasure, to moral living, and to the future. Love then, in Herrick's view, has a quasi-religious function. This function is emblematically represented in some of Herrick's love poems through the allegory of "love's religion."

V   *The Religion of Love*

Although the concept of a religion of love was a fairly commonplace one in the Elizabethan poetry that Herrick must have read, he himself uses the term "*Loves Religion*" only once in *Hesperides*—in a poem entitled "*To his Mistresse objecting to him Neither Toying or Talking.*" The occasion of this poem is suggested by its title; its theme is expressed in the speaker's oath: "By *Loves Religion*, I must here confesse it, / The most I love, when I the least expresse it" (lines 5–6). The lady is guilty of the false assumption that demonstrativeness and articulateness indicate sincerity of feeling. Her complaint, however, is understandable; moreover, it brings up a problem with which poets as well as lovers have long wrestled—how can the feelings of love be expressed in a fresh, significant manner? The "religion of love," though it is more of an artistic construct than an authentic faith, provides one answer. And even though it is a poetic device and was by Herrick's time no longer a new one, in his hands it (like pastoral) proves to be an effective means of articulating certain aspects, emotions, and concepts of the amatory experience. A case in point is the poem "*To* Julia, *the* Flaminica Dialis, *or* Queen-Priest" in which an invitation to love is submerged beneath an elaborate and quasi-Roman ceremony of the religion of love.

This poem begins with the speaker admonishing Julia, who, as the title indicates, is seen here in the role of a high priestess of love:

> THOU know'st, my *Julia*, that it is thy turne
> This Mornings Incense to prepare, and burne.
> The Chaplet, and *Inarculum here be,
> With the white Vestures, all attending Thee.
>
> > * A twig of a Pomgranat, which
> > the queen-priest did use to weare
> > on her head at sacrificing [Herrick's
> > note].

The stately language of these lines and the meticulousness with which the ceremonial garb is stipulated lend an air of gravity to the rites, whose specific purpose is to propitiate Venus for the failure of Julia and the persona to worship her properly:

> This day, the *Queen-Priest,* thou are made t'appease   5
> Love for our very-many Trespasses.
> One chiefe transgression is among the rest,
> Because with Flowers her Temple was not drest:
> The next, because her Altars did not shine
> With daily Fyers: The last, neglect of Wine: 10
> For which, her wrath is gone forth to consume
> Us all, unlesse preserv'd by thy Perfume.

These lines can be taken at least two ways. As has been previously noted, ceremony for Herrick is a means by which human actions are sanctified, are given form and meaning. To neglect the rites due to Venus, as the persona and Julia have done, is then to reduce love to the level of the merely physical. On the other hand, since the religion of love is itself a metaphor for human love, the flowers, fires, and wine to which the persona refers can be taken as standing for various amatory delights. Hence these lines would imply that Julia and the persona have for a time neglected love itself, and this lapse has aroused the ire of love's goddess.

In these terms the poem's concluding lines can be read as comprising a covert invitation to Julia to love:

> Take then thy Censer; Put in Fire, and thus,
> *O Pious-Priestresse!* make a Peace for us.
> For our neglect, Love did our Death decree,   15
> That we escape. *Redemption comes by Thee.*

Here again the formal diction and the other ceremonial trappings (like the pious homily of line 16 which parallels, in

effect, the scholarly footnote of line 3) give the poem a deceptive solemnity—deceptive because the prayer for intercession is
really a request to Julia to rekindle her passions ("Put in
Fire"). A renewal of their love will, it is implied, save them
both from the death of a loveless existence. But Julia herself is
The Way, as the parody of Christian dogma in the poem's final
line emphasizes. Without her, the heaven of love is unattainable. Whether it be viewed as a physiological fact or as a romantic hypothesis, the importance of the lady to her lover is conveniently and flatteringly expressed in the mode of love's religion by elevating her (as here) to priestess or even to saint (as
is intimated at the close of "Flaminica Dialis" and is specified in
"To Silvia" [I and II] and in "The Transfiguration").

Although its title has recognizably Christian connotations and
it is full of Biblical echoes, "The Transfiguration" is another
amatory poem addressed to the ubiquitous Julia. It is, however,
a considerably more serious love poem than "Flaminica Dialis,"
though it too functions as a kind of panegyric to her:

> IMMORTALL clothing I put on,
> So soone as *Julia* I am gon
> To mine eternall Mansion.
>
> Thou, thou are here, to humane sight
> Cloth'd all with incorrupted light;   5
> But yet how more admir'dly bright
>
> Wilt thou appear, when thou art set
> In thy refulgent Thronelet,
> That shin'st thus in thy counterfeit?

The difference which the speaker marks out between Julia and
himself is that he, like all mortal men, will put on incorruption
only at death, whereas Julia is pure and bright in this life. The
primary tension in the poem, however, is between Julia present
and Julia future: even her refulgence and purity as a mortal
comprise but a "counterfeit," an inferior physical representation
of the idea and the ideal of Julia, the quintessential Julia who
eventually will be enthroned in heaven.

In "The Transfiguration" the three streams of orthodox Christianity, Neo-Platonism, and love's religion converge in a poem
which, though a far cry from Herrick's Cavalierly flippant and

sensuous love lyrics, is nonetheless an interesting illustration of his synthesis of the "cleanly" and the "wanton." For even though it smacks more of the former than the latter, it is still a poem in praise of a lady who is earthly and—to judge from many of Herrick's other Julia poems—earthy. While he is no true Platonist, Herrick does write some poems about love that are even more abstract than this one. As is inevitable, however, they tend to be epigrams rather than lyrics.

Very early in *Hesperides* Herrick attempts a definition of love in the plainly titled epigram "*Love what it is*": "LOVE is a circle that doth restlesse move / In the same sweet eternity of love." Although the poem is as cryptic as its title is straightforward, a hypothesis as to its meaning can be constructed: the circle is, of course, the perfect figure and is thus as apt an emblem for ideal love as it was for the ideal life in Herrick's poems on the country life. Furthermore, God, who is from all eternity, is love; out of love He created the circle of the universe. If these inferences from Herrick's abstract and ambiguous image are valid, then the poem affirms that love makes not only the world go round but even the universe and eternity itself. This interpretation receives some support from a comment of Robert Burton's which was likely the source not only of this epigram, but of a slight variation upon it with the simple title of "*Upon* Love" [VIII]. In Burton's definition love is "*Circulus a bono in bonum,* a round circle still from good to good; for love is the beginner and end of all our actions, the efficient and instrumental cause, as our poets in their symbols, impresses, emblems of rings, squares &c. shadow unto us. . . ." [10] To Burton's diction Herrick adds symbol and movement in "*Upon* Love": "LOVE is a Circle, and an Endlesse Sphere; / From good to good, revolving here, & there." It is a far cry from this universalizing of love's influence to the recrimination of the following couplet from one of the concluding poems of *Hesperides,* "*On Himselfe*" [XVI]: "IL'E write no more of Love; but now repent / Of all those times that I in it have spent."

But both these lines and those of "*Upon* Love" merely exemplify different poems in different moods that happen to occupy opposite ends of the spectrum of Herrick's amatory verse. As such, they must be viewed in perspective—as must the couplet that concludes Herrick's secular volume: "To his Book's end this last line he'd have plac't, / *Jocond his Muse was; but his Life was chast.*" There are good reasons why it would be a mistake to read these lines as either straightforward autobiography or an ultimate rejection of love. They are, for one thing, written in a long tradition of poetic retractions of what Chaucer referred to as his "many a song and many a leccherous lay." [11] And for another, this, the final couplet of *Hesperides*, serves Herrick as an appropriate transition from his "profane" to his "noble" numbers, from a volume vibrant with "cleanly-*Wantonnesse*" to a volume quickened by love of God.

CHAPTER 5

The White Island *and* This Sacred Grove: *The Theme of Faith*

IT is an axiom of seventeenth-century studies in literature that Herrick's collection of religious poems, *His Noble Numbers,* fares rather poorly in comparison with the devotional verses of Donne, Herbert, and other eminent poets of his time.[1] That these "Pious Pieces," furthermore, are generally inferior to his secular poems has also been taken to be almost self-evident. These generalizations are more accurate than most of those that have been circulated about Herrick; and yet, as this chapter attempts to show, they too require some qualification.

This chapter does *not* particularly address itself to one question with which students of Herrick have too frequently bedeviled themselves—why this poet, an English parson, a "religious man," was so often successful when he turned his hand to "profane" verse—and particularly verse that often was of an erotic or "pagan" cast—and only infrequently successful at writing "Christian poetry"? There are at least two things wrong with this question. First, it assumes that, because he was an English parson, Herrick *was* a "religious man." But this there is no way of knowing. History provides after all more than a few examples of churchmen who were "religious" in very few senses of that word. It is also a fact that, in the seventeenth century, there were few professions other than the clergy open to educated but impecunious young men. Economic necessity rather than deep-seated conviction may have motivated Herrick to take holy orders.

Second, even if it is assumed that the poet was a sincerely Christian man—which is also quite possible—the question posed above assumes that sincerity somehow automatically produces effective poetry. But anyone who has ever tried to express his own deep feelings by writing a "great" poem should be able to recognize the fallaciousness of this assumption. As Northrop Frye has observed, when we say that a poem "seems sincere," all that we can mean is that it communicates its emotions effectively.[2] Thus, to puzzle over the question of the "sincerity" of Herrick's Christian faith is not only useless but diversionary since the debate detracts from his poems themselves.

Raising the shibboleth of sincerity can, for example, confuse the issue in the case of the very first poem of *His Noble Numbers*—"*His Confession*":

> Look how our foule Dayes do exceed our faire;
> And as our bad, more then our good Works are:
> Ev'n so those Lines, pen'd by my wanton Wit,
> Treble the number of these good I've writ.
> Things precious are least num'rous: Men are prone   5
> To do ten Bad, for one Good Action.

Is Herrick, with this poem, "sincerely" rejecting as much as two-thirds of his entire creative output? Is he casting out "*Corinna's going a-Maying*," his many "Julia-poems," the "sack-poems"—all those works of "wanton Wit" by which his reputation as a poet must have been made and is now sustained? When we consider that verse confessions of this kind were traditional, that Herrick did ultimately allow the "rejected" poems to be published, and that "*His Confession*" must serve esthetic as well as spiritual purposes by providing a transition from one collection to another published in the same volume as *Hesperides,* from one complex of tone, mood, and subject area to another, it seems unnecessary to take this poem to heart.

"*His Confession*" can be somewhat misleading in yet another way: from it a reader who is only slightly familiar with Herrick might infer that *Hesperides* is wholly lacking in verse of a religious character. While it is true that there are relatively few poems in that volume which could be classified as orthodoxly Christian works, *Hesperides* does contain a number of poems that are "religious" in the broadest sense of that term. It is with a few of the more interesting examples of such poems that the two sections which follow deal.

I   *The Uses and Abuses of Religion*

Although Herrick was born, bred, and ordained in the Church of England, *His Noble Numbers* is not a noticeably sectarian collection. And even his "profane" verse, like the prose of Sir Thomas Browne, is surprisingly free from the kind of malice toward all

other sects that was commonplace in literature written in this period—a period whose greatest tensions were inspired by religious
controversy in general and by sectarianism in particular. There
are, however, a few exceptions, one of which is a curious poem
entitled *"The Christian Militant."* Here the tendency of Herrick to
blend Christian and "pagan" elements (a tendency that has been
the despair of some of his Victorian critics) manifests itself in
satire.

From a historical point of view, the title of this poem is more
reminiscent of the spirit of seventeenth-century English Puritanism than of Anglicanism. It recalls, for example, Puritan tracts like
John Downame's *The Christian Warfare* (1604) and such phrases
as "the true warfaring Christian" from the *Areopagitica* (1644) of
the great Puritan, John Milton.[3] For Milton, such a Christian is
one who tests his faith, reason, and virtue by confronting evil in
all of its guises and overcoming it—an active as opposed to a pas-
sive Christian. That Herrick is attempting a similar definition in
this poem seems to be indicated by its opening lines; the true
"Christian Militant," he asserts, is—"A *man* prepar'd against all
ills to come, / That dares to dead the fire of martirdome."

The couplet is deceptive. To be prepared for possible misfor-
tunes is common sense, but to be prepared for *all* possible misfor-
tunes smacks of an excess of caution and of pessimism; and it also
suggests a lack of the faith that "God will provide." Furthermore,
one so completely prepared runs small risk of being truly tested,
of being thrown wholly upon his own resources. Thus he "deads"
or extinguishes "the fire of martirdome" that could provide the
ultimate tempering of his faith. Such a man would enjoy the kind
of physical security depicted in the next couplet, the security of
one—"That sleeps at home; and sayling there at ease, / Feares not
the fierce sedition of the Seas."

There is irony in the fact that this security is juxtaposed with
the reference to martyrdom in the preceding line. Furthermore,
sleeping at home is a luxury seldom actually enjoyed by truly militant types; and sailing the dangerous ocean vicariously—by perus-
ing maps—is scarcely the mark of an active man. On the contrary,
as Chapter 3 made clear, both activities are those enjoyed by the
contemplative man, the man who values quietude, security, and
retirement, and seeks these in the country life. This life, of course,
has a powerful appeal for a moderate Anglican like Herrick, but

it would be despicable to a crusading Puritan. Therefore, the character who has been described thus far is a contradiction, an unmilitant militant, and thus a figure of fun.

This fun—or more accurately, ridicule—is further manifested in this couplet by Herrick's wordplay. For "sedition," the act of revolting against lawful authority, is rather an unusual metaphor for the action of the sea—unless "Seas" is a pun for "sees," referring to the offices or powers of bishops. In the earlier seventeenth century, of course, one of the chief sources of conflict between non-Anglican Protestants and the Church of England was the latter's ecclesiastical hierarchy, with its strength and influence centered in its bishops. To many of the Puritan persuasion the Anglican bishops, like their Roman Catholic counterparts, were attempting to usurp the office of Christ as mediator between God and man. Such an act would, to a rigid Protestant, fully merit the charge of "sedition."

Further confirmation that Herrick's poem is a veiled satirical portrait of the arch-Puritan is to be found in lines 5-12, where the *Christian Militant* is described as one—

> That's counter-proofe against the Farms mis-haps,   5
> Undreadfull too of courtly thunderclaps:
> That weares one face (like heaven) and never showes
> A change, when Fortune either comes, or goes:
> That keepes his own strong guard, in the despight
> Of what can hurt by day, or harme by night: 10
> That takes and re-delivers every stroake
> Of Chance, (as made up all of rock, and oake:).

The portrait that is developed here, if taken out of context, could be regarded as a flattering one that describes a man who confronts the flux of human existence with courage and Stoic-like equanimity. And this is just the point: Herrick's *Christian Militant* appears in these lines to be considerably less a Christian and less a militant than he is a Stoic. Indeed, it is this Stoical quality, arising from a fundamental belief in restraint and temperance and carried to the extreme of asceticism, that is often associated with seventeenth-century English Puritanism. The Puritan is traditionally depicted as one who is defensive and pessimistic about life, who expects and finds evil in everyone and everything, who tries to react to life no more than does an insensate rock or tree. This kind of Stoicism, which results in a negation rather than an affirmation of life, is in all important respects the antithesis of Herrick's own vein of Stoicism, extensively modified as it is by his Neo-Epicureanism.

The incongruities of the poem peak in its two concluding couplets. Like the passage above, these lines, taken out of context, would seem to comprise a conventional description of the Christian martyr; they become suspect, however, when viewed in relation to the poem as a whole, melodramatically showing as they do the *"Christian Militant"* to be one—

> That sighs at others death; smiles at his own
> Most dire and horrid crucifixion.
> Who for true glory suffers thus; we grant   15
> Him to be here our *Christian Militant*.

A sigh can, it is true, be heartfelt; but it seems a trifling response, if one is to respond at all, to "[an]others death." And for a person to smile at his own crucifixion seems at best grotesque; even an unshakable faith in one's ultimate salvation can scarcely justify such a response, as may be inferred from the Biblical descriptions of Christ's reactions on the cross. Furthermore, the likelihood that Herrick's "Christian Militant"—domestic, withdrawn, secure— would suffer so dramatic a fate, and in particular, so archaic a torture as crucifixion (except in his own dreams of martyrdom), is so small as to make the image preposterous.

The careful reader of this poem must then be left with one of two impressions—that its incongruities are unintentional and thus it is a badly flawed work, or that they are deliberate. In the latter case, their purpose would be to create a caricature of the kind of Puritan satirized by Herrick's mentor, Ben Jonson, in the person of "Zeal-of-the-Land Busy" (of *Bartholomew Fair*). Besides the evidence of the poem itself, the latter interpretation finds some support in the simple fact of Herrick's craftsmanship, a craftsmanship which occasionally errs, but never blunders as outrageously as it might seem to here. Also, outside the poem itself, but of possible relevance, is the fact that Herrick was after all an Anglican and a Royalist and one who was forcibly removed from his parish by the Puritans. What could be more likely than that he would give vent to his feelings by one of the few means left open to him—verse satire? And finally, it should be noted that *"The Christian Militant"* is not the only poem of *Hesperides* in this vein. Another is one of Herrick's longer works, "*The Fairie Temple: or, Oberons Chappell. Dedicated to* Mr. John Merrifield, *Counsellor at Law.*" "*The Fairie Temple,*" however, is a satire not of Puritanism but of Roman Catholicism.

So familiar and so fully developed in the British Isles was the myth of the fairies and the fairie kingdom that poets of the English Renaissance like Shakespeare (in *A Midsummer Night's Dream*, c.1595), Michael Drayton (in *Nimphidia, the Court of Faery*, 1627) and Ben Jonson (in his masque, *Oberon the Faery Prince*, 1611) were accustomed to draw heavily upon it. The popularity of the genre and the challenges it extended to a poet's ingenuity and imagination clearly struck a responsive chord in Herrick, for four longer fairy poems in addition to "*The Fairie Temple*" are scattered throughout *Hesperides*.[4] But the satiric as well as the picturesque potentialities of the genre are best realized in his poem for Merrifield.

"*The Fairie Temple*" has two formal divisions, the first of which is a six-line dedication that calls attention to the differences between real temples made of "Lime, or Wood, or Stone" and this one, a product of the creative imagination. Merrifield is challenged to say if he has seen an actual temple "more fine / Then this" and then is presented with *The Temple* itself, which is the main body of the poem. The dedication thus also serves thematically as an affirmation of art and dramatically as an *entrée* into the imaginary temple itself. It resembles, in function if not in texture, "The Church Porch," George Herbert's induction to his book of sacred poems, *The Temple*.

In his "*Temple*" Herrick describes the chapel's decor, fixtures, and services in considerable detail and in addition catalogues its "ecclesiastical staff." Some passages are mainly descriptive; in these Herrick plays the miniaturist in verse, carving out images with exquisite workmanship and on the smallest possible scale. There are, for example, his lines on the fairies' altar:

> The Altar is not here foure-square,
> Nor in a forme Triangular;   55
> Nor made of glasse, or wood, or stone,
> But of a little Transverce bone;
> Which boyes, and Bruckel'd children call
> (Playing for Points and Pins) *Cockall.*
> Whose Linnen-Drapery is a thin   60
> Subtile and ductile Codlin's skin;

> Which o're the board is smoothly spred,
> With little Seale-work Damasked.

The tiny altar is made of a knuckle-bone (*"Cockall"*) of the kind used in the games of grimy ("Bruckel'd") children and is covered with a figured cloth made from the skin of a moth. To make it even rarer, richer, and more exquisite, the cloth is fringed with a "Spangle-work of trembling dew." In passages such as these, Herrick lives up to Douglas Bush's description of him as "the goldsmith's apprentice, the master of filigree." [5] Yet even here Herrick is more than a mere skilful artisan in verse. As L. C. Martin has pointed out,[6] the poet's reference to the shape and composition of the altar slyly alludes to a theological controversy about the proper shape, composition, and location of the church altar—one of those minor conflicts that added fuel to what would become the fire of the great Civil War.

"The Temple" is full of satire of this and the more obvious type, with most of the latter being directed against Roman Catholicism. Herrick goes so far as to claim in lines 22–25 that the faith of the fairies is "a mixt Religion . . . Part Pagan, Part Papisticall," and to assert in lines 109–110 that ". . . if their Legend doe not lye, / They much affect the *Papacie*." The very coupling of ancient polytheism and Romanism is in itself a criticism, but Herrick goes further by combining external elements of both religions in his description of the physical aspects of the chapel. The opening lines of the poem, for example, portray a *"Temple of Idolatry"* where Oberon "of *God-heads* has such store, / As *Rome's Pantheon* had not more" (lines 5–7). Here insects—"Idol-Cricket," *"Idol-Beetleflie,"* *"Idol-Canker"* (a worm) and the "golden god, *Cantharides"* (a beetle)—serve as the graven images of the gods. Herrick creates the impression that the temple is not only overcrowded with these god-heads, but also overdecorated with ikons of fairyland's "saints"—"Saint *Tit,* Saint *Nit,* Saint *Is,* Saint *Itis"* and numerous others (lines 28–32). The absurdity of the saints' names compounds the absurdity of the catalogue and, by implication, that of the whole canonical apparatus.

Nor does Herrick handle fairyland's holy men more gently. One "little-Puppet-Priest" "squeaks" his exhortations (lines 39–40), another "pules" or whines his (line 43), while the chief priest stands at the altar "off'ring up the Holy-Grist: / Ducking in Mood, and Perfect Tense, / With (much-good-do't him) reverence" (lines

51–53). The service, in other words, is in Latin, with much bowing and nodding in response to the grammar of the liturgy, with its imperatives, subjunctives, and the like.

On other counts also Herrick scores Roman Catholicism. The fairies' faith is, he implies, highly doctrinaire: they worship by the book—by "their Book of Canons," "their Book of Articles," and "their Book of Homilies" (lines 78–82). Their services are depicted as being overly elaborate, with special candles, ornate robes, and ceremonial fixtures, all of which are foolishly supposed to lend "sanctity" to the occasion (lines 91–102). Also coming in for ridicule are the ecclesiastical hierarchy—with its "many *mumbling Masse-priests,*" "many a dapper *Chorister,*" "*Canons*" and "*Cloyster-Monks*"; the Church's practice of selling "Their *Pardons* and *Indulgences*"; and its paraphernalia of rosaries, relics, and incense (lines 113–24).

The very length of Herrick's catalogue reinforces the impression of the absurdity of the fairies' religion, and the very minuteness of the items catalogued takes away from whatever impressiveness and significance they might otherwise possess. And, finally, the point of view which the reader of "*The Temple*" must infer is confirmed by Herrick's diction—by his use of verbs like "squeaks" and "pules" to describe the voices of the fairy-priests and of nouns like "trifle" and "trinket" to describe the "holy" relics. Nonetheless, the tone of this poem is essentially good-humored. In an age when to be a Catholic was sometimes analogous to being a subversive, when Catholics were persecuted by deed and by word, Herrick's satire is more humorous than malicious.

Elsewhere in *Hesperides* Herrick pays his respects to Roman Catholicism, its ceremonies and its symbols, by employing them to lend dignity and significance to poems such as "*The Funerall Rites of the Rose.*" This work has been regarded by so notable a commentator as F. R. Leavis as a trifle, an extended and merely witty conceit based upon the resemblances between flowers and maidens.[7] But Leavis seems less than cognizant of the thematic weight such an analogy can and does bear in this poem. The theme of the transiency of life, which is implicit in its opening line, "THE Rose was sick, and smiling di'd," is strengthened rather than diluted by the very delicacy of Herrick's trope. The sickness of the rose, and the fact that, ironically, she smiles as she dies, personify her and thus call the reader's attention to his own flower-

like fragility. The presence of friends lends even more poignancy
to this condition:

> And (being to be sanctifi'd)
> About the Bed, there sighing stood
> The sweet, and flowrie Sisterhood.
> Some hung the head, while some did bring   5
> (To wash her) water from the Spring.

The Catholic associations of the noun "Sisterhood" transform the
flowers that surround the rose into brightly habited nuns who respond to her death by performing the appropriate rituals: some
droop as if in prayer, while others bathe her with their tears,
which are the dew-drops collected from "the Spring"—a punning
metaphor for that season of the year which provides life-giving
moisture to blooming flowers. But, in the case of the rose, these
waters offer only sanctification, not renewal.

Other preparations completed, the rose is arrayed for burial,
and her sister-flowers begin a series of quasi-Catholic devotions.
They keep "a solemne Fast"; sing funeral songs, "The sacred
Dirge and *Trentall*"; and they expend, as incense, their natural
fragrance: "But ah! what sweets smelt every where, / As Heaven
had spent all perfumes there." The sense of finality in the verb,
"spent," anticipates the performance of the last rites:

> At last, when prayers for the dead,
> And Rites were all accomplished;
> They, weeping, spread a Lawnie Loome,   15
> And clos'd her up, as in a Tombe.

The rose is returned to the earth from which she arose, and the
reader is reminded that "ashes to ashes, dust to dust" is a prophecy for him also.

In spite of the fact that Roman Catholic forms figure importantly here and are employed in a wholly different manner than
they are in *"The Temple"* (where they serve to heighten the reader's sense of the ridiculous), this poem fails to generate a strong
sense of Christian optimism. These forms sanctify death and con-
sole the survivors, but they work no change upon the rose herself
—she is "clos'd . . . up" in the finality of the tomb. One critic has
argued that the rose transcends the flux of nature through the art
of these rituals,[8] yet neither the optimism of art nor that of Chris-

tianity seems manifest in the closing lines. The former type of
optimism *is* strongly in evidence in other poems of *Hesperides*, as
Chapter 6 will demonstrate; and orthodox Christian optimism of
course pervades *His Noble Numbers*. But a number of the "religious" poems of Herrick's profane volume adhere to the pattern of
"The Funerall Rites of the Rose" in that they embody an approximate balance at least between Christian and pagan elements—almost as if Herrick were in his art following the Scholastic principle of John Donne: "What ever dyes, was not mixt equally." [9]
Such balancing is a function of Herrick's artistic and intellectual
poise, but generations of Christian critics have viewed the very
juxtaposition of Christian and pagan as smacking of a quintessential paganism. They are right, but for the wrong reasons. The
Herrick of *Hesperides* is in the final view a pagan because of his
assumptions and the attitudes which follow from them, not because of his poetic technique. As the next section shows, his eclecticism and his synthesizing artistry are more significant than his
supposed heresy.

II   *Christian and Pagan*

The reader who returns to Herrick's complete works for the second time will, if he is observant, perceive foreshadowings of *His
Noble Numbers* throughout the *"Sacred Grove"* of his *"secular"*
poems. That they are indeed foreshadowings is, however, far from
self-evident; Herrick's insistent paganism can easily detract one's
attention from them. For example, one of Herrick's double poems,
"Mattens, or morning Prayer" and *"Evensong,"* takes its titles from
two Anglican services, yet its texture is heavily interwoven with
non-Christian strands. In *"Mattens,"* the speaker's final charge to
his pious audience echoes Revelation v.8, and its allegations concerning the interdependence of one's soul, one's actions, and one's
ends or aims seem to reflect a Christian orientation:

> Next to the Altar humbly kneele, and thence,   5
> Give up thy soule in clouds of frankinsense.
> Thy golden Censors fil'd with odours sweet,
> Shall make thy actions with their ends to meet.

Yet the same speaker's initial injunction, "First wash thy heart in
innocence, then bring / Pure hands, pure habits, pure, pure every
thing" (lines 3–4), echoes Tibullus (ii.I.13–14) and is reminiscent

of the ancient Roman ceremonies dramatized in Jonson's *Sejanus* (v.174–5).

"*Evensong*" also echoes a passage from Revelation—"I am Alpha and Omega, the beginning and the end, the first and the last" (xxii.13)—but the persona speaks of Jove rather than Yahweh: "*Jove's* is the first and last." While "Jove" is, of course, a stock epithet for "God," its presence in a poem that seems from its title to treat an everyday Anglican ritual is an index of Herrick's sometimes surprising eclecticism.

A more subtle example of this tendency of the poet is one of his numerous occasional pieces, "*A Dirge upon the Death of the Right Valiant Lord,* Bernard Stuart." A proper dirge, this work is intended to be sung—according to Herrick's directions—by three soloists and a chorus. It opens with the first soloist intoning, with priestly severity, a ritual banishment of those who would profane the solemnity of the occasion with noise: "HENCE, hence profane; soft silence let us have; / While we this *Trentall* sing about thy Grave." The mood thus set, the second soloist sings a panegyric to the fallen lord, a panegyric couched in such terms as to suggest Stuart's resemblance to the risen Lord:

> 2. Had Wolves or Tigers seen but thee,
>   They wo'd have shew'd civility;
>   And in compassion of thy yeeres,   5
>   Washt those thy purple wounds with tears.
>   But since th'art slaine; and in thy fall,
>   The drooping Kingdome suffers all.

Like Adam and the second Adam, Stuart possessed the kind of radiant innocence that could make wild beasts "civil," or tame and harmless. The implied comparison verges on the heretical, but it is only implied; Herrick insures his technical orthodoxy by making it clear that the miracle described did not in fact occur. However, Stuart is also like Christ in that he suffered "purple" or vivid wounds, underwent a "fall" (as did the first Adam), and by his death affected the future of a "Kingdome."

The response of the chorus to this account is sacramental: it offers tears to wash the fallen's wounds and to substitute for the holy water which must daily be sprinkled o'er the tomb; and if tears are not enough, the singers offer their own souls in sacrifice. This heavy emphasis upon the performance of the appropriate rituals of death is more pagan than Christian, as is the assurance of lines 13–14, which has the effect of laying the potentially uneasy shade of Stuart to rest: "Sleep in thy peace, while we with spice perfume thee, / And *Cedar* wash thee, that no times consume thee." The very allusion to the possibility of the flesh's decay, however, gives rise to a ringing affirmation of the incorruptibility and immortality of the soul in the song of the third soloist:

> 3. Live, live thou dost, and shalt; for why?   15
>   *Soules doe not with their bodies die:*
>   Ignoble off-springs, they may fall
>   Into the flames of Funerall:
>   When as the chosen seed shall spring
>   Fresh, and for ever flourishing.   20

Lines 15–16 seem to lend a distinctively Christian note to this lyric proclamation; yet, as Martin has noted, both Ovid and Tacitus make similar statements.[10] An additional qualification of the Christian tenor of these lines is contained in the reference to the pagan custom of cremating bodies on funeral pyres. Also, the conception that human bodies are gross—"Ignoble off-springs"—in comparison to souls has its roots in Platonism as well as in Christianity. The image of the souls as "the chosen seed," the seminal and eternal elements of man's being, recalls not only Deuteronomy iv.37 but also Plato. Finally, the affirmation of the poem's climactic couplet—that Stuart will become a legendary figure—casts him in a mold that is, on the one hand, "heroic" (and thus somewhat pagan) but, on the other, saintly (and thus vaguely Christian):

> *Cho*[rus]. And times to come shall, weeping, read thy glory,
>   Lesse in these Marble stones, then in thy story.

These lines at least approach the kind of grandeur that Milton achieves in a much longer poem, *Lycidas;* and the achievement of this quality is to some extent the result of the union, in both poems, of Christian and pagan consolations.

If decorum allows that a Christ-metaphor is appropriate for celebrating a fallen nobleman, it also requires that a humble poet choose a more modest trope to dramatize his own existence. Thus, as Milton in *Lycidas* adopts the guise of a simple shepherd, so Herrick in *"On himselfe"* [IV] assumes the role of the ordinary pilgrim. But even though the title of the latter poem invites an autobiographical interpretation, a first reading yields little that would identify its speaker as Robert Herrick and Robert Herrick alone; his sense of decorum, as usual, requires him to keep, to some degree, his distance. In the first four lines, for example, the speaker merely indicates by his garb and equipment that he is indeed a pilgrim:

> HERE down my wearyed limbs Ile lay;
> My Pilgrims staffe; my weed of gray:
> My Palmers hat; my Scallops shell;
> My Crosse; my Cord; and all farewell.

The hat with its palm leaves signifies that its wearer has visited the Holy Land, and the shell is a kind of identification badge of the pilgrim. The act of laying these and his other impedimenta aside and bidding them farewell signifies, of course, that he forsees the end of the pilgrimage of life:

> For having now my journey done,
> (Just at the setting of the Sun)
> Here I have found a Chamber fit,
> (God and good friends be thankt for it)
> Where if I can a lodger be
> A little while from Tramplers free;   10
> At my up-rising next, I shall,
> If not requite, yet thank ye all.

An autobiographical reading of these lines would hold that the poem was likely written while Herrick lived in his quiet, isolated parsonage at Dean Prior. More important, however, is the poet's successful re-creation of the mood of one weary of life and longing for rest but not unmindful of the blessings he has enjoyed.[11] It is in the spirit of gratitude that Herrick the pilgrim thanks his friends for their kindnesses, but Herrick the poet cannot resist the opportunity for a pun; thus the metaphor of lying down in death becomes the metaphor of "up-rising" in eternal life. It is as both holy man and poet that he offers one last gift:

> Mean while, the *Holy-Rood* hence fright
> The fouler Fiend, and evill Spright,
> From scaring you or yours this night.   15

The triplet is a charm or versified spell to keep off evil. As such, it is a fitting conclusion to this little poem, for it is the one fairly substantial link between the work's persona and its poet: on several occasions Herrick tried his hand at the genre of the charm.[12] For this poet, as Chapter 6 will show, poetry itself is a kind of charm or "incantation"; also, it is one of Herrick's customs to write poems as gifts for his friends, as the "pilgrim" does.[13] But the main effect of this modest Christian allegory is to communicate a sense of simple and sincere religious faith, the kind of faith dogmatized and intensified in *The Pilgrim's Progress*.

While the charm that climaxes *"On himselfe"* [IV] has reference to a context in which religion is mixed with superstitions that are often pagan in origin, the poem has an unmistakably if not blatantly Christian character. This character is strengthened by the basic assumptions—that life is a trial and death is a release—which are embodied in the metaphor of the pilgrimage to the shrine of eternal life. These assumptions, as will be seen, are more central to *His Noble Numbers* than to *Hesperides;* but *"On himselfe"* [IV] is by no means the only poem of the latter volume in which they figure. They are self-evident, for example, in such epigrams as *"Comforts in Crosses,"*

> BE not dismaide, though crosses cast thee downe;
> Thy fall is but the rising to a Crowne,

and *"Sufferance,"*

> IN the hope of ease to come,
> Let's endure one Martyrdome.

Likewise foreshadowing the spirit and the intellectual orientation of *His Noble Numbers* is a poem in a very different mode, *"Comfort to a youth that had lost his Love."* Although, from its title, this poem might appear to be one of Herrick's conventional and Neo-Elizabethan love complaints, it turns out to be something quite different. Indeed, *"Comfort"* may appear to be a rather strange work to a modern reader. Purporting to be a poem of simple consolation to the bereaved, its tone is so curt and its utterances so brutally frank that it is difficult to see how it could possibly serve its purposes.

Part of the poem's abrupt quality undoubtedly comes from its

prosody: though not divided into proper stanzas, it is actually
composed of six quatrains, each of which consists of three lines of
iambic dimeter and one of iambic monometer, rhyming *a-b-b-a*.
Herrick uses very short lines more frequently than any other important English poet—the extreme example is "*Upon his departure hence,*" which is written in iambic monometer exclusively.
One reason for Herrick's employment of such tactics in "*Comfort,*"
at least, may be found in the place of consolation in Christian
doctrine. Since death, for the believing Christian, is not an end
but a beginning, not the loss of life but the gaining of eternal life,
not the loss of love but the refinding of God's love, excessive grief
upon the death of a loved one becomes a kind of heresy. Thus, a
poetic consolation in the Christian mode will invariably be required in cases of extreme sorrow, in cases where human emotions
are on the verge of overwhelming faith. Hence a firm tone, such
as we find in the very opening lines of Herrick's poem, becomes
theologically as well as psychologically necessary:

> WHAT needs complaints,
> When she a place
> Has with the race
> Of Saints?

"Saints," of course, makes the Christian identification; and the
poem's theme is, indeed, summed up in these four lines. The
youth is told: "Cease grieving, for grief is now inappropriate—one
does not grieve for the blest." But since both this argument and its
object are bound up in emotions, the poem itself can only be an
effective antidote to grief if it is persuasive, if it functions as an
appeal to the emotions—and not to the reason—of the addressee.
This is precisely what Herrick makes it do.

In the two quatrains that follow, he asks the forlorn youth to
visualize his lady as a "saint" in heaven, as one whose essence (as
well as whose being) has been transfigured:

> In endlesse mirth,   5
> She thinks not on
> What's said or done
>   In earth:
> She sees no teares,
> Or any tone
> Of thy deep grone   10
>   She heares.

The vision of heaven projected here is not at all sentimental, but it is affecting. The traditional conception of heaven as a type of "*Sacred Grove*"—a place where one is reborn merely as a perfected version of what he was on earth and where one retains his emotional involvement with those he has left behind—is shattered. It is replaced by a conception in which heaven and its occupants resemble abstractions (even "endlesse mirth" seems hypothetical at best) and are clearly abstracted. This heaven makes inevitable and thus understandable what would otherwise appear to be the strangely cruel detachment of the youth's dead mistress:

> Nor do's she minde,
> Or think on't now,
> That ever thou   15
>   Wast kind.
> But chang'd above,
> She likes not there,
> As she did here,
>   Thy Love.   20

Because transfiguration is so radical a process, the lady has transcended not only her lover, but their love; in her, as in the rest of the "Saints," the old doctrine of *contemptus mundi* is perfectly fulfilled.

Up to this point Herrick's poem parallels the heavily Christian close of *Troilus and Criseyde,* in which Chaucer describes the newly slain Troilus as looking down from his vantage point in heaven and despising "This wrecched world" and its folly. Troilus contrasts mundane existence with "the pleyn felicite / That is in hevene above . . . (v.1818–19) and even mocks those who loved him: "And in hymself he lough right at the wo / Of hem that wepten for his deth so faste" (v.1821–22). Herrick, however, elects to bring his argument-by-persuasion to a close on a note which suggests that all passions now are spent and only sweet reasonableness remains:

> Forebeare therefore,
> And Lull asleepe
> Thy woes and weep
>   *No more.*

Here, within the very tight limitations of his form, Herrick suddenly but successfully modulates his poem's dominantly stern tone: line 21 is firm, hortatory and logical, but the soft consonants and long vowels of lines 22–24 imply compassion. And the words themselves suggest that, while woes are inevitable and weeping natural, both must have an ending. Dogma is thus ultimately mollified by humanity, a tendency which, as shall be indicated, is general in Herrick's *Noble Numbers*.

III   *Religious Variety and Unity*

If the very variety of the "religious" poems of Herrick's "secular" volume is evidence of his doctrinal and esthetic eclecticism, an eclecticism controlled by his synthesizing poetical imagination, the unity of *His Noble Numbers* is evidence of his willingness and ability to subdue that eclecticism and that imagination in the interests of more conventional religious impulses. But though Herrick, through the former group of poems, helps prepare his reader for the latter, the alteration in the texture of his poetry that results from the subordination of his *"Hesperidean"* impulses is immediately noticeable.

It has already been noted, for example, that the opening poem of his sacred volume, *"His Confession,"* is an implied rejection of most of those poems which Herrick himself, in the subtitle to his book, dignified with the adjective "humane." But even more surprising to the reader who has joined the ranks of Herrick's admirers *because* of "those Lines" penned by his "wanton Wit" will be *"His Prayer for Absolution,"* the companion-piece to *"His Confession."* In *"His Prayer"* the implicit rejection is made explicit, and in no uncertain terms:

> For Those my unbaptized Rhimes,
> Writ in my wild unhallowed Times;
> For every sentence, clause and word,
> That's not inlaid with Thee, (my Lord)
> Forgive me God, and blot each Line   5
> Out of my Book, that is not Thine.
> But if, 'mongst all, thou find'st here one
> Worthy thy Benediction;
> That One of all the rest, shall be
> The Glory of my Work, and Me.   10

But here, as in the case of *"His Confession,"* it would be a mistake to read too literally. Even though the first couplet implies that the poet's "wild unhallowed Times" are a thing of the past, it is by no means certain that all of the poems of Herrick's profane volume were necessarily written before those of *His Noble Numbers*.[14] Furthermore, that the intent of the poem is to communicate strong religious feeling rather than intellectual conviction may be deduced from the fact that, although God is called upon to "blot" or erase lines not informed with the Holy Spirit, it is clear that it was Robert Herrick who saw the book through the presses—and with relatively few blottings. The request to God (lines 7–10) to act as critic is similarly metaphoric (as well as being borrowed, most likely, from the apostrophe, "To the King"—see Chapter 1), for it carries out the main intention of the poem—to dramatize the state of complete dedication of one's art and thus of one's self to God.

   While the introductory pieces of *His Noble Numbers* appear to be, more than anything else, poetic formalities, this is not to say that Herrick's sacred volume is merely a collection of exercises in the modes of religious verse. While it is, as one scholar calls it, "a large, metrical prayer book [containing] creeds and graces, confessions and thanksgivings, litanies and dirges, nativity and circumcision songs, anthems and carols, plus a large body of near-catechetical wisdom," [15] this "prayer book" possesses both a conceptual unity and an emotional harmony that it in part derives from its Anglican Protestant orientation. This orientation, which explicitly and implicitly manifests itself in poems throughout *His Noble Numbers*, is expressed in general terms in a succinct and simplified summary of Protestant doctrine entitled *"His Creed."* Like a number of Herrick's "profane" meditations, this poem opens with the speaker contemplating his own death. The striking difference is that the speaker raises his mind's eye from the event of death to a vision of an afterlife:

> I DO believe, that die I must,
> And be return'd from out my dust:
> I do believe, that when I rise,
> Christ I shall see, with these same eyes:
> I do believe, that I must come,   5
> With others, to the dreadful Doome:
> I do believe, the bad must goe
> From thence, to everlasting woe:
> I do believe, the good, and I,
> Shall live with Him eternally.   10

The oblivion that succeeds death in *Hesperides* is here replaced
by the conscious and active existence postulated by Christianity as
commencing with Doomsday: souls are reunited with bodies,
Christ comes as judge, and the great and terrifying confrontation
occurs. What happens next is presented in terms that are breath-
takingly simple: individuals are classified as "the bad" or "the
good," with the speaker—completely unselfconsciously and confi-
dently—including himself among the latter. The destination of
each group of souls remains ambiguous: there is no suggestion of
a Dantean vision of nine circles of Hell or of a Bunyanesque vision of a heavenly city.

The specifically Protestant nature of Herrick's creed is further
suggested by the next couplet: "I do believe, I shall inherit /
Heaven, by Christ's mercies, not my merit." Salvation is by faith
alone and through grace; one cannot by his "merit" earn his way
into heaven. Christ is the key, as the poem's climactic lines emphasize:

> I do believe, the One in Three,
> And Three in perfect Unitie:
> Lastly, that JESUS is a Deed
> Of Gift from God: *And here's my Creed.*   15

Though these doctrines are not simple, they are basic; and they
are acknowledged in a spirit of simplicity so complete as to seem
almost innocent, almost childlike. And just these qualities, according to some students of Herrick, pervade *His Noble Numbers* and
allow for the drawing of unfavorable comparisons between Herrick's devotional verses and those of the major religious poets of
his day—Donne, Herbert, and Milton. According to Mr. John
Press, for example, "We shall, indeed, not find in [Herrick]
Donne's passionate apprehension of Christian dogma, Crashaw's
fervent devotional mysticism, Milton's exaltation of God's majesty
or Herbert's unfeigned desire to attune himself to God's will." [16]
Press is undoubtedly correct: as a maker of religious verse, Herrick is Herrick and not a Donne, a Herbert, or a Milton. Neither in
quantity, in quality, nor in kind does his devotional poetry approach the stature of theirs. Yet, as the remaining sections of this
chapter suggest, *His Noble Numbers* merits scrutiny for the insights it offers into Herrick's poetical character, for its exemplifica-

tion of a non-metaphysical mode of seventeenth-century religious verse, and for the more than a few poems of genuine artistic merit that it contains.

IV *God and the Individual*

A reading of the first few poems of *His Noble Numbers* disabuses the careful reader of the notion that the religious orientation of Herrick's devotional poetry is intellectually merely orthodox and emotionally almost childlike. For, following hard upon the two poems analyzed earlier, *"His Confession"* and *"His Prayer for Absolution,"* is a series of epigrams which come to grips with that most complex yet most fundamental of theological problems —the nature of God—and which, taken together, resolve it in a way that is at once original and poetic. In the first of them, *"To finde God,"* Herrick sets up the problem by constructing a verse argument, the purpose of which is to show, by the *reductio ad absurdum* of a catalogue of impossibilities, that God can not be apprehended by man's crude sensibilities. Herrick has used this technique twice before in his *Hesperides* to develop love complaints (*"His Protestation to Perilla"* and *"Impossibilities to his friend"*) in the manner of Donne's "Goe, and catche a falling starre," and once (in *"Proof to no purpose"*) to dramatize the finality of death and the completeness of oblivion. In *"To finde God,"* however, Herrick is no longer the lover or the gloomy Stoic; his role is that of the Christian metaphysician. As such, his speech is dialectical and systematic. He lists impossibilities, for example, according to the classifications of the four elements—fire ("WEIGH me the Fire"); air ("measure out the Wind"), water ("Distinguish all those Floods"); and earth ("Tell [measure] me the motes, dust, sands and speares / Of Corn, when Summer shakes his eares." In its directness and in the dramatic grotesqueness of its challenges, however, the speaker's charge is passionate as well as systematic. Thus the end of the poem—where he deftly exposes illogic by using logic, by leaping from the hypothesis of lines 1–14 to the conclusion of lines 15–16 ("This if thou canst; then shew me Him / That rides the glorius *Cherubim*")—comes as the climax of an emotional as well as a logical development. The *actual* conclusion of Herrick's argument, however, takes place in the silence after the poem's last line, in which the inner voice of the reader's reason confirms the impossibility of meeting the challenges enumerated and thus the impossibility of any sensory apprehension of the Almighty.

To accept this is not to admit that God is wholly unknowable. The Christian may draw upon his faith, his reason, and the *Holy Bible* to enable him to find God, as Herrick does in the epigrams that follow. But even these resources have their limitations, as is paradoxically suggested in *"What God is"*: "GOD is above the sphere of our esteem, / And is the best known, not defining him." Even the title of this epigram is paradoxical for it does not tell what God is at all; it claims that, since God is so much beyond man, he can know Him better by not imposing the abstraction and oversimplification of a definition upon Him. The implication is that human hearts rather than human minds are the best means of apprehending God.

Yet Herrick reveals his essential rationality by disregarding his own exhortation in the very next epigram in the series, *"Upon God"*: "GOD is not onely said to be / An *Ens*, but *Supraentitie*." The couplet is prosaically rational: it is "scholarly" ("is . . . said to be"), not personal; and it employs the kind of classification essential to logical definition ("*Ens*" is an Aristotelian term for the category, "being," and "*Supraentitie*," of course, means "the Being beyond being"). God, then, is The Great Paradox—He is being itself, the essence of existence, and yet He is also quintessential and above existence.

In the next two epigrams Herrick moves from the abstract and the authoritative to the emotional and the traditional, for each deals with qualities of God that are associated with the New and the Old Testaments, respectively—His benignity and His wrath. The first of these is an epigram in the allegorical mode, *"Mercy and Love"*:

> "GOD hath two wings, which He doth ever move,
> The one is Mercy, and the next is Love:
> Under the first the Sinners ever trust;
> And with the last he still directs the Just.

Since "Sinners" and "the Just" can never, in the view of any Christian, be mutually exclusive categories, it is not the case that Herrick is here subscribing to any Puritan classifications of the Elect and the Damned; he is emphasizing the benignity with which

God directs both the more and the less sinful. Indeed, the Anglican orientation of his theology is suggested in the next epigram, "*Gods Anger without Affection*," which gives the other side of the coin. Whereas the more radical Protestants of the earlier seventeenth century (Puritans and Presbyterians) tended to emphasize the God of Wrath more than the God of Love, the very title of Herrick's poem shows the reverse trend. The poem itself stresses that the Eternal is unchanging, that "His wrath is free from perturbation," or true passion, and that, if we think otherwise, "The alteration is in us, not Him."

Herrick's preliminary attempt to define God is summarized in "*God not to be comprehended*": " 'Tis hard to finde God, but to comprehend / Him, as He is, is labour without end." This couplet, as it harks back to the first of these linked epigrams, unifies the series; and, as it envisions a quest, it looks ahead to other poems throughout *His Noble Numbers*. All of the latter are attempts by a rational, sensitive human being to comprehend the incomprehensible, a task that his reason insists is impossible and that his heart insists he must try. Persisting as it does from the very beginning of Herrick's sacred volume to its final epigraph, this quest for God lends thematic unity to the variety of *Noble Numbers* and seriousness and elevation to its texture. Furthermore, its presence is evidence that, however orthodox, however childlike Herrick may appear to be in some poems of that collection, he is—as Miss Starkman also avers—far from being childish.[17] A hundred-odd couplets, for example, "turn on the fundamental axis of salvation and damnation. These couplets are, indeed, simple, but they are scarcely naïve; they represent, rather, a reduction to, an achieved, simplicity."[18] In these and other "Pious Pieces" Herrick is still the intellectual and emotional pilgrim, searching for a fuller comprehension of the Truth in accordance with the Protestant principle that each living soul must make his own way to that Truth which is God. The corollary of this principle—that God will come part way to meet the soul who seeks after him—is the assumption of "*To God*" [XII].

Coming as it does near the end of *His Noble Numbers*, this poem is an apt exemplar of that volume's evolved conception of the ideal relationship between man and God. Herrick visualizes this relationship as personal and intimate; the word he uses in this poem is "familiar" but the term has no connotation of "lacking in respect." Accordingly, the poem opens with a moving if negative plea—that God not come to the persona in the shape of Yahweh, the God of Wrath:

> COME to me God; but do not come
> To me, as to the gen'rall Doome,
> In power; or come Thou in that state,
> When Thou Thy Lawes didst promulgate,
> When as the Mountaine quak'd for dread,   5
> And sullen clouds bound up his head.

Both the mighty God of the Day of Judgment and the giver of the Commandments to Moses, the God of "thunders and lightnings," are more awful than the persona can bear. He is no Moses, and he knows it; he asks that God respond to his weakness:

> No, lay thy stately terrours by,
> To talke with me familiarly;
> For if Thy thunder-claps I heare,
> I shall less swoone, then die for feare.   10

His fear of God, an inevitable emotional effect of his faith, needs no reinforcement; it is the antidote to that fear—God's love—that he particularly seeks:

> Speake thou of love and I'le reply
> By way of *Epithalamie,*
> Or sing of *mercy,* and I'le suit
> To it my Violl and my Lute:
> Thus let Thy lips but love distill,   15
> Then come my God, and hap what will.

To suggest the harmony implicit in his hoped-for relationship with his God, the persona promises to assume the role of a musician-poet. If God responds to the plea of the poem with love and thus furthers the eventual marriage of his soul with Him, the poet, as is most fitting, will render an epithalamium or nuptial song. If God Himself will sing and sing of mercy (which is evidence of his concern for mankind), the musician will demonstrate his own grateful concern by accompanying the song. This vision of the harmony of his soul with God transforms the initial insecurity of the persona into ultimate trust, one so complete as to precipitate a complete surrendering of his self into God's hands—"hap what will."

The blessed assurance that man is the continual recipient of such love and mercy is reiterated throughout Herrick's *Noble Numbers*—reiterated, indeed, to the extent that it sets that volume's tone. Though the converse of this conception—that man is continually judged and sometimes scourged by God—makes its appearance in poems like *"Whips," "To his angrie God,"* and *"Gods Anger,"* a title like *"To his ever-loving God"* is still more representative of the faith exemplified and dramatized in the collection.

L. C. Martin has pointed out that the latter poem echoes several other of Herrick's works,[19] but the one which it most calls to mind is the poem discussed earlier in this chapter, *"On himselfe"* [IV]. The central metaphor of both is the quest or the journey of life. In *"On himselfe,"* this metaphor is couched in terms of a pilgrimage, but it becomes, in *"To his ever-loving God,"* simply a trip on foot. But here too the persona, the ordinary traveller, finds the way to be hard:

> CAN I not come to Thee, my God, for these
> So very-many-meeting hindrances,
> That slack my pace; but yet not make me stay?
> Who slowly goes, rids (in the end) his way.

The question raised in lines 1–3 is answered in line 4: the obstacles that life places between man and God may slow man's journey to Him, but they need not halt it. The reason this should be so is couched in homely and proverbial terms: "slow but sure makes progress" ("rids . . . his way"). Certain progress, however, depends, like all else, upon God; thus the traveller next offers up a prayer for divine assistance:

> Cleere Thou my paths, or shorten Thou my miles,   5
> Remove the barrs, or lift me o're the stiles:
> Since rough the way is, help me when I call,
> And take me up; or els prevent the fall.

The assumption behind the prayer is that God's love is personal, that He has a concern for the individual traveller and will manifest that concern by removing some of the obstacles between man and Him. The references to bars and stiles lend the realism of detail to the metaphor and, in addition, give a rural English character to the setting. So too does the image of the traveller's destination:

> I kenn my home; and it affords some ease,
> To see far off the smoaking Villages.　　　　　10
> Fain would I rest, yet covet not to die,
> For feare of future-biting penurie.

The archaic verb "kenn," meaning "catch sight of," reinforces the rustic, familiar qualities of the context; the sense of assurance and peace that is thus generated is crystallized in the identification of heaven with "home." This identification is dramatically and vividly confirmed in the image that follows in which Herrick envisions heaven—not as a celestial metropolis (in the manner, for example, of Bunyan)—but as a typical rural village, the English complement of the "*Sacred Grove.*" With the smoke curling reassuringly from the chimneys (suggesting the light and warmth to be found within), the image perfectly renders the emotional qualities that are at the base of Herrick's faith.

His weary traveller, however, cannot rest, cannot die, even though he has his goal in sight, because, by implication, he is impoverished—he has not yet been able to lay up for himself treasures in heaven. Should death come to him while this is his condition, his future—the life everlasting in his heavenly home—might be put in jeopardy. It is this, which translates into his love of God and not some pagan love of life, that impels him to continue his journey: "No, no, (my God) Thou know'st my wishes be / To leave this life, not loving it, but Thee." The apostrophe, "(my God)," as it echoes the same phrase in line 1, brings the poem full circle and reminds the reader that, though it takes the form of an allegory, "*To his ever-loving God*" is also a colloquy between one man and his God. As such, it is particularly effective in communicating the sense of warm familiarity which for Herrick is not only possible but eminently desirable in such a relationship. This is also the sense of the poet's "*A Thanksgiving to God, for his House,*" which defines this relationship in highly personal and even amusingly familiar terms.

Although it takes the form of a prayer and would be expected to be a conventionally Christian exercise in this form, "*A Thanks-*

giving" at bottom contains some of the philosophical assumptions
which, as we have seen, Herrick shares with the school of Epicurus:

> Lord, Thou hast given me a cell
>   Wherein to dwell;
> And little house, whose humble Roof
>   Is weather-proof;
> Under the sparres of which I lie   5
>   Both soft, and drie;
> Where Thou my chamber for to ward
>   Hast set a Guard
> Of harmlesse thoughts, to watch and keep
>   Me, while I sleep.   10

The emphasis in these lines is three-fold: upon the humbleness of
the persona's situation, upon the security and general satisfaction
he derives from this situation, and upon his indebtedness to God
for it all. And though the image evoked here suggests the village
rather than the open countryside, the cottage rather than the "*Sacred Grove,*" its tone and texture are reminiscent of the pastorals of
Herrick's *Hesperides.* Furthermore, the philosophical conception
which undergirds these verses is the same as that of the poet's
bucolics—the conception of moderation, the principle of nothing
in excess. The consanguinity of Roman moderation and hospitality (which Herrick so effectively celebrates in "*A Panegerick to Sir
Lewis Pemberton*") and Christian humility and humanity is exemplified in lines 11–16:

> Low is my porch, as is my Fate,
>   Both void of state;
> And yet the threshold of my doore
>   Is worn by'th poore,
> Who thither come, and freely get   15
>   Good words, or meat.

The good shepherd feeds his sheep both literally and figuratively;
he remains, withal, merely good and merely a shepherd.

Since both moderation and humility have reference not only to
the quality of a life but to the quantities of wordly goods by
which that life is sustained, the persona, by means of a catalogue
like that of "*The Fairie Temple,*" demonstrates the modesty of the

lot which contents him: his parlor, hall, and kitchen are all
"small"; his buttery or storehouse, his storage bin, and even his
bread are all "little." And only a few sticks make an adequate fire,
"Close by whose living coale I sit, / And glow like it." The warmth
of the fire is complemented by the inner radiance of a man at
peace with himself and with his God.

The final movement of the poem reaffirms that all blessings
come from God and are clear examples of His goodness and
mercy. Even the plain vegetables that grace the persona's board—
the "Pulse" (peas and beans), "Worts" and "Purslain" (herbs),
"Water-cresse," and "my beloved Beet"—he acknowledges, "of
Thy kindnesse Thou hast sent." And they are seasoned by their
recipient's "content"—his spiritual and physical satisfaction. But
God's benignity extends further than providing mere subsistence;
indeed, he leavens the loaf of life with good cheer:

> 'Tis Thou that crown'st my glittering Hearth
> With guiltlesse mirth;
> And giv'st me Wassaile Bowles to drink,
> Spic'd to the brink.   40

Though the poem is a prayer, it concludes with the persona reading a lesson for himself from the catalogue of his blessings:

> All these, and better Thou dost send
> Me, to this end,
> That I should render, for my part,
> A thankfull heart;
> Which, fir'd with incense, I resigne,   55
> As wholly Thine;
> But the acceptance, that must be,
> My Christ, by Thee.

Here the poem moves beyond any Roman context: in return for
hospitality, it is sufficient to render thanks; in return for the manifold blessings of this life, man must render unto God that which is
God's—his heart. The poem thus moves from receiving to giving,
from grateful acceptance to the grateful giving of all that man can
give and God accept. And it is this offering and the spirit in which
it is made that set "A Thanksgiving" apart from Herrick's other
Neo-Epicurean affirmations of the good life, however else it may
resemble them.

V *Holy Living and Holy Dying*

Committed as Herrick is to the conception of a God of Love
and Mercy, it is understandable that the figure of Christ, the historical exemplar of these qualities, should loom large in *His Noble
Numbers*. It is, however, worthy of note that, of the thirty-seven
poems in this collection which deal to some extent with Christ, a
large majority of them treat only two events in the Savior's life—
His nativity (eight poems, appearing mainly toward the beginning of the volume) and His crucifixion (sixteen poems, appearing mainly towards its end). The remaining thirteen tend to present Christ in abstract rather than dramatic and poetic terms.
What significance this division has is a matter for conjecture.
While it is true that Christ's birth and his death are the two most
dramatic events of his earthly sojourn, there are other incidents
that are apt for poetical rendering. Perhaps Herrick consciously or
unconsciously focused upon these two events because for him
they showed divine love and mercy to their best advantage. Perhaps too as a poet with a particular sense for the drama, significance, and form present in ritual, Herrick was powerfully drawn
to the original and the traditional ceremonial aspects of these
events. This last conjecture gains some weight from the fact that
the element of ritual dominates many of these poems—as, for example, "*A Christmas* Caroll."

The full title of this poem—"*A Christmas* Caroll, *sung to the
King in the Presence at* White-Hall"—is one of the few pieces of
evidence extent that Herrick did have a public for some of his
poems, and a distinguished one at that. Further evidence that he
was not merely an obscure versifier is found in the footnote ap-
pended to the poem: "*The Musicall Part was composed by*
M. Henry Lawes." Lawes, composer of the music for Milton's
masque, *Comus,* was one of the distinguished musicians of the
period, as Herrick himself proclaims in "*To* M. Henry Lawes, *the
excellent Composer of his Lyricks.*" And music, indeed, receives
the emphasis in "*A Christmas* Carroll," which Herrick has arranged as a production featuring four solo voices and a chorus
(perhaps composed of the soloists themselves). It is the chorus
that begins the carol, in a seven-line stanza both proclaiming the
purpose of the ritual—to celebrate the birth of the Christ-child
(which is referred to in the historical present, as if it had just
occurred)—and setting the joyful mood:

>   *Chor.* WHAT sweeter musick can we bring,
>   Then a Caroll, for to sing
>   The Birth of this our heavenly King?
>   Awake the Voice! Awake the String!
>   Heart, Eare, and Eye, and every thing   5
>   Awake! the while the active Finger
>   Runs division with the Singer.

The unique prosody of this stanza merits some attention. Its first
five verses, in iambic tetrameter mainly, all conclude with the
same masculine rhyme, whereas lines 5–6 comprise a distich with
feminine rhymes. However, the rhyming words "Finger" and
"Singer" possess initial morphemes that also happen to rhyme
with the masculine rhyme of the preceding five lines. Though it is
elaborately wrought, this pattern is not at all intrusive; indeed, it
lends to these lines a certain formalism that controls but does not
dampen their enthusiasm.

The choral song is followed by the solos, the first two of which
are in tercets and have as their theme the tradition celebrated by
Milton in his ode *"On the Morning of Christ's Nativity"*—that
Christ's first coming brought not only peace on earth and good
will toward men but also, as a symbol of the new dispensation, a
miraculous reversal of the natural order. Thus the first soloist ban-
ishes night, which is associated with sin, and welcomes the day,
the natal day itself, and also Christ, the Son who is the bringer of
light:

>   I Dark and dull night, flie hence away,
>   And give the honour to this Day,
>   That sees *December* turn'd to *May*.   10

By transforming the month of December, which marks the death
of the year and the dead of winter, into May, the month of the
rebirth of the natural world and of man's good spirits and natural
vitality, Christ's birth has actually accomplished that which the
pastoral myth has always promised—to endow man spiritually
and actually with a perpetual spring. Not comprehending this ful-
fillment, the second soloist asks:

>   2 If we may ask the reason, say;
>   The why, and wherefore all things here
>   Seem like the Spring-time of the yeere?

This question is dramatically reiterated in the third solo in which Judea and the English countryside meet in the fragrance of a pastoral image; its answer, however, is not given until the fourth solo:

> 3 Why do's the chilling Winters morne
>   Smile, like a field beset with corne?   15
>   Or smell, like to a Meade new-shorne,
>   Thus, on the sudden? 4. Come and see
>   The cause, why things thus fragrant be:
>   'Tis He is borne, whose quickning Birth
>   Gives life and luster, publike mirth,   20
>   To Heaven, and the under-Earth.

The reason why the hour and even the season have been transfigured is that Christ's birth is a "quickning" or life-giving birth, one which reverses the trend of the hour and the season toward death. Furthermore, it is a cosmic birth, illuminating heaven as well as the earth. The star in the East sheds some light upon the scene, but the Son will illuminate the whole world.

The reaction of mankind (represented by the singers) to this cosmic event constitutes the closing movement of the carol:

> *Chor.* We see Him come, and know him ours,
>   Who, with His Sun-shine, and His showers,
>   Turnes all the patient ground to flowers.   25
>
> I   The Darling of the world is come,
>   And fit it is, we finde a roome
>   To welcome Him. 2. The nobler part
>   Of all the house here, is the heart,
>
> *Chor.* Which we will give Him; and bequeath
>   This Hollie, and this Ivie Wreath,   30
>   To do Him honour; who's our King,
>   And Lord of all this Revelling.

In the tercet (lines 23–25) Christ becomes the true Apollo who, by blessing the earth with his "Sun-shine" (a pun, perhaps?), makes earth a new Eden, a revitalized *Sacred Grove.*

But Christ has come primarily to renew men, not nature. Thus there is deliberate irony in the first soloist's exhortation that a room be found for Him for whom there was none. But the irony is

resolved in terms of the familiar Biblical metaphor: the body is
the temple of the holy spirit and the heart is the *sancta sanctorum*
of that temple—hence it is the most suitable locale of all for
Christ's dwelling-place. The metaphor also bridges the chronological gap between the actual event and the celebration: if Christ
lives now as He lived then, He lives in men's hearts. Therefore,
the singers enthrone Him in their surrendered hearts and mark
His reign over themselves, as well as over the celebration, by
tendering Him the traditional Christmas plants. Thus this intricately fashioned lyric has moved from a triumphal chorus to a
semi-pastoral interlude to a ritual dedication. And it climaxes in a
worshipful but high-spirited salute to one who is an earthly as
well as a heavenly king and a master of human revels as well as of
human hearts.

In inevitably sharp contrast to the mood of *"A Christmas*
Caroll" is *"Good Friday:* Rex Tragicus, *or Christ going to His*
Crosse." Here, as in the former, Christ is king—but a tragic king.
And whereas Herrick's carol is a lyrical ritual, *"Good Friday"* is a
theatrical one: its action, its language, and its dominant metaphors are dramatic. The poem as a whole is an apostrophe to
Christ by the persona, who may be visualized as one of the Savior's followers who waits on Golgotha with his master. That the
reader, as a witness to the event, is observing the death of a king
is made clear from the start:

> PUT off Thy Robe of *Purple,* then go on
> To the sad place of execution:
> Thine hour is come; and the Tormentor stands
> Ready, to pierce Thy tender Feet, and Hands.

The robe of purple designates a monarch, which makes the actions contemplated by the "Tormentor" particularly outrageous
and unjust—if all kings rule by "divine right," overthrowing this
one is doubly unjust because he is divine right personified. Furthermore, if a king is a link between God and man, "breaking" this
one is doubly irreligious because he *is* God and man. This iniquity
and this irony will, however, be lost on the brute masses who constitute the audience and upon the minor players, who are all too
eager to fulfill their odious roles:

> Long before this, the base, the dull, the rude   5
> Th'inconstant, and unpurged Multitude

> Yawne for Thy coming; some e're this time crie,
> How He deferres, how loath He is to die!
> Amongst this scumme, the Souldier, with his speare,
> And that sowre Fellow, with his *vineger*,   10
> His *spunge*, and *stick*, do ask why Thou dost stay?

Herrick's image of the common people is extraordinarily vivid, and possibly a reflection of his Royalist sympathies; yet it is achieved—not through the use of detail—but by an ingenious selection and combination of adjectives ("unpurged," "sowre"); action-expressing verbs ("Yawne," "deferres"); and bitter humor (the boredom of the waiting "*Skurfe* and *Bran*"—the mere chaff of the human race; the appropriateness of the nature of the "vinegar man"). The humor is not at all out of place; it is like the humor of Herrick's ironic meditation, "*His Letanie, to the Holy Spirit*," in the sense that it is the effect of being able at last to see the world as it really is (because one's illusions are dispelled by the imminence of death)—which is to see its absurdity.

Having increased the irony of the scene by showing that this most momentous of dramas will be played out before an audience that is not only unsympathetic but hostile, not only unattentive but ignorant, Herrick turns the attention of *his* audience (who might be struck by the parallels between themselves and the audience described) to the protagonist. Christ is addressed as if he were a tragic actor who must purge this audience of its spiritual pity and terror:

>   . . . Go Thy way,
> Thy way, Thou guiltlesse man, and satisfie
> By Thine approach, each their beholding eye.
> Not as a thief, shalt Thou ascend the mount,   15
> But like a Person of some high account:
> The *Crosse* shall be Thy *Stage;* and Thou shalt there
> The spacious field have for Thy *Theater.*
> Thou art that *Roscius,* and that markt-out man,
> That must this day act the Tragedian,   20
> To wonder and affrightment. . . .

Herrick is not usually given to elaborate conceits, and the success of this one can be debated. It may appear to be overly ingenious or even precious; it may be regarded as at best incongruous and at worst blasphemous. But even in the context of the *Noble Num-*

bers, the latter criticisms are irrelevant: regardless of one's view of
actors, all men play roles all the time, and the *Bible* itself is the
authority for the conception that, in Christ, God is playing the
role of Man. The former charges, since they have to do with taste,
are both more and less easily dismissed; what *can* be urged in
defense of Herrick's conceit is that it is presented with the dignity
and seriousness that the persona perceives in Christ and that it is,
in a sense, faithful to the event: here God only *appears* to suffer,
only *appears* to die. Nonetheless, like Roscius (a great actor),
Christ gives this drama its animation and its significance—"this
Scene from Thee takes life and sense" (line 26).

The poem concludes with the persona's exhortation: "Why then
begin, great King! ascend Thy Throne, / And thence proceed, to
act Thy Passion." Out of this tragedy will come a triumph of cosmic proportions, one that will eventually transform "Hell, and
Earth, and Heav'n," including even the base multitudes "who see
Thee nail'd unto the Tree." Through the workings of "The Lawes
of Action,"—on one level, the principles of tragic acting; on another, the divine laws that ordained this tragedy—this audience
will be purged. It will at last understand the emotions of Christ's
followers, who carry out the denouement of the drama by seeing
that the tragic actor, who is actually to live and die his part, is
"sweetly buried." The incident thus ends as it began, in quietude
and resignation; but the quietude and resignation are measurably
elevated by the expectation of the triumph of this tragedy's final
act.

Although "Good Friday" is a dramatic and—one might even
say—theatrical monologue, it is far from being strident, declam-
atory, or bathetic. The situation is vividly realized but artistically understated, and this very understatement lends added force
and dignity to the poem. This act of dramatically re-creating one
of the events in the life of Christ in order to impress its significance upon one's mind and heart is not one that, in the Renaissance, was confined to poets. On the contrary, such exercises, which
came to be known as "meditations," were recommended to all
Christians. Formulated, apparently, by St. Ignatius Loyola, meditations had, according to Louis L. Martz,[20] gained such currency
in England by the end of the sixteenth century that they were to
influence significantly the devotional poetry of John Donne and
his disciples. Although, as has elsewhere been noted, Herrick can
hardly be numbered among the latter, at least one poem of *His*

Noble Numbers, "*His Meditation upon Death,*" is evidence that
he was aware of the meditative tradition, its practices, and its uses
for poetry.

The formal steps of the meditative exercise, for example, to a
considerable extent regulate the structure of Herrick's poem. They
are preceded, however, by an introductory passage in which the
persona puts death in context by philosophizing about life, and in
the process reveals something of himself:

> BE those few hours, which I have yet to spend,
> Blest with the Meditation of my end:
> Though they be few in number, I'm content;
> If otherwise, I stand indifferent:
> Nor makes it matter, *Nestors* yeers to tell,   5
> If man lives long, and if he live not well.
> A multitude of dayes still heaped on,
> Seldome brings order, but confusion.
> Might I make choice, long life sho'd be with-stood;
> Nor wo'd I care how short it were, if good: 10
> Which to effect, let ev'ry passing Bell
> Possesse my thoughts, next comes my dolefull knell.

The self-portraiture of these lines reveals a familiar face, the face
of one who is aware that life is short but confronts the fact with
equanimity; who is content with whatever life is allotted to him;
and who is more concerned with the quality of his hours than with
their quantity. He seems, of course, to be very like the Neo-
Epicurean persona of *Hesperides.* And so he is—but with this
difference: to help insure the quality of his life he reverts, not to
an active affirmation of it, but to the contemplation of his death.
For him, as a true Christian, this is a compelling duty and a continual one: it will be performed each time he hears the melancholy tolling of the funeral bell, a bell which the persona, like
John Donne, will imagine tolls for *him.* Yet the persona is quite
unlike the Donne of the famous seventeenth "Meditation": the
latter is confident in his faith, but the former seems to be confident in his philosophy. The significance of this attitude of Herrick's persona is indicated below.

The first step of the meditative process is the recreation of some
significant event in the mind of the meditator by the concerted
application of his powers of imagination. This event might be the
Crucifixion, into which scene the meditator would imaginatively

project himself—much in the manner of the persona of *"Good Friday."* In the case of this poem, however, the event is the persona's own death, of which he is reminded by the all-too-frequent death knell and by his nightly retirement to his bed:

> And when the night perswades me to my bed,
> I'le thinke I'm going to be buried:
> So shall the Blankets which come over me,   15
> Present those Turfs, which once must cover me:
> And with as firme behaviour I will meet
> The sheet I sleep in, as my Winding-sheet.

In order to perform this first step of the meditation—this "composition of place," as it is called—the meditator must be as sensitive and imaginative as an improvising actor. The familiar objects of the ritual of sleep become his props, but the "play" is not a game—the metamorphosis of the comfortable into the fatal carries with it a certain shock value, and deliberately so. By the repetition of such shocks one reinforces his "firme behaviour," the Stoical element that is so conducive to the Christian makeup.

Though Herrick is rarely an innovator, he is an inveterate experimenter with poetic forms. This tendency of his shows up in *"His Meditation,"* where, instead of moving on to the next step of the exercise, he institutes a second "composition of place." He has his persona visualize his awakening from sleep; by means of an analogy between that event and his eventual resurrection, he begins to meditate upon the latter. He visualizes the Day of Judgment, "that *Gen'rall Doome,* / To which the Pesant, so the Prince must come" (lines 23–24). The terrible democracy of that event, the dread impartiality of the Judge, the weakness of mere tears as a defense, and the horrible vision of the penalty for guilt, force the persona into the next step of the meditation, the analysis of the implications of these experiences for him:

> Let me, though late, yet at the last, begin
> To shun the least Temptation to a sin;   30
> Though to be tempted be no sin, untill
> Man to th'alluring object gives his will.

Although a trace of the philosopher is visible in lines 31–32, the persona is clearly no longer the almost worldly, almost bored Neo-Stoic of the opening lines of the poem; the effect of the meditation has been to transform him into one who is concerned, not just with living and with dying, but with holy living and with holy dying.

The final step of the meditation involves a colloquy or dialogue in which the tensions evoked by the composition and by the analysis are resolved. Though such colloquies are usually imagined conversations with God, they can take the form of dialogues with one's self,[21] as is the case here:

> Such let my life assure me, when my breath
> Goes theeving from me, I am safe in death;
> Which is the height of comfort, when I fall,   35
> I rise triumphant in my Funerall.

This resolution is, of course, triumphantly orthodox in its affirmation of the Christian paradox of life in death. But the final effect of the poem is psychological as well as theological: the meditation resembles a play in that it evokes fears in order to purge them and psychiatric therapy in that it elicits mental images in order to ease the anxieties which lie behind them.

For complete liberation from his fears and anxieties, of course, the true believer must wait for his "rise triumphant," for his own ascension into heaven. It is worth noting that while Herrick, in his *Hesperides,* is preoccupied with the problem of the nature of heaven-on-earth and ultimately resolves that problem in terms of the "*Sacred Grove,*" the country life refined by art, in *His Noble Numbers* he hardly treats the subject of heaven at all. Its existence, as we learn from "*His Creed*" is, of course, accepted; its possible nature is seriously examined only in a poem called "*The white Island: or place of the Blest.*" And interestingly enough, the image of the island developed in this poem, with its connotations of remoteness, security, and peace, draws together the conventional Christian vision of heaven and the idea and ideal of pastoral toward which Herrick aspires in *Hesperides.* The opening stanza, however, purports to contrast the "white island" of heaven with the ephemeral "island" of this world:

> IN this world (the *Isle of Dreames*)
> While we sit by sorrowes streames,
> Teares and terrors are our theames
>   Reciting.

The image of the *"Isle of Dreames"* and its imputation of an illusory nature to this world calls to mind Plato's "Myth of the Cave," in which that existence man calls "reality" is depicted as merely the shadow of a higher reality. This shadow-world, with its "sorrowes streames," also recalls the Classical vision of the underworld where all is insubstantial and where the dominant "theames" do indeed seem to be unhappy or even fearful ones—the Elysian Fields, after all, are only for the few.

Stanza II is transitional, transferring the focus of the poem from the here and now to the hereafter, "the white island" of Stanza III:

> But when once from hence we flie,   5
> More and more approaching nigh
> Unto young Eternitie
>   Uniting:
>
> In that *whiter Island,* where
> Things are evermore sincere;   10
> Candor here, and lustre there
>   Delighting.

There is a kind of whimsy in the reference to "young Eternitie"—young because it never grows old; because in eternity time, the force that ages, no longer exists. Yet eternity is also young in the more serious sense that it unites the blest with the lost virtues of their youth—innocence, sincerity, joy, and brightness.

Herrick does not attempt to portray "the white island" in really graphic detail: his image is as deliberately vague as Milton's image of God. Heaven is a place of whiteness ("Candor"), suggesting pervasive purity, and brightness ("lustre"), suggesting ubiquitous holiness, a place where things are always what they seem to be (and thus are "sincere")—an implied contrast with the *"Isle of Dreames,"* where distinctions between appearance and reality are at best difficult to make. Possessing these qualities, the island or its atmosphere casts off any impurities:

> There no monstrous fancies shall
> Out of hell an horrour call,
> To create (or cause at all)   15
>   Affrighting.

Sin, like Macbeth, murders sleep; thus the sleeping (like many of
the waking) dreams of the inhabitants of the *"Isle of Dreames"*
become nightmares. But the blest, being without sin and without
labor, have no need of sleep; eternal vigilance is the price of
heaven, but it is vigilance over immortal pleasures:

> There in calm and cooling sleep
> We our eyes shall never steep;
> But eternall watch shall keep,
>   Attending   20
>
> Pleasures, such as shall pursue
> Me immortaliz'd, and you;
> And fresh joyes, as never too
>   Have ending.

There is a disturbing aspect to the image of Stanza V; while it is
easy enough to accept *intellectually* the hypothesis that heaven is
itself "calm" and "cooling" as earthly sleep cannot always be, Herrick's very manner of presenting the latter makes the prospect of
never again tasting the joys of sleep *emotionally* less than appeal-
ing. Hardly more attractive is the prospect of being eternally
watchful and eternally happy. There is, in short, a sense of strain
in these stanzas which debilitates the ultimate effectiveness of the
poem. It can be conjectured that this strain comes from the poet's
basic inability to deny the existence of the concrete and the value
of being, to deny life in the affirmation of afterlife, to renunciate—
in Emily Dickinson's phrase—"A Presence—for an Expectation." [22]
Some confirmation of this conjecture may be found in the poem's
emphasis upon the minimization of pain and maximization of
pleasure, as if Herrick's vision of heaven makes it easier for his
Christianity to come to terms with his Neo-Epicureanism. For
John Press, Herrick's Christianity in fact surrenders to Neo-Epicureanism here; "the white island," he says, "is simply the Earthly
Paradise indefinitely prolonged and rendered a shade more
edifying by the apparent absence of wine and sex. . . ." [23]

This criticism is well taken; the vision of "the white island" does
appear rather "tepid" when placed side by side with Herrick's vision of the *"Sacred Grove."* The poem is a minor technical master-
piece, with its tetrameter triplets and linking monometer fourth
lines, its strict economy and precise diction; but ultimately its thematic and emotional complex breaks down. This breakdown,

however, is specific—confined to this poem—not general. As a whole, the *Noble Numbers* is a success—a modest success in many ways, but still a success—because it contains enough affecting, well-executed sacred verses to have insured the reputation of whoever had composed them, even if he did not also happen to be the author of "Corinna's *going a Maying.*"

For Herrick, as a devotional poet, is more than Press would have him be—one who glosses over his essential paganism with a veneer of ritualism.[24] As has been suggested above, ritual for Herrick is meaning, feeling, and form, the very stuff of the religious *and* the esthetic experience. Because ritual shapes his art and renders it generally less intense and complex than that of the Donnes and the Herberts, it does not follow that the religious experience which gave rise to such art was somehow invalid or ineffectual. This charge, however, is substantially Press's when he alleges that "Herrick's intellectual and emotional resources are too meagre to sustain him when he exiles himself from the delicious pagan landscape and attempts to survey the divine order of the universe." [25] But this statement, surely, is an exaggeration; otherwise one could legitimately charge Herbert, Vaughan, and Crashaw with being seriously deficient in "intellectual and emotional resources" because none of them wrote secular verse to compare with Herrick's best.

Religious experience and secular experience are not always that distinguishable nor are the impulses and techniques whereby they are transformed into poetry. It may be that, as Press claims, the bulk of *Noble Numbers* is made up of a "succession of dull, mechanical pieces," [26] yet the presence of more than a few interesting, well-executed, and even affecting poems *does* make up for the rest and *does* demonstrate that Herrick—far from being some kind of esthetic schizophrenic—will not necessarily disintegrate into a bad poet when he turns his hand to devotional verse. The presence of effective and essentially religious poems in *Hesperides* is further evidence that he is one poet, not two. Furthermore, as has been indicated above, there is no unresolvable schism between Herrick's philosophy and his religion because, on the one hand, Christian humanism had long since absorbed the elements of Stoicism and Epicureanism that are of importance to Herrick; and, on the other hand, Herrick—much like Sir Thomas Browne—when necessary had the "capacity to live in divided and distinguished worlds, and to pass freely to and fro between one and another, to be capable of many and varied responses to experience, instead of being confined to a few stereotyped ones." [27] But while faith mediates for Browne between these divided and distinguished worlds, it is art that mediates for Herrick. Indeed, as the next chapter shows, Herrick can be distinguished from Browne and from all the rest of his contemporary artists, major and minor, in the extent to which he makes a religion of his art.

The Pillar of Fame *and* This Sacred Grove: *The Theme of Immortality*

ROBERT HERRICK has sometimes been rebuked for having had what some scholars appear to regard as the bad taste to have published his *Hesperides* in the very midst of England's most catastrophic civil war. This book, it is charged, is an anachronism—a mere collection of "pastoral ditties" by a man born too late, a man with the world view and artistic temperament of an Elizabethan. So absorbed was he in the world of his art, the charge continues, that he remained blithely unaware of the "real world" going up in flames all around him.

The naïveté of this view is at least equal to that it imputes to Herrick. While there is some validity in classifying Herrick as an Elizabethan in temperament—for he does show the lyricism, the richness, the vitality, and the variety which are generally associated with that period—the fact is that his poetry does *not* merely regress to a happier age; rather, as has been suggested earlier, it *mediates* between "dull *Devon-shire*," the world as it really is, and the "*Sacred Grove*," the world as it might be. Indeed, Herrick's involvement in "the real world" can be demonstrated by reference to a number of poems that deal specifically with the Civil War. There are, for example, occasional verses on the political and martial fortunes of King Charles,[1] poems which refer to particular events of the war,[2] and others which mourn specific persons fallen in the Royalist cause.[3] The very existence of these seems to be ignored by Herrick's critics.

The poet's involvement as a person and as an artist in the events that were shaping his age is, furthermore, demonstrated less obviously but more poetically in such works as "*Farwell Frost, or welcome the Spring*" and "*The bad season makes the Poet sad.*" The latter is a hybrid poem, being half occasional and specific, half general and ambiguous. Its first couplet, for example, admits to at least three levels of interpretation: "DULL to my selfe, and almost dead to these / My many fresh and fragrant Mistresses." The tone

of these lines, which is triggered by the alliterating "DULL" and
"dead," suggests that the poem is to be a complaint, and—as
would seem from the reference to the persona's "Mistresses"—a
love complaint, specifically. But, if the poem is read in the context
of Herrick's *Hesperides,* it becomes possible for these sweet ladies
to be the Julias, Corinnas, and Electras of his other poems; and it
may even be that these "Mistresses" are personifications of his
lyrics themselves. Proof that the poem is more than personal and
amatory is to be found in lines 3–6, where the causes of the persona's condition are adduced:

> Lost to all Musick now; since every thing
> Puts on the semblance here of sorrowing.
> Sick is the Land to'th'heart; and doth endure   5
> More dangerous faintings by her des'prate cure.

Here England has become the foremost of his "fresh and fragrant
Mistresses," but with her heartsickness and her faintings, she appears more pathetic than provocative. Yet the persona, as a lover
of both women and his country, cannot help but respond to her
plight. His response, however, is a negative one—the loss of his
"Musick," his artistic creativity, and the loss of any innocence with
regard to the salutary effects of civil war.

The situation thus set, the second movement of the poem expresses a desperate hope for the future through an invocation of
the past, a cry for a return to prewar days—days which Herrick
envisions in terms of a golden age:

> But if that golden Age wo'd come again,
> And *Charles* here Rule, as he before did Raign;
> If smooth and unperplext the Seasons were,
> As when the *Sweet Maria* lived here: 10
> I sho'd delight to have my Curles halfe drown'd
> In *Tyrian Dewes,* and Head with Roses crown'd.
> And once more yet (ere I am laid out dead)
> *Knock at a Starre with my exalted Head.*

Although, with its reference to actual personages, this passage
deals with historical reality, that reality is framed in terms of art.
As Virgil in his fourth eclogue looked forward to an idyllic time
when a marvellous infant would bring pastoral serenity and peace
to the world, so Herrick looks forward to the re-establishment of

the reign of Charles I and thus to an age in which the seasons (political, it can be inferred, as well as climatological) again will be bucolically tranquil. Herrick's remembrance of things past is of course artistic and nostalgic rather than historical; his impulse is to raise historical reality, life, to the height of his poetic ideal. This tendency is also observable in lines 11–12 whose action, arising as it does out of Anacreon, is more a metaphor for happiness than it is a description of an actual response, and in lines 13–14 which, in imitation of Horace, depict the return to the animation and sensitivity (and on the next level to creativity, to the making of poems) that the initial couplet had indicated were lost. The ultimate effect of this poem then is to affirm the humanity of the artist. It suggests that, in Herrick's own view, the poet is not a star dwelling apart; he is a human being whose sensibilities and, consequently, whose creativity, are particularly responsive to the external world. Thus a "bad season," whether it be bad meteorologically or bad politically, can make itself felt in the world of his art. The "*Sacred Grove*" is not inviolable.

In "*Farwell Frost, or welcome the Spring*" Herrick's pastoralism mediates between art and life to demonstrate the life in art and the art in life. It is a vital and an artful poem which brings the fond hopes of "*The bad season*" into focus: it predicates the eventual amelioration of England's condition upon the analogy of the cycle of the seasons rather than upon nostalgic wishes for the restoration of the political past. Here, as elsewhere, conventional pastoral (in which spring is eternal) does not suit Herrick's purposes; therefore, he modifies the bucolic vision to bring it to terms with life, and in particular the life of the English countryside— where the cycle of death and rebirth is dramatically and picturesquely illustrated every year:

> FLED are the Frosts, and now the Fields appeare
> Re-cloth'd in fresh and verdant Diaper.
> Thaw'd are the snowes, and now the lusty Spring
> Gives to each Mead a neat enameling.
> The Palms put forth their Gemmes, and every Tree   5
> Now swaggers in her Leavy gallantry.
> The while the *Daulian Minstrell* sweetly sings,
> With warbling Notes, her *Tyrrean* sufferings.

Herrick's use of personification enables him at once to set the scene and give it animation: the frosts, which have, like unwelcome suitors, been besieging Dame Nature, have been driven off by "the lusty Spring," Nature's true paramour. As a consequence, Nature comes forth once again, her beauty enhanced by the trappings with which her lover has be-decked her. She is draped in her gown of multipatterned green cloth ("Diaper") and furnished with gemlike blossoms and leaves. Providing the musical background to her progress is the nightingale, "the *Daulian Minstrell*," who also—according to tradition—endured suffering because of another's unlawful passions.

The contrast between the present spring and the past winter is sharpened by the contrast between love and lust: the Spring, like a true lover, has clothed and fostered Nature, but Winter was her ravisher:

> What gentle Winds perspire? As if here
> Never had been the *Northern Plunderer*   10
> To strip the Trees, and Fields, to their distresse,
> Leaving them to a pittied nakednesse.

Winter's agent in this crime is the North Wind, "the *Northern Plunderer.*" If we recall that some of Charles' strongest opposition also came from the north, Herrick's epithet can be seen to contain his first hint as to the structure of meaning of the entire poem. This structure eventually becomes apparent as the simile of lines 13–22 steadily expands:

> And look how when a frantick Storme doth tear
> A stubborn Oake, or Holme (long growing there)
> But lul'd to calmnesse, then succeeds a breeze   15
> That scarcely stirs the nodding leaves of Trees:
> So when this War (which tempest-like doth spoil
> Our salt, our Corn, our Honie, Wine, and Oile)
> Falls to a temper, and doth mildly cast
> His inconsiderate Frenzie off (at last)   20
> The gentle Dove may, when these turmoils cease,
> Bring in her Bill, once more, *the Branch of Peace.*

The war has been like a force of nature, "spoiling" or destroying the plenty of the "*Sacred Grove*" that is England; but it is also human in its madness, its "Frenzie." And as destructive natural forces eventually yield to benign ones and hysteria succumbs to calmness, so there is hope for the nation. These parallels are completed and summarized in the bird images, with the nightingale, a symbol of suffering, giving way to "the gentle Dove," a symbol of peace.

At this point it is possible to look back over the poem and see that its first movement can be read as a type of submerged allegory: "the *Northern Plunderer*" can be the invading Scots and Nature is England herself; the "stubborn Oake" of the second movement, the monarch of the forest, may be the king and "the *Daulian Minstrell*" of the first may well be Herrick himself, the poet sorrowfully responding to the plight of his native land.

I *Art as Response*

The criticism that Herrick as poet lives largely in the world of his own imagination is further called into question by the evidence of two of his poems about rural Devonshire, where he lived as a parish priest for all of thirty-one of his eighty-three years. "*Discontents in Devon*," for example, is grounded in a paradox: Devonshire to him is "dull," a place that makes him sad and discontented, yet he is forced to admit that he "ne'r invented such / Ennobled numbers," such inspired poetry, as he has amid these apparently uncongenial surroundings. In short, he sees very clearly the discrepancy between the English countryside and the "*Sacred Grove*"; what he does not indicate is that it may be this very discrepancy that impels him to compose his "Ennobled numbers."

"*His Lachrimae or Mirth, turn'd to mourning*" reveals Herrick in another mood: the West-country, to which he has in effect been banished, has so dampened his good spirits and so deadened the "Organ" of his creativity that he is unable to "rehearse / A Lyrick verse, / And speak it with the best." His frustrated state is mirrored not only in the sporadic movement of the poem's meter but in the fact that its third stanza contradicts to some extent its first by attributing the loss of his poetic powers to the passage of time. The contradiction between these two poems, however, is not a troublesome one. They are written in different moods, but both represent a familiar phenomenon: the artist's continual awareness of the mystery of his own creativity and, in particular, the problem of the link between that creativity and the world of which he is a part. As was indicated earlier, the tension between the latter world and the world of art, between what may be called a lower and a higher reality, helps both to unify and to define *Hes-*

perides. In Herrick's "Pious Pieces" the higher reality to which he aspires is the artifact of the Christian heaven, which the poet transmutes into the image of "the white island." This mythopoeic impulse is also in evidence in his "Humane Works," where the higher reality is symbolized by the myth of the *"Sacred Grove"*— where Nature or life has been, not transcended, but translated by art. Similar to this pastoral myth, and like it hinted at as early in *Hesperides* as *"The Argument of his Book,"* is the myth of the land of faerie. The pivotal image of one of Herrick's double poems, *"The meddow verse or Aniversary to Mistris* Bridget Low-man" and *"The parting verse, the feast there ended,"* is based upon this familiar English metaphor.

The particulars given in the first title indicate that an actual event is being celebrated, but this poem, like most of Herrick's occasional pieces, goes beyond the actual to the universal. Both halves of the poem are in the form of an apostrophe, with *"The meddow verse"* being essentially a poetic speech of invitation and welcome. Although it is not an invitation to love, it is like many poems in this vein, blithely flattering; Mistress Lowman is invited to "Come with the Spring-time, forth Fair Maid, and be / This year again, the *medows Deity."* The occasion might well be May Day, for the time is spring; it is therefore appropriate that, like Proserpine, she come forth and be goddess and queen. "This flowry Coronet," the speaker says, will designate her to be "the Prime, and Princesse of the Feast." The demonstrative "This" may contain an implicit stage direction, but it may suggest on another level that the poem itself is the coronet. Similarly, the phrase "this Fairie land" in the lines which follow may suggest not only the actual fields where the celebration takes place but Herrick's *Hesperides* itself, the half-actual, half-artificial land in which the event of the poem occurs:

> This is your houre; and best you may command,
> Since you are Lady of this Fairie land. 10
> Full mirth wait on you; and such mirth as shall
> Cherrish the cheek, but make none blush at all.

The final couplet, a type of punning benediction, wishes that she may have the kind of sport that will "Cherrish" (meaning both to caress and to make cherry-colored) her complexion. The contrast between innocent mirth such as this and the kind which results in a blush of shame symbolizes the contrast between "this Fairie land," or the "*Sacred Grove*," and the world of objective reality.

The mood is altered from *allegro* to *penseroso* in "*The parting verse*," which effectively communicates the depression of the spirits that can follow hard upon the ending of some revels because of the realization that anniversaries mark ends as well as beginnings:

> Loth to depart, but yet at last, each one
> Back must now go to's habitation:
> Not knowing thus much, when we once do sever,
> Whether or no, that we shall meet here ever.

The long vowels and short words of these lines reinforce the sense of regret conveyed; the jocund Herrick of "*The meddow verse*" seems not only melancholic but perceptibly older:

> As for my self, since time a thousand cares   5
> And griefs hath fil'de upon my silver hairs;
> 'Tis to be doubted whether I next yeer,
> Or no, shall give ye a re-meeting here.
> If die I must, then my last vow shall be,
> You'l with a tear or two, remember me,   10
> Your sometime Poet. . . .

The hyperbole of "a thousand cares" and the melodramatic references to his imminent death and to his last vow are signs that the speaker's mood is an exaggerated (and perhaps a drunken) one, redolent of the infinite sadness that the end of an affair can entail. Since he is therefore at the bottom of one cycle, it comes as no surprise that the speaker begins to swing back toward the mood of "*The meddow verse*" in the concluding moments of the poem:

> . . . but if fates do give
> Me longer date, and more fresh springs to live:
> Oft as your field, shall her old age renew,
> *Herrick* shall make the meddow-verse for you.

As is customary with the Herrick of the secular poems, fate is a consideration; but there is hope in the cycle of nature and in poetry. The meadows may die but they are born again; the fairy land may fade, but the poem that contains it may endure. The "*Sacred Grove*" reflects a world in flux, but is itself stasis—a world where Nature can be heightened and made permanent by Art. And for Robert Herrick this accomplishment is "a consummation devoutly to be wished."

II *Art as Nature Refined*

As one student of Herrick has phrased it, the poet "wishes to unite art and nature which he finds interrelated yet disparate." [4] This disparity exists because Nature (all that makes up the physical world, man included) is flawed; and it is marred because it is "fallen." For behind even Herrick's secular poems lies the Christian assumption that God once created a perfect world as well as a perfect man and woman and that, when Adam and Eve sinned and fell, this world fell with them. A corollary of this assumption is that man and his world since that time have continually degenerated. As a believer, Herrick could only accept this situation and receive consolation from the promise of eternal life in another perfect world; but, as a poet, he could also create his own, near-perfect world. And from these philosophical, psychological, and mythopoeic impulses comes Herrick's pastoralism, to be crystallized in the symbol of the *"Sacred Grove."* Partaking as it does of both objective reality and the poet's vision of the ideal, this perfected world mediates between the two; and, as such, it acts both as a sanctuary and as a model for those who seek a creative transcendence (or at least an artistic amelioration) of a fallen world and a fallen race of men. It reconciles "an idealized concept of nature and actual existence, and [the] conflict between the search for simplicity and a complex, pressing society. . . ." [5]

Thus the following pattern, which Harold E. Toliver sees in the poems of Andrew Marvell, is also apparent in *Hesperides:* "Overwhelmed by the existent, the pastoral poet frequently retreats from the 'red and white' world into the 'green' world. In poems of 'pastoral success' . . . he often consolidates gains, becomes reoriented toward the world, and finally re-enters society. The general pattern varies from poet to poet and from poem to poem, but is remarkably persistent." [6] This tendency, this "need to synthesize art and nature to achieve an idealism appropriate to humanity," is, as R. J. Ross notes, "Herrick's persistent theme." [7] The point from which this theme departs is indicated in a poem entitled *"Upon Man."*

One of Herrick's more abstract and prosaic epigrams, *"Upon Man"* does not readily admit of an interpretation:

> MAN is compos'd here of a two-fold part;
> The first of Nature, and the next of Art:
> Art presupposes Nature; Nature shee
> Prepares the way to mans docility.

The main difficulty resides in the question of Herrick's use of the term "Art." If "Nature" refers to "physical man," "Art" may be understood as representing "intellectual man"—that combination of intelligence, sensitivity, and perhaps spirituality which is an aspect of, but only partially dependent upon, man's physical being. (The adverb, "here," it should be noted, by its emphasis permits the inference that *elsewhere,* in heaven, man may be different.) Lines 3–4 then may be paraphrased as follows: "Man's corporeality, his 'lower' form of existence, is a necessary condition of the 'higher' form, his intellectual and imaginative existence; hence his very corporeality renders man capable of being instructed ('docile') and thus improved." The thrust of this paradox is ultimately that, in the words of Sir Thomas Browne, ". . . Nature is not at variance with Art, nor Art with Nature. . . . Art is the perfection of Nature. . . ." [8] Or, as Herrick's mentor, Ben Jonson, puts it: ". . . without Art, Nature can ne're bee perfect; &, without Nature, Art can clayme no being." [9] This relationship is regarded as true whether the object for consideration is human nature or the whole world of physical reality.

These conceptions, as has been suggested, are synthesized by Herrick into fundamental principles of his comprehensive esthetic. But, in spite of the seriousness of their implications, he can advance them quite without solemnity—in some of his poems on the subject of women's clothes, for example. Trivial as these "meditations on the psychology of dress" may appear to be, they are (as John Press points out) "a mark of [Herrick's] interest in aesthetic theory and a pointer to the nature of his poetic endowment." [10]

One such "meditation" is *"Delight in Disorder,"* a poem probably in imitation of the second stanza of Jonson's lyric, "Still to be neat, still to be drest." Yet Jonson's lines are an endorsement of complete naturalness,

> Give me a looke, give me a face,
> That makes simplicitie a grace;
> Robes loosely flowing, haire as free:
> Such sweet neglect more taketh me,   10

and a blanket condemnation of "all th'adulteries of art." But *"Delight in Disorder"* calls for a compromise between complete naturalness and total artfulness. Working backwards from effects to causes, Herrick's poem opens with a description of the kind of response such a compromise can evoke in the speaker: "A sweet disorder in the dresse / Kindles in cloathes a wantonnesse."

To the conventionally minded, "a sweet disorder" would be a paradox; the main effect of the poem as a whole, however, is to demonstrate that it is *not*—that it is, rather, the esthetic achievement of the Golden Mean. But, at this early stage of the poem, the speaker only implies that the erotic potentialities of women's garments are realized when those garments achieve a look of studied carelessness. It would be a mistake, however, to take "wantonnesse" only in its strongest sense, connoting qualities of lewdness or lasciviousness. The "disorder" is after all "sweet"—Herrick is commending, not condemning, it; it "kindles" rather than "inflames." Furthermore, as the analysis of the phrase, "cleanly-*Wantonnesse*," in Chapter 4 indicates, "wantonnesse" can also bear the more innocent connotations of "sportive," "gay," and "lively." [11] None of these meanings is entirely amiss here and the last is particularly apt, for Herrick uses subtle personification to suggest that animation is lent to clothes by proper arrangement.

The remainder of the poem is taken up by a catalogue of specific examples of "sweet disorder" and by a restatement of their effect:

> A Lawne about the shoulders thrown
> Into a fine distraction:
> An erring Lace, which here and there   5
> Enthralls the Crimson Stomacher:
> A Cuffe neglectfull, and thereby
> Ribbands to flow confusedly:
> A winning wave (deserving Note)
> In the tempestuous petticote: 10
> A carelesse shooe-string, in whose tye
> I see a wilde civility:
> Doe more bewitch me, then when Art
> Is too precise in every part.

The "Lawne," or linen stole, is only apparently "thrown" about the shoulders: its disorder is "fine"—carefully achieved as well as pleasing—and it attracts while appearing distracted. The "erring

Lace" recalls the "erring" garment of the poem "Julia's *Petticoat*"
—it too wanders here and there as if lost, but it also errs in the
sense of being somewhat "wanton," for it "enslaves" the "Crimson
Stomacher," a decorative covering worn by seventeenth-century
ladies under the lacing of their bodices.

As rivers seem to flow aimlessly, so should cuffs and ribbons,
and the larger bulk of the petticoat should be as natural as the sea
itself in its surging movement. In short, the artifact—even if it be
a mere shoelace—must come to terms with, or appear to come to
do so, with the natural. "Art"—that which is "civil" or controlled—
must be qualified by Nature, that which is "wilde" or free. Perfection is attained when the subject is neither too "precise," too
"wilde," nor too "middling." "BEAUTY," as Herrick says in *"The
Definition of Beauty,"* "no other thing is, then a Beame / Flasht
out between the Middle and Extreame." This epigram lends credence to the inference that the esthetic principle elucidated in
"Delight in Disorder" is generally corollary to Herrick's philosophical doctrine of moderation. In this connection it is interesting to note that the poem occupying the place opposite to *"Delight
in Disorder"* in *Hesperides* is *"To* Dean-bourn" (discussed in
Chapter 3) in which Herrick complains about the "warty incivility" that Devonshire men share with the river that runs through
their land. Upon them neither the arts of living nor the fine arts
have worked their necessary refinements. Thus they are possessed
by "wildness" but have no redeeming "civility." They are living
examples of excess, of extremism.

The paradox of "wilde civility" also figures importantly in another of Herrick's "aesthetic meditations," *"Art above Nature, to
Julia."* As L. C. Martin has noted, in this poem—as in numerous
others—Herrick is indebted to Robert Burton, a passage of whose
Anatomy of Melancholy (3.2., 2.3.) reads as follows: "It is a question much controverted . . . whether naturall or artificiall objects be more powerfull? . . . for my part I am of opinion, that
though beauty it selfe be a great motive . . . artificial is of more
force, and much to be preferred. . . ." Rhetorically, Herrick's
poem takes the form of a conditional statement that also functions
as an argument. The persona itemizes a number of female fash-
ions but witholds his reason for calling attention to them until the
last couplet, where—with some humor—that reason turns out to
be esthetic as well as sensual.

Implicit in the poem, however, is an analysis of the relationship between Art and Nature, one that is carried on in Herrick's meta-phors. In the first couplet, for example, Julia's hat can be seen as exemplifying an agreeable synthesis between the artful and the natural; "When I behold a Forrest spread / With silken trees upon thy head" shows Art—in the form of green, silken ribbons curled to form treelike pyramids—imitating Nature, the "Forrest." Next, in ten lines of unusual (for Herrick) ambiguity and awkward-ness, Julia's lace is compared to the white peaks of mountains and her braided hair to geometrical circles and squares.

The poem concludes with an unstated comparison resembling that of lines 7–10 of *"Delight in Disorder"* (Herrick imitates him-self almost as frequently as he imitates other writers):

> Next, when those Lawnie Films I see
> Play with a wild civility:
> And all those airie silks to flow,   15
> Alluring me, and tempting so:
> I must confesse, mine eye and heart
> Dotes less on Nature, then on Art.

Julia's linens and silks, artifacts of human society, billow and flow like nature's own winds and waves. They thus imitate, in Ben Jonson's phrase, "that orderly disorder, which is common in Nature." [12] But while the final couplet gives the nod to Art, throughout the poem the persona has taken pains to show that it is Art which achieves effects like Nature that so sways him. Ulti-mately, however, the impact of the poem is more sensuous—in its savoring of shapes, textures, and movement—than sensual; per-haps it is for this reason and the ambiguities of lines 3–8 that it is finally unsuccessful. Its undoubted charm, which is mainly real-ized in its second half, is insufficient to make up for the poem's unconvincing emotions and rhetorical opaqueness. Despite its popularity with anthologists, *"Art above Nature"* is primarily of interest as a dramatization of Herrick's esthetic.

The direct application to poetry of the principles implicit in "a wilde civility" is made by Herrick in *"A Request to the Graces."* In this poem, the Graces, "the companions of the Muses . . . and the close associates of all the other powers who make life delight-ful," [13] are invited to examine Herrick's *"Numbers"* as critics—*"Ponder* my words, if so that any be / Known guilty here of in-civility" (traces of raw naturalness)—and if such be found, to lend them the artfulness they require:

> Let what is graceless, discompos'd, and rude,
> With sweetness, smoothness, softness, be endu'd.
> Teach it to blush, to curtsie, lisp, and shew   5
> Demure, but yet, full of temptation too.

It is possible to feel uncomfortable about Herrick's metaphor and his diction in these lines but, at the same time, to recognize their relevance, not only to erotic verse, but to poetry in general. Indeed, discomfort is a part of the intended effect of this quite unsolemn poem, whose humorous tone is set by the poet's pun in requesting the Graces to grace his "graceless" verse. In point of fact, relatively few of Herrick's poems are actually graceless, or actually comparable to young ladies in urgent need of a finishing school. But, at the same time, not many of them are merely "pretty" either, merely sweet and smooth and soft (though some critics tend to think otherwise). What Herrick is trying to do here then is to suggest once again that the Beautiful is only achieved through the refinement of Nature by Art.

There is also more than meets the eye in the gnomic couplet— *"Numbers ne'r tickle, or but lightly please, / Unlesse they have some wanton carriages."* These lines are less a justification for erotic verse (poetry, like all art, can "please" in a number of ways) than they are an unsolemn assertion of a solemn principle—that poetry must provide Delight as well as Instruction. Herrick is, of course, entertaining himself with the idea of his poems as coquettes or worse, but his metaphor is based upon accepted esthetic theory.

From what has been said thus far, it is evident that Herrick gave considerable thought to his art, arrived at certain conclusions about it, and attempted to put these conclusions into practice in his own verses. The latter process, involving the actual craft of poetry, is the subject of several of his notable poems.

III   *Art as Craft*

In his *Discoveries*, Herrick's acknowledged master, Ben Jonson, writes that "For a man to write well, there are required three Necessaries. To read the best Authors, observe the best Speakers: and much exercise of his owne style." [14] While there is no way of knowing whether or not Robert Herrick was able to follow the second piece of advice—though as a young man about Cambridge and London he must have heard some excellent speeches—it is absolutely certain that he followed the other two. The more than fourteen hundred poems of his *Hesperides* and the evidence of his revisions of a number of them prove that Herrick extensively "exercised" his style. And with regard to Jonson's first precept, not only Herrick's reading of the classics (whether in the original or in translation is not of major consequence), but his *absorption* of them, his sensitivity to their spirit and their modes, have been universally acknowledged and admired. Furthermore, as an examination of L. C. Martin's notes to the Oxford edition of Herrick's works makes clear, the poet's reading was not confined to the "Ancients," but extended to the prose, poetry, and drama of the "Moderns." Jonson himself is, of course, among the latter; and, if some of the poems which Herrick dedicated to him are taken at even an approximation of their face value, it was chiefly from this "rare Arch-Poet" that he learned his craft.

"*Upon Master* Ben. Johnson" is classified as an epigram, but in some ways it resembles a highly compressed elegy. To praise Jonson, it purports to describe the fate of the theater after the dramatist's death:

> The Sock grew loathsome, and the Buskins pride,
> Together with the Stages glory stood
> Each like a poore and pitied widowhood.

The synechdoche of sock and buskin has the effect of confirming Jonson's own claim that he was the modern heir of the Classical dramatists. This glory and honor—to be, in effect, an "Ancient" —Herrick clearly concedes to him. The loss of such a genius inevitably affects the actors, who seem to be no better and no worse than their material: "For men did strut, and stride, and stare, not act." The strong alliteration of this line is an indication that the poem's satiric vein is gaining in intensity, gaining indeed to such an extent that it begins to approximate the bite of some of Herrick's more Juvenalian epigrams.

One of the bases for the literary compatibility Herrick obviously feels for Jonson is implicit in lines 13–14: "*Artlesse the Sceane was;* and that monstrous sin / Of deep and *arrant ignorance* came in." It was, of course, Jonson himself who praised William Shakespeare's apprehension of "Nature," but added a qualification:

> Yet must I not give Nature all: Thy Art,
>   My gentle *Shakespeare,* must enjoy a part.
> For though the *Poets* matter, Nature be,
>   His Art doth give the fashion.
> > ("To the Memory of My Beloved, the Author
> > Mr. William Shakespeare: And What He Hath
> > Left Us," lines 55–58)

Herrick's tribute contains no hint of the charge—issued by modern as well as seventeenth-century critics—that Jonson possessed rather more Art than Nature; indeed, in lines 5–8 Herrick implies that with Jonson's death all naturalness has gone out of the theater. Herrick is also more generous to Jonson than Jonson was to Shakespeare in the matter of the learning of poets; the famous attribution to the Bard of "small *Latine,* and lesse *Greeke*" (though qualified by the claim that Shakespearean lines threaten "the eyes of Ignorance") is in sharp contrast to Herrick's implication that his learned mentor, like a literary St. George, single-handedly kept the dragon Ignorance from the theater's door.

The memory that this hero's "unequal'd Play, the *Alchymist*" was hissed at caps Herrick's growing sense of outrage; he excoriates Ben's critics:

> > Oh fie upon 'em! Lastly too, all witt
> > In utter darkness did, and still will sit
> > Sleeping the lucklesse Age out, till that she
> > Her Resurrection ha's again with Thee.   20

The curse has a catharthic effect; the image of the present and future Dark Ages of the theater is forbidding but subdued. The hope of the rebirth of dramatic art through the intervention of a saintlike Jonson recalls the conventional elegiac conclusion, with the subject of the elegy transfigured in heaven and ready to exercise his good offices on behalf of the faithful who remain below. Though it is an angry poem, as elegies frequently are, the consolation embodied in this "epigram's" final image to some extent mitigates that anger. In other poems, in which this consolation becomes part of a full-blown religion of art, it serves to mitigate the poet's rage not only against critics but against death itself.

The almost mystical aspect of Herrick's conception of poetry is also observable in another poem on Ben Jonson, *"An Ode for him.*" The latter is paired in *Hesperides* with a highly conventional and somewhat impersonal epitaph entitled "*Upon* Ben. Johnson." The ode, however, is in every respect—form, diction, tone, and meter—unique. As its opening line indicates, it is to be a highly personal representative of its genre:

> Aн *Ben!*
> Say how, or when
> Shall we thy Guests,
> Meet at those *Lyrick* Feasts,
> Made at the *Sun,* 5
> The *Dog,* the triple *Tunne?*
> Where we such clusters had,
> As made us nobly wild, not mad;
> And yet each Verse of thine
> Out-did the meate, out-did the frolick wine. 10

Herrick's recollection in tranquillity of the revels of past years enhances them with an almost Roman dignity. The *Sun, Dog,* and "triple *Tunne*" are London taverns where Jonson reigned over a court of admiring literati—his "sons"—but the feasts are more poetic bacchanals than they are alcoholic ones. The celebrants are made ecstatic by "clusters" of poems rather than by wine. Now whether Jonson's entertainments of his "sons" were really thus is of little consequence; more important is that, to Herrick, Jonson's was an art that inspired art, that proceeded not from some strange madness (as Plato held) but from powerful yet "noble" aspects of human awareness. This art, like all good art, not only could communicate but could *involve* its audience in its communication.

The first stanza is really an invocation of the past; the second, of the future:

> My *Ben*
> Or come agen:
> Or send to us,
> Thy wits great over-plus;
> But teach us yet 15
> Wisely to husband it;
> Lest we that Tallent spend:
> And having once brought to an end
> That precious stock; the store
> Of such a wit the world sho'd have no more. 20

Here the first stanza's metaphor of poetry-as-wine is domesticated to a semireligious, semiagrarian context; and the mood of the poem is thus somewhat subdued. Jonson is asked to intercede, like a saint, on behalf of those he left behind; this intercession would take the specific form of his endowing his "sons" with merely his superfluous talent. Like a fine old wine, it will be enough for them if they limit their consumption of it. As the hyperbole of the compliment in Stanza I is balanced by the Classical allusion, so the extravagancy of the ultimate compliment is tempered both by its metaphors and by their association with the Biblical parable of the talents (John: xxv). Such unity in variety makes Herrick's ode doubly a compliment—because it flatters and because it is a successful poem; it is doubtless the kind of compliment Jonson would have most appreciated.

Though Herrick admired Jonson as Jonson admired Shakespeare—"this side Idolatry"—he must have appreciated the wisdom of Jonson's dictum that, while the poet should hold the great masters up as his models, he must regard them as "Guides, not Commanders." [15] The poet, in short, must be open to instruction, but he must also be his own man. Whatever he takes from his literary predecessors (and both Jonson and Herrick took much), he must re-create so that something new is made from something old. As Jonson phrases it, the poet must "bee able to convert the substance, or Riches of an other *Poet,* to his owne use. . . . Not, to imitate servilely, as *Horace* saith, and catch at vices, for vertue: but, to draw forth out of the best, and choisest flowers, with the Bee, and turne all into Honey. . . ." [16] This dictum indeed is the theme of Herrick's epigram, *"Upon his Verses:*

> WHAT off-spring other men have got,
> The how, where, when, I question not.
> These are the Children I have left;
> Adopted some; none got by theft.
> But all are toucht (like lawfull plate)   5
> And no Verse illegitimate.

The metaphor of his verses as his children, his flesh and his blood, communicates something of Herrick's pride in his craft and his fondness for the products of that craft. But one is no craftsman unless he can point to his products and say, "All my own work."

Thus Herrick makes a point of stressing the difference between mere "adoption"—Imitation—and "kidnapping," plagiarism. His verses have been tested upon the touchstone of the principle of Imitation (as gold and silver "plate" were rubbed as a test of quality) and have been certified as the poet's own. Here, as in most cases where Herrick refers to himself and to his art, his description is an accurate one. Though he frequently imitates, occasionally translates, and in a few instances borrows directly, the great majority of his verses are originals—lines which the poet has made uniquely his own through his personal inspiration and the application of his own genius.

Inspiration, according to the shepherd-persona of Milton's pastoral elegy, *Lycidas,* has its own catalyst:

> *Fame* is the spur that the clear spirit doth raise   70
> (That last infirmity of Noble mind)
> To scorn delights, and live laborious days.

Though it is expressed with considerably less grandeur, Herrick makes a similar claim in *"Fame makes us forward":*

> To Print our Poems, the propulsive cause
> Is Fame, (the breath of popular applause.)

Herrick's criticism is more severe than Milton's. While the latter views Fame with mixed emotions—it is a weakness or sickness (but the kind to which only exalted beings are prone)—the former seems to depict it as an almost mechanical force ("the propulsive cause"). Still, fame is quite insubstantial, an airy nothing expelled, not by the judicious, the "fit audience though few," but by the uncritical masses. There are good reasons then why poets are "forward" or presumptuous when they rush into print with their poems. Despite such cynicism, however, Herrick includes himself ("us," "our Poems") in his condemnation. He too has done what no true gentleman and artist (according to the mores of the seventeenth-century literati) would do—publish his poems. Evidently fame—or something analogous to it—*is* the spur.

That something may be what Herrick in some contexts calls "Glorie," which may be defined as honorable or justified fame— the fame beyond *mere* fame. Unlike common fame, "Glorie," as an epigram with that title complains, is difficult for poets to come by in their lifetimes: "I MAKE no haste to have my Numbers read. / *Seldome comes Glorie till a man be dead.*" From a historical point of view, Herrick treats himself more fairly in this epigram than in the one above; he did not after all rush into print, but waited until he was fifty-seven years old—apparently long after many of his poems were written. His prophecy is also accurate: it was indeed long after his death—over one hundred fifty years—that he finally began to acquire his "Glorie." This historical fact compounds the irony already present in his poem about unfavorable critics, "*Upon the same [the Detractor]*":

> I ASK'T thee oft, what Poets thou hast read,
> And lik'st the best? Still thou reply'st, The dead.
> I shall, ere long, with green turfs cover'd be;
> Then sure thou't like, or thou wilt envie me.

The very existence of *Hesperides,* however, is sufficient evidence that his cynicism toward the world of letters, or some aspects of it, must have been too localized and occasional to weaken Herrick's ultimate faith in poetry, in his appreciation of his own genius, and in his concern for his craft. Indeed, a sense of his dedication to that craft in particular and to art in general can be inferred not only from the temper and texture of his book as a whole, but from particular poems about poetry. The craftsman's dedication to excellence, for example, is the theme of "*His request to Julia*":

> JULIA, if I chance to die
> Ere I print my Poetry;
> I most humbly thee desire
> To commit it to the fire:
> Better 'twere my Book were dead,   5
> Then to live not perfected.

The address to Julia, the premonition of death, and the gnomic quality of the last couplet lend an air of convention to the poem; furthermore, in view of his even artistic temper and his philosophy of moderation, it seems rather unlikely that Herrick himself would urge so rash and irrevocable an act as the one alluded to. Yet the essential point is still well taken: the craftsman must have the *desire* to bring his work as close as possible to perfection even though he knows it to be unattainable. He must *care* about his book because it is very much alive, not "dead"; and, like all living things, the fewer its defects, the more certain it is to endure. That, in spite of the conventions of *"His request,"* such concerns are for Herrick very real is confirmed by his practice of revision. What he preaches in the epigram, *"Parcell-gil't* [partially gilded]-*Poetry,"* he himself practices: "LET's strive to be the best; the Gods, we know it, / Pillars and men, hate an indifferent Poet." Following Horace, Herrick here claims that all three levels of being—the divine, the human, and the inanimate (the pillars, according to Patrick, are those columns around whose bases book-sellers displayed their wares)[17]—reject mediocrity. The pillars may also represent posterity, which manages eventually to distinguish between artistic excellence and that which falls short of it.

Although a casual reader might not expect Herrick as he wrote to have been, like the great Milton, highly conscious of the future generations who would read his works, such a poem as *"Lyrick for Legacies"* reveals him to have been thoroughly cognizant of his relationship to posterity:

> GOLD I've none, for use or show,
> Neither Silver to bestow
> At my death; but thus much know,
> That each Lyrick here shall be
> Of my love a Legacie,   5
> Left to all posterity.
> Gentle friends, then doe but please,
> To accept such coynes as these;
> As my last Remembrances.

Like coins, poems are artifacts and symbols both; as a coin counterfeits the head of a king, for example, so a poem imitates life; as a coin stands for value, so a poem represents a value placed upon some aspect of life. But a legacy of coins is a limited one, expressive of love among a few people; a poem, however, is expressive of a love for *"all"* posterity." A poem is also in two senses a "remembrance": as a means by which the poet remembers posterity, it causes him to look beyond the narrow confines of the present, and as a means by which posterity will remember the poet, it is a living memorial to his genius. That the value of this gift outright is for Herrick self-evident is suggested by the very simplicity of his poem.

The poet has as much need of memorials as other men; he is,

like them, mutable. He lives—as Herrick expresses it in "*A Lyrick to Mirth*"—only "WHILE the milder Fates consent." He may exhort others to "Drink, and dance, and pipe, and play; / Kisse our *Dollies* night and day," yet he recognizes that such "affirmations" of life only prolong pleasure; they do not perpetuate the poet. Just as the shepherd-persona of Milton's *Lycidas* finally recognizes that even Apollo's son, Orpheus himself, could not be saved and thus he, a human poet, is doomed, so the persona of Herrick's poem realizes that even Anacreon and Horace can only be resurrected through their poetry and therefore he himself cannot expect more: "Death will come and mar the song." "Then," he goes on, "shall *Wilson* and *Gotiere* / Never sing, or play more here." Possibly it is with an eye toward posterity that Herrick names two actual artists of his own time; the fact that posterity would be likely to forget the musicianship of Wilson and Gotiere (as it has) reinforces the point of the poem. Yet Anacreon and Horace *are* remembered—and in this fact lies the hope of Herrick the poet. It becomes the primary consolation of his art and the basis of a religion that co-exists with Christianity and Neo-Epicureanism in his *Hesperides*—the religion of art.

IV   *Art as Religion*

Although the religion of art has no bible, no volumes of history and dogma, no organized priesthood or congregations of worshippers, and no temples, it is an ancient faith. And although its origins are unknown, its creed can be traced back at least to the first century, B.C., and more specifically to the poets of Rome's Silver Age—Horace, Ovid, Catullus, Tibullus, and Martial. Martial expresses the first article of that creed—that literature alone is immortal—in the concluding verse of Epigram 2 (Book X): *solaque non norunt haec monumenta mori*. Likewise, it is with this article of faith that Herrick concludes one of his best-known poems, "*To live merrily, and to trust to Good Verses*": ". . . onely Numbers sweet, / With endless life are crown'd." The effect of these lines, however, can only be measured by a consideration of the poem as a whole, for its patterns of thought, emotion, and action are intricately constructed to build up to a climax that must thoroughly convince the reader of the validity of its insight.

In addition to setting an exuberant tone for the poem, the title of course announces its dual themes, the first of which is dramatized in Stanzas I–X and the second in the final three stanzas.

Herrick's craftsmanship is very much in evidence here (though not intrusively so): the poem's organization is at once "dramatic" —based upon the ritual of the toast as it is performed at the kind of "*Lyrick* Feasts" to which Herrick refers in his ode to Jonson— and "thematic," following the logical development of the precepts enunciated in the title. In the twelve short lines of Stanzas I–III the scene and mood are set:

> Now is the time for mirth,
>   Nor cheek, or tongue be dumbe:
> For with the flowrie earth,
>   The golden pomp is come.
>
> The golden Pomp is come;   5
>   For now each tree do's weare
> (Made of her Pap and Gum)
>   Rich beads of *Amber* here.
>
> Now raignes the Rose, and now
>   Th'*Arabian* Dew besmears   10
> My uncontrolled brow,
>   And my retorted haires.

Although this is to be a "lyric feast," the setting appears to be the "*Sacred Grove*" rather than Ben Jonson's rooms in "The Triple Tun." From all indications—the references to spontaneous mirth and music and to spring's onset, plus the almost erotic personification of the trees—this is to be a pastoral poem. Yet, as it turns out, this element of the poem functions only as setting; for, as early as Stanza III, the mood becomes more specifically Dionysian than bucolic. The texture, however, remains literary: from the pun on "raignes" (to rule and to shower "*Arabian* Dew"—perfume) to the self-conscious ecstatics of the frenzied brow and the unkempt locks, the stanza is Anacreontic. A sense of excitement, however, is communicated from the exhortation of the first line of the poem and it builds effectively to the action of the succeeding stanzas.

As is customary at Dionysian rites, wine—"the drink of Gods and Angels"—figures importantly here, serving ceremonial as well as lubricational purposes. For the carousing, neither indiscriminate nor unedified, takes place according to a prescribed ritual: each draught is preceded by a dual toast—to the wine itself and to one of the Classical poets. Though each poet is duly honored in his toast, the toastmaster, in the spirit of the occasion, cannot resist having some fun; and, as is frequently the case at bacchanals, the fun can border on crudity. For example, the toastmaster ventures to announce that the wine is so potent that, were Homer to imbibe it, the blind Greek bard would have his sight restored:

> *Homer*, this Health to thee,
>   In Sack of such a kind,
> That it would make thee see,   15
>   Though thou wert ne'r so blind.

By playing upon the resemblance between the names "Virgil" and "Virginia," the toastmaster suggests that the wine is as rich as an empire in the "Indies," the New World:

> Next, *Virgil*, Ile call forth,
>   To pledge this second Health
> In Wine, whose each cup's worth
>   An Indian Common-wealth.   20

Publius Ovidius Naso ("Nose"), best known as Ovid, is the butt of Herrick's next rhetorical joke:

> A Goblet next Ile drink
>   To *Ovid;* and suppose,
> Made he the pledge, he'd think
>   The world had all *one Nose*.

As Martin paraphrases the stanza, "The wine has an aroma (line 26) so rich that Ovidius Naso, sensing it, would think he was using everyone's nose."[18] No such foolery, however, marks the toast to the Roman lyrist, Catullus:

> Then this immensive cup   25
>   Of *Aromatike* wine,
> *Catullus,* I quaffe up
>   To that Terce Muse of thine.

Catullus is the first poet toasted to be identified as such (and, unlike Virgil and Homer, he may require such identification); furthermore, he is paid the compliment of having his muse character-

ized as "Terce" or polished and refined—high praise from a poet
who seeks such qualities in his own verse.

Four generous toasts having been drunk, the progression of the
poem is as this point dramatically interrupted. The toastmaster, at
last feeling the effects of his imbibing, cries out to the god of
wine:

> Wild I am now with heat;
>   O *Bacchus!* coole thy Raies!
> Or frantick I shall eate
>   Thy *Thyrse,* and bite the *Bayes.*

The warmth generated by the alcohol threatens to turn the toastmaster into a low comic fool who, instead of wearing a lamp-
shade, will eat the pine cone atop Bacchus' symbolic Thyrsus, or
staff, and the bays, or laurel wreaths, the symbolic crowns of the
poet. But even though he is in a state of almost total inebriation,
as the first line of the next stanza humorously suggests, the persona is not so overcome as to forget that he has been in the process of toasting the Classical poets:

> Round, round the roof do's run;
>   And being ravisht thus,
> Come, I will drink a Tun   35
>   To my *Propertius.*

This gesture in honor of one of the minor Roman poets is quickly
followed by another to Tibullus: "Now, to *Tibullus,* next, / This
flood I drink to thee."

It is worth noting at this point that the humor of the poem is
not all slapstick and questionable puns. There is, for example, a
nice subtlety in the progression of the toasts: the poets are cited in
a generally descending order of literary importance—from Homer
to Tibullus—but the toasts drunk to each are quantitatively in an
inverse proportion to that order since Homer and Virgil, of epic
fame, rate only a cup each while Ovid merits a goblet; Catullus,
an "immensive cup"; Propertius, a "Tun" or huge cask; and Tibullus, a veritable flood. The ironic humor would of course be compounded by Herrick's own awareness that he is rather more the
kindred spirit of Tibullus and of the other minor poets than he is
of Homer or Virgil.

It is Tibullus, however, who inspires the second interruption of the poem's progress. His name recalls something to the toastmaster's wine-soaked brain, and with the excessive wisdom, earnestness and sobriety of the very drunk, he sees the opportunity to turn priest: "But stay; I see a Text, / That this presents to me." The "Text" or passage of scripture is given in Stanza XI and it is taken, not from the *Bible*, but from Ovid's *Amores* (III.9:39–40). The "sermon" of which the "Text" is the subject comprises the two concluding stanzas of the poem:

> Behold, *Tibullus* lies
>   Here burnt, whose smal return
> Of ashes, scarce suffice
>   To fill a little Urne.
>
> Trust to good Verses then;   45
>   They onely will aspire,
> When Pyramids, as men,
>   Are lost, i'th'funerall fire.
>
> And when all Bodies meet
>   In *Lethe* to be drown'd;   50
> Then onely Numbers sweet,
>   With endless life are crown'd.

There is an ironic overtone to the "Text": all that is left of Tibullus, who once lived and breathed and wrote poetry and who was thus a man of consequence, is a small urn of ashes. Yet this irony is qualified by the fact that the name of Tibullus *is* remembered and his verses are still read. Thus the main point of the "sermon" is well taken, even though it has been made by an inebriated "priest": successful poetry ("Numbers sweet") does indeed outlive its maker. As Hippocrates most succinctly puts it—*ars longa, vita brevis.*

This theme is validated logically and historically by the toasts to the Classical poets in the poem's second movement, for no more convincing proof of the eternizing power of verse could be demonstrated than this ritual itself, in which the "Ancients" are honored by the "Moderns." Thus not only are "Numbers sweet" crowned with "endless life," but they themselves confer crowns upon their makers. Though poets are mortal, their "Glorie," or deserved fame, is immortal. It is this form of immortality—of one's name and spirit rather than of one's soul or body—that is promised by art's religion; and it is promised even to lesser poets like Tibullus (and Robert Herrick himself). While this promise may be readily secured by an epic or a verse tragedy, it may be forthcoming on the strength of so modest a poem as *"To live merrily, and to trust to Good Verses"*; for the latter's effectively dramatic development and its forceful communication of its double theme and its mixed emotions make it likely that, had he written little else, Herrick would still be read and remembered for this poem.

While Herrick can not be directly identified with the persona of *"To live merrily . . . ,"* in two poems he does formally adopt the role of a priest of the religion of art. In *"An Hymne to the Muses,"* for example, in four triplets he honors the demi-goddesses of the title who, he says, "still inspire me"; he invokes their aid for his "measures ravishing"; and he concludes by requesting that they confer upon him the immortal badge of the poet:

> Then while I sing your praise,   10
> My *Priest-hood* crown with bayes
> Green, to the end of dayes.

It is as such a priest of poetry that Herrick offers *"His Prayer to Ben. Johnson"*:

> WHEN I a Verse shall make,
> Know that I have praid thee,
> For old *Religions* sake,
> Saint *Ben* to aide me.

Patrick conjectures that "Religion" here may refer to a vow (as of friendship) or to the tradition of loyalty to one's friends,[19] but a consideration of the poem as a whole suggests otherwise: as even the first stanza makes clear, Jonson's spirit is invoked in moments of creativity rather than at times of more conventional need. Furthermore, while Ben is literally a "saint," being one who has passed on and is enjoying his reward in heaven, he is more significant as a saint of the religion of art, for his influence and inspiration have been experienced and can still be invoked—as they are in Stanza II:

> 2. Make the way smooth for me,   5
>   When I, thy *Herrick*,
>   Honouring thee, on my knee
>   Offer my *Lyrick*.

In most religions a part of one's blessings should be offered up in gratitude and in the hope of future blessings; since the grace that is given to the adherents of the religion of art is inspiration, it is appropriate that poems—the fruits of such inspiration—be the sacrifices. On this basis, Stanza III may be read allegorically:

> 3. Candles Ile give to thee,
>   And a new Altar;   10
>   And thou Saint *Ben*, shalt be
>   Writ in my Psalter.

It is most likely that the "Psalter" is the yet-to-be published *Hesperides* itself, in which Jonson's name will indeed figure prominently; if this be so, the candles and altar may represent specific poems in honor of him (such as the two that follow *"His Prayer," "Upon* Ben. Johnson" and *"An Ode for him"*).

While it is unnecessary to take either Herrick's "prayer" or his "hymn" with the utmost seriousness (nor are they so intended), this is not to suggest that the religion of art is for the poet merely a useful and charming fiction. It *is* a fiction, but one which approaches the stature of a myth; and, like most myths, it serves as a metaphor for a great truth or for a series of truths. Such myths can then be of the utmost significance and relevance for men, and this significance and relevance must be in part due to, not in spite of, the fiction by which they are communicated. The fact that the myth of the religion of art is neither so institutionalized nor so well-known as others in no way invalidates its use in poetry.

The religion of art also resembles other "faiths" in that it can become a state religion, which another poem entitled *"On him-selfe"* [VIII] indicates is indeed the case with regard to the *"Sacred Grove,"* the world of Herrick's *Hesperides:*

> Live by thy Muse thou shalt; when others die
> Leaving no Fame to long Posterity:
> When Monarchies trans-shifted are, and gone;
> Here shall endure thy vast Dominion.

The slow and dignified measures of these heroic couplets (as opposed to the more familiar nervousness of Herrick's usual tetrameter couplets) give the poem the effect of being a type of ritual response, an article of faith of sufficient importance to be solemnly chanted. That this effect is the result of more than Herrick's prosody is evident when it is noted that here three major themes of *Hesperides* meet: the transiency of the natural world—which is opposed by the permanence of the world of art—and the transcendence of that transiency which the artist may achieve through the creation of his own world of art. The latter vision is rendered in almost surrealistic terms in one of Herrick's most ambitious and effective poems, *"The Apparition of his Mistresse calling him to Elizium."*

"The Apparition" is in a sense the counterpart in *Hesperides* of the poem, *"The white Island"* in *His Noble Numbers:* it represents an alternative (which, in view of Herrick's ultimate reconcilement of his art and his Christianity, must be regarded as a complement) to the particular vision in *"The white Island"* of the Christian heaven. In form *"The Apparition"* is a hybrid: a combination of the "dream vision" and the invitation-poem. While it is never made explicit that the ghost of his lady appears to Herrick in a dream, the event does take place (as the end of the poem discloses) at the time of night when most people are asleep. But, unlike the usual dream-vision, *"The Apparition"* is not an allegory; and, unlike the usual invitation poem, the invitation, issued by the shade of the lady and not by a living lover, is an invitation to love after death rather than to love in life. Furthermore, the pleasures promised are ultimately more esthetic and intellectual than amorous.

Three main movements constitute the poem: a description of Elizium; an account of the inhabitants of the place and their activities there; and the hurried conclusion of the lady's narrative occasioned by the coming of the day. To evoke the mood and setting of the Classical myth—according to which Elizium was that paradisiacal part of Hades reserved for those favored by the gods— Herrick calls upon his pastoral muse. The delicate beauty of the lady's invitation adds to the enticement:

> COME then, and like two Doves with silv'rie wings,
> Let our soules flie to'th'shades, where ever springs
> Sit smiling in the Meads; where Balme and Oile,
> Roses and Cassia crown the untill'd soyle.

The simile of the souls as birds is not an unconventional one. As Martin has noted, it is an echo of Psalm lxviii.13, *"yet shall ye be as* the wings of a dove covered with silver," and the identical image is employed by Andrew Marvell in a famous passage of *"The Garden"*:

> My Soul into the boughs does glide:
> There like a Bird it sits, and sings,
> Then whets, and combs its silver Wings;
> And, till prepar'd for longer flight,   55
> Waves in its Plumes the various Light.

Marvell's *"Garden,"* like Herrick's *"Sacred Grove,"* is paradise regained, a triumph of "a green Thought in a green Shade" over a fallen world. In *"The Apparition,"* however, the vision of the *"Sacred Grove"* is transferred from this world to the next. The lady's choice of similes is apt, for it translates death, the one means by which movement between these worlds is possible, into the romance and beauty of flight.

Elizium itself emerges as a conventionally pastoral landscape, much like the one pictured in Michael Drayton's *"The Description of Elizium,"* the prelude to *The Muses Elizium* (1630). Herrick's Elizium is also a land of milk and honey, of oils and spices, of supremely sensuous beauty—

> Where no disease raignes, or infection comes   5
> To blast the Aire, but *Amber-greece* and *Gums.*
> This, that, and ev'ry Thicket doth transpire
> More sweet, then *Storax* from the hallowed fire:
> Where ev'ry tree a wealthy issue beares
> Of fragrant Apples, blushing Plums, or Peares: 10
> And all the shrubs, with sparkling spangles, shew
> Like Morning-Sun-shine tinsilling the dew.

The distance between this world and the one of objective reality is somewhat greater than that between the latter and the *"Sacred Grove."* Elizium, as might be expected, has evolved into a higher state of physical and spiritual perfection. Nonetheless, both imaginary worlds possess the lushness of Ovidian pastoral, a quality communicated in olfactory images (the all-permeating fragrance of the gum, *"Storax"*) and visual ones (the "blushing Plums"), and in metrical effects (the alliteration of "shrubs, with sparkling spangles, shew"). Unfortunately, in the case of line 11, Herrick succumbs (as he does not often do) to the excesses to which exotic pastoral is prone. In the context of the poem, however, any excesses can be attributed to Nature, for she, through her agents, is the architect and the artist of this world:

> Here in green Meddowes sits eternall May,
> Purfling the Margents, while perpetuall Day
> So double gilds the Aire, as that no night   15
> Can ever rust th'Enamel of the light.

It is May who frames this picturesque landscape—figuratively, as Elizium's dominant season; literally, in her act of "Purfling the Margents" ("richly embroidering the meadows' edges").[20] Day provides the finishing touches by gilding the entire scene with the golden glow of sunshine.

To complete this scene, one which a seventeenth-century artist of the "Picturesque" like Poussin might have painted, Herrick adds idealized human figures. These, with their youth and beauty and by their decorous yet subtly erotic activities, both complement the sensuousness of Elizium and call to mind Herrick's amatory ideal of "cleanly-*Wantonnesse*":

> Here, naked Younglings, handsome Striplings run
> Their Goales for Virgins kisses; which when done,
> Then unto Dancing forth the learned Round
> Commixt they meet, with endlesse Roses crown'd.   20

This description not only completes the physical setting but facilitates a shift of narrative focus from Elizium itself to Herrick and his persona-mistress, for the actions of the young men and women may be taken as constituting an allegory of love—with the games and kisses suggesting courtship; the performance of the elaborate dances, the rites of marriage; and the mingling of the couples, the rites of love itself.

That lovers are not only present in Elizium but are crowned with roses suggests that the gods look favorably upon them; but lovers must be united, as Herrick and his lady are not. Hence the invitation must proceed from its first promise, that of a new life in an idyllic realm, to its second, that of a renewed and ideal love. That such a love will give them entrée into Elizium is implied in lines 21-24:

> And here we'l sit on Primrose-banks, and see
> Love's *Chorus* led by *Cupid;* and we'l be
> Two loving followers too unto the Grove,
> Where Poets sing the stories of our love.

Here the two protagonists are subtly transformed from mere observers of Elizium to participants in it: they join the procession of lovers led by the God of Love himself and the progress of this ritual carries them into the poet's sector of Elizium where their love will be immortalized. The ritual of immortalization is the ultimate one, the ceremony that caps the rest of the amatory rites; as such, it becomes the agency of transition between the two major movements of the poem.

The second movement of *"The Apparition"* in effect dramatizes an important corollary of the doctrine of the religion of art which has it that poets are persons favored by the gods—the fond expectation that this favoritism will extend to the afterlife. Indeed, the third promise implicitly made by the apparition is that, if he follows his mistress, he will surely enjoy not only an idyllic existence and an idyllic love but an equally great blessing, perpetual consort with the great poets of history. These poets, who by no coincidence are mainly "Ancients" (plus a few honored "Moderns"), are next catalogued in roughly chronological order, beginning with the half-legendary Musaeus, who was believed to be the author of "Hero and Leander," the saga of two lovers who—like the poet and his mistress—were separated by death. The list continues with Homer, who is enthroned as the monarch of all poets: ". . . then," promises the persona, "Ile bring / Thee to the Stand, where honour'd *Homer* reades / His *Odisees,* and his high *Iliades,*"

> About whose Throne the crowd of Poets throng
> To heare the incantation of his tongue.   30

The phrase, "the incantation of his tongue," reflects another doctrine of the religion of art—that poetry is a kind of magic, for it is capable of altering or appearing to alter the very laws of nature, so completely does it enthrall the consciousness of its hearer.

Among the poets who follow in the lady's catalogue, particular attention is given to Anacreon to whose bacchanalian verse Herrick has paid the sincerest form of flattery.[21] Speaking through the persona of the apparition, Herrick returns the compliment to himself by suggesting that, in Elizium, Anacreon will recite *his* (Herrick's) poems:

> Ile bring thee *Herrick* to *Anacreon*,
> Quaffing his full-crown'd bowles of burning Wine,
> And in his Raptures speaking Lines of Thine,
> Like to His subject; and as his Frantick-   35
> Looks, shew him truly *Bacchanalian* like,
> Besmear'd with Grapes; welcome he shall thee thither,
> Where both may rage, both drink and dance together.

The warmth of this image and the coolness of the "Pleasures" and "fresh joyes" alluded to in "*The white Island*" provide one indication of the extremes of temper exemplified in Herrick's profane and sacred volumes.

Ovid, to whom Herrick is indebted for the lush and overtly erotic spirit of some of his amatory poems, is also singled out in a particularly affecting image; but the great Virgil, with whom Herrick has less in common, is merely mentioned:

> Then stately *Virgil*, witty *Ovid*, by
> Whom faire *Corinna* sits, and doth comply   40
> With Yvorie wrists, his Laureat head, and steeps
> His eye in dew of kisses, while he sleeps.

This vignette reverses the circumstances of "*Corinna's going a-Maying*" and its sensuality is far more muted; as a compliment to Ovid, it has the beauty of its own restraint.

The other Roman poets get shorter shrift, but it is nonetheless made clear that all truly inspired poets, those who are "fill'd" with divine "Rage," will have their places in the perpetual sun of Elizium. "Thou shalt there / Behold them," the apparition reassures Herrick, "in a spacious Theater." Whether this theater is a natural amphitheater or an edifice is left ambiguous so that a transition between the "*Sacred Grove*" and the stage, and between Classical poets and modern playwrights can be effected. What may come as a surprise to the modern reader is that the authors singled out for praise are two whose names are known today mainly to students of the drama:

> Among which glories, (crown'd with sacred Bayes,
> And flatt'ring Ivie) Two recite their Plaies,   50
> *Beumont* and *Fletcher*, Swans, to whom all eares
> Listen, while they (like Syrens in their Spheres)
> Sing their *Evadne*. . . .

Collaborators in numerous tragedies (such as *The Maid's Tragedy*, in which the title-figure is named *Evadne*), tragicomedies, and comedies, Beaumont and Fletcher were more highly regarded in the seventeenth century than they are today. Indeed, in the eyes of some critics they were viewed as having eclipsed Shakespeare himself. That Robert Herrick subscribed to this view is indicated not only by the passage quoted above, but by the fact that an earlier version of the same passage had honored Shakespeare along with Beaumont; here the persona had pointed with pride to—

> *Shakespeare* and *Beamond,* Swans, to whom all eares
> Listen, while they call back the former yeares
> To teach the truth of Seenes. . . .[22]

While the lines are ambiguous, they appear to ground their praise in the axiom of dramatic criticism that plays instruct as well as delight. Paraphrased the passage might read: "The plays of Shakespeare and Beaumont capture the attention of all because, in their recreation of human events, they communicate new insights into the truths inherent in those events." The revised version is, of course, a more conventional compliment to the sweetness and musicality of Beaumont and Fletcher's dramatic verse; but it also reads more clearly and poetically. Whatever treason this version does to the memory of the Bard, and whatever doubts it may raise as to Herrick's capabilities as a drama critic, it does represent an improvement over the ambiguity of the earlier version.

There is, however, one reputation that remains constant with Herrick throughout *Hesperides*—that of Ben Jonson. And it is the possibility of Herrick's being united with his literary "father" that is held out by the apparition as the ultimate inducement. After explaining that Elizium holds more delights for him than he can imagine, the lady says:

> . . . Doe but come,   55
> And there Ile shew thee that capacious roome
> In which thy Father *Johnson* now is plac't,
> As in a Globe of Radiant fire, and grac't
> To be in the Orbe crown'd (that doth include
> Those Prophets of the former Magnitude)   60
> And he one chiefe. . . .[23]

Here Herrick's mythopoeia acquires a specifically historical orientation as the vision of Elizium becomes in essence an idealized re-creation of the past, with "Father *Johnson*" once again presiding as poet-prophet over his literary progeny in the old Sun Tavern, here apotheosized into "a Globe of Radiant fire."

At this climactic point, where a beautifully idyllic but vague bucolic vision becomes an opportunity for actually reliving the memorable past, the narrative is interrupted by a reminder of the passage of time in the real world:

> . . . But harke, I heare the Cock,
> (The Bell-man of the night) proclaime the clock
> Of late struck one; and now I see the prime
> Of Day break from the pregnant East, 'tis time
> I vanish; more I had to say;   65
> But Night determines here, Away.

Since the lady is, after all, a ghost, she must obey the supernatural law that orders all spirits to their resting places before the dawning of the day. But the interruption is, of course, deliberate and dramatic. Although the Latin tag, *Desunt nonnulla* ("some things are missing"), precedes the main body of the poem, it is complete in all important respects. By his unification and development of form, structure, and theme, Herrick has created an original poetic genre out of two conventional ones; and, by his presentation of one of the motifs of the religion of art, he exemplifies its vitality as myth. The poem itself particularly exemplifies the special imaginative bent of its creator: if wishes are revelations of the self, this poetically realized wish-fulfilment reveals an imagination that is unique in the power of its response to nature and to love but, beyond both of these, to art.

V   *Art as Salvation*

Although *"The Apparition"* is a notably successful poem, its subject—what might be called "true immortality"—occupies far less of Herrick's attention than that form of immortality which is the result of achieving well-merited fame or "Glorie" on earth, and which is therefore more susceptible to rational and pragmatic analysis. He makes much, for example, of the doctrine that to have one's name mentioned in a poem is not only an honor but a guarantee that one's memory will be perpetuated. This doctrine follows from an assumption that is so basic to Herrick that he states it as the very motto of his *Hesperides—Effugient avidos Carmina nostra Rogos—*"Our songs shall escape the eager funeral pyres." Herrick affirms and reaffirms this article of faith in poem after poem—among which is the epigram, "*Verses*": "WHO will not honour Noble Numbers, when / Verses out-live the bravest deeds of men?"

Logically, it follows that, if poems are indeed "eternal" (in the sense that they will last as long as men endure), the memory of those whose names are embedded in poems like lillies in crystal will be similarly eternal. As lillies thus preserved possess a kind of life, so will those souls fortunate enough to have been honored by poets. At first glance this may appear to be merely a fond hope, but history confirms that it is actually a fact. For poetry *can* keep this promise; its "eternizing power" is real. Because of Homer, even Odysseus' faithful dog is remembered; what is more likely then than that men can be immortalized? Accordingly, throughout *Hesperides* it is possible to encounter poems which serve not only to immortalize Herrick's relatives and friends but to reaffirm his faith in the religion of art and to emphasize the importance of this religion.[24] A typical example is "*To the most accomplisht Gentleman Master* Michael Oulsworth":

> NOR thinke that Thou in this my Booke art worst,
> Because not plac't here with the midst, or first.
> Since Fame that sides with these, or goes before
> Those, that must live with Thee for evermore.
> That Fame, and Fames rear'd Pillar, thou shalt see   5
> In the next sheet *Brave Man* to follow Thee.
> Fix on That Columne then, and never fall;
> Held up by Fames *eternall Pedestall.*

The wit that makes this poem more than a piece of hack-work resides in its central conceit: the poem is positioned near the conclusion of the published volume and thus Oulsworth is among the last to be honored; but, since the book is a type of pantheon, the

"Fame" of those to whom early dedicatory poems were written precedes them, while it "sides" with those whose dedicatory poems come in the "midst" of the volume. Thus Oulsworth has really been given a place of honor: from his niche, he can see "In the next sheet" (the sheet of paper adjacent to the one on which his poem is printed) that which supports the whole pantheon, "Fames rear'd Pillar"—a reference to the "pattern poem" known as *The Pillar of Fame*," which looms so dramatically on the last page of Herrick's secular volume. As this pillar-poem, representing the eternizing power of poetry, gives structural integrity to *Hesperides*, it insures the perpetuation of Oulsworth's name and memory.

The grace, good humor, and wit of the above poem are the characteristics of Herrick's most successful dedicatory pieces—like *"To his worthy Kinsman, Mr.* Stephen Soame." Here Christianity and the religion of art are yoked together in such a way that those mentioned in *Hesperides* become the poet's "righteous Tribe," his chosen people whom he, godlike, has elected to "canonize" in the "eternall Calender," of his book. Another is *"To his faithfull friend, Master* John Crofts . . ." in which Crofts and the poet's other *"Immortals"* become stars in the heaven of *Hesperides*. The success of *"To Mistresse* Katherine Bradshaw, *the lovely, that crowned him with Laurel*," however, rests less upon the ingenuity of its central conceit (which is the familiar one of *Hesperides* as a pastoral world) than upon a simplicity that conveys a sentiment while avoiding sentimentality. Although the poem appears in the first third of *Hesperides*, its opening lines seem to be based upon the assumption that the reader has already accepted Herrick's classification of himself as a pastoral poet:

> My Muse in Meads has spent her many houres,
> Sitting and sorting severall sorts of flowers,
> To make for others garlands; and to set
> On many a head here, many a Coronet.

If Herrick's signs are interpreted correctly, it becomes evident that he is constructing a pastoral allegory about the eternizing power of poetry. Through his shepherd-persona he in effect says: "My creative spirit has for some time impelled me to seek out the proper words to honor various persons." These compliments, however, have not been returned; none of these worthies has given his own Muse "a day of Coronation," "Till you (sweet Mistresse) came and enterwove / A *Laurel* for her, (ever young as love)." If Herrick's allegory is consistent, the meaning of these lines is that the lady has publicly affirmed him to be a man of letters and has also immortalized him by writing a poem honoring him as a poet. He will then reciprocate with this, his own poem: "You first of all crown'd her; she must of due, / Render for that, a crowne of life to you." The quietly supreme confidence of this utterance may well suggest the assurance with which the doctrine behind it is held.

If poems outlive men and if men named in poems "outlive" ordinary mortals, it follows that the makers of poems will also be granted "immortality." The importance of this principle to Herrick can scarcely be underestimated. As Leah Jonas has observed: "despite Sidney's jesting reference to it, the Renaissance poet was inclined to take rather seriously the concept of poetic immortality: 'Exegi monumentum aere perennius.' That monument, or pillar, or pyramid became a commonplace of later-day theory, a solace to poets, an inducement to patrons, and in some cases, notably those of Drayton and Herrick, a force determining the nature of their work." [25]

This force, it must be recognized, ultimately comes into some conflict with the force of Herrick's Neo-Epicureanism, for as Epicurus himself says in his epistle to Menoceus, ". . . a right understanding that death is nothing to us makes the mortality of life enjoyable, not because it adds to it an infinite span of time, but because it takes away the craving for immortality." [26] Yet the conflict is not an irreconcilable one. Herrick does not—in *Hesperides* at least—crave immortality as Epicurus understands it, as a state of actual eternal life after death. Rather, for the English poet poetic immortality is "a solace" and hence a form of pleasure. It might not be sophistry then to contend that Herrick's striving to attain such a good could conceivably receive Epicurus's blessing.

Herrick's commitment to the doctrine that poetry immortalizes its maker is expressed figuratively in *"Upon himself"* [VII] and literally in *"Poetry perpetuates the Poet,"* Herrick's Hesperidean equivalent of *"His Creed"* of *Noble Numbers.* The conceit of *"Upon himself"* yokes together the religion of art and Biblical pastoralism:

> TH'ART hence removing, (like a Shepherds Tent)
> And walk thou must the way that others went:
> Fall thou must first, then rise to life with These,
> Markt in thy Book for faithfull Witnesses.

The first line echoes Isaiah xxxviii.12—"Mine age is departed, and is removed from me as a shepherd's tent"—with its calm (almost Stoical) apprehension of increasing age and approaching death. But the Christian overtones dominate initially in *"Upon himself"*: the verb, "Fall," suggests an analogy between the speaker and the first Adam, whose "fall" doomed every man to sin and death, while the phrase, "rise to life," of course, suggests the salvation which Christ, the second Adam, made possible. The last line, however, unexpectedly makes it clear that "with These" refers not to everyman but only to those whom the speaker has chosen to "save" in his dedicatory poems. His book then becomes an analogue of the heavenly register, and the poet himself becomes a type of Christ. This is parody, of course, but it is scarcely blasphemous: in Herrick both of these faiths co-exist, and here he is simply using the diction of one to reinforce the authenticity of the other.

"Poetry perpetuates the Poet" is a less elaborate but no less ingenious poem, for its central metaphor is struck off in a single word:

> HERE I my selfe might likewise die,
> And utterly forgotten lye,
> But that eternall Poetrie
> Repullulation gives me here
> Unto the thirtieth thousand yeere,   5
> When all now dead shall re-appeare.

The sonorous Latin word "Repullulation" ("regeneration" or "the act of budding and flourishing again"), as it is used here, combines Herrick's pastoral sense of the affinity between man and nature and his faith in the eternizing power of verse: like nature's blossoms, the poet dies only temporarily. He is reborn time and time again in his verse—"here," on earth. Such "immortality," it is implied, will suffice until true immortality becomes possible—upon the Day of Judgment. The period of time referred to in the final couplet is called "that great Platonick yeere" in *"His Winding-Sheet."* Originally conceived of as a cycle of thirty thousand years "in which the heavenly bodies were supposed to go through all their possible movements and return to their original relative positions (after which, according to some, all events would recur in the same order as before) . . . ,"[27] this pseudo-scientific, pagan hypothesis became integrated with the Christian conception of Doomsday, as it is in both of Herrick's poems. To flourish—even figuratively—for this entire cycle is to gain for oneself the kind of immortality that purely natural objects inherit. And herein may lie the resolution of the irony that permeates Herrick's pastoral vision: through his imitation and refinement of self-regenerating nature in his art, the artist, in other respects a mere mortal, can also become self-regenerating.

This perpetuation is possible—according to *"His Poetrie his Pillar"*—only through art. No deeds, however great, no monuments, however grand, can perpetuate one's memory without the assistance of art. To validate this argument, Herrick begins by evoking that sense of the imminence of death and of the transiency of life which characterizes so many of his meditations:

> 1. ONELY a little more
>   I have to write,
>   Then Ile give o're
> And bid the world Good-night.
>
> 2. 'Tis but a flying minute,   5
>   That I must stay,
>   Or linger in it;
> And then I must away.

Since this poem is positioned rather early in *Hesperides,* the foreshortening of lines 1–2 seems intended to reinforce the sense of life's brevity. Herrick's Neo-Epicureanism makes itself felt in the metaphor of the sleep of death in lines 3–4—death becomes as natural an act as sleep—but the limitations of this consolation are distinctly underscored in the second stanza's restressing of the fact of human transiency. Then, like a priest making universal applications from the example of himself, Herrick goes on to the second stage of his argument:

> 3. O time that cut'st down all!
>   And scarce leav'st here   10
>   Memoriall
>   Of any men that were.

4. How many lye forgot
   In Vaults beneath?
   And piece-meale rot   15
   Without a fame in death?

The phrase, "that cut'st down all," obviously suggests the image of
Time as the grim reaper; cruel and indiscriminate, it obliterates
all the traces of men's lives except the horrible trash of the charnel
house. Death then is the great obscenity, an event over which a
concern for the inherent decency and value of human life demands transcendence.

This demand, Herrick avers, can be met in but one way:

5. Behold this living stone,
   I reare for me,
   Ne'r to be thrown
   Downe, envious Time by thee.   20

6. Pillars let some set up,
   (If so they please)
   Here is my hope,
   And my *Pyramides.*

Logically Herrick has begged the question, for he has simply as-
serted, not proved, that his *Hesperides* is an indestructible monument to his memory, an irrevocable guarantee of his fame. Yet he
can do no other because this claim, his consolation and his faith,
can be validated only by history, not by logic.

As it so happens, over three hundred years of history indicate
that Herrick's trust was reasonably well reposed. While the hope
that he expressed in an epigrammatic aside *"To his Booke"* [IV]
—"THOU art a plant sprung up to wither never, / But like a Laurell, to grow green for ever"—has turned out to be somewhat sanguine (the "Laurell" of *Hesperides* for a time did fade), it is flourishing now and there is every prospect that it will continue to do
so. In a sense, Herrick's book is the ultimate and broadly unifying
symbol of his poetry. Whether he represents it as a "Laurell" ever
green, as a *"Sacred Grove,"* as a calendar of "saints," or as a monu-
mental pillar, it serves as the sacred repository of his faith and his
works. It is the subject of his opening poem, of poems strategically
placed throughout the 1648 volume, and of *"The pillar of Fame,"*
the climactic poem of his "Humane Works." That this poem

stands as Herrick's ingenious variation upon Horace's grand theme, *Exegi monumentum aere perennius*—"I have achieved a monument more enduring than brass"—is then altogether fitting and proper. Although the vision of his *Hesperides* has seemed to some an insubstantial pageant, it was for Herrick a thing of Truth and Beauty and the source of his "Glorie." To him it represented the primacy of art over nature, of stasis over flux, of man over time. To make quite certain that even the most casual reader of his book would carry this much at least away with him, Herrick shaped his affirmation into a "pattern poem"—one which, when printed, assumes the outline of its subject:

> FAMES pillar here, at last, we set,
> Out-during *Marble, Brasse,* or *Jet,*
>   Charm'd and enchanted so,
>   As to withstand the blow
>   Of   overthrow:
>   Nor shall the seas,
>   Or   OUTRAGES
>   Of storms orebear
>   What we up-rear,
>   Tho Kingdoms fal,   10
>   This   pillar   never   shall
>   Decline or waste at all;
> But stand for ever by his owne
> Firme and well fixt foundation.

But more than its outward shape and its crucial position make this poem a fitting conclusion to Herrick's secular volume: *"The pillar of Fame"* both crystallizes the major problem of *Hesperides*—How is death to be confronted?—and proclaims the doctrine of the immortalizing power of poetry, Herrick's triumphantly poetic resolution of that problem.

CHAPTER 7

The *"Criticks" and* This Sacred Grove:
Herrick's Reputation

THERE has seldom been a poet more acutely concerned about his "Fame"—his reputation as an artist—than Robert Herrick, or one with fewer illusions about the readers upon whom that fame depends. Several of his poems wryly allude to assorted "criticks," "detractors," and "soure" readers; and others view with alarm what must happen to his *Hesperides* when it should come before the public eye. In this regard he was a good prophet, for it was to be his fate, first, to be ignored; second, to be either damned with faint praise or nearly sanctified by uncritical praise. It may indeed be said of the criticism of Robert Herrick that it has been consistent only in its contradictions.

Today, for example, Herrick's reputation is as high in some critical circles as it was in 1625 when he was ranked side by side with a great man of letters, Ben Jonson, and with a poet of widely recognized merit, Michael Drayton.[1] Yet, in other circles, he is passed over with as little attention as was accorded his *Hesperides* when it was published in 1648. By no means has he been shown the kind of critical consideration that has been lavished upon the two poets of the earlier seventeenth century to whom he is closest in real stature, George Herbert and Andrew Marvell. L. C. Martin explains why Herrick was the victim of such "sour neglect" in his own age:

The neglect is not surprising. Herrick was 57 when his poems were published and many of them belong to an earlier taste as well as to an earlier time. Their directness and apparent ease would be generally much less attractive in 1648 than the ingenuities and 'strong lines' of the metaphysical poets, whom Herrick had not greatly cared to imitate. And when the mid-century modes faded out or were absorbed in the Augustan order, the change brought him no advantage. It was too late to accept his poetry without question and too soon to realize that some of it is timeless.[2]

Near-oblivion was the result. Except for a few cursory and obscurely placed references, Herrick seems to have been largely unknown to the ages of Pope, Swift, and Johnson. The resurgence of interest in him that began very late in the eighteenth century was the result of antiquarian rather than critical interest. And it did not begin promisingly. Early in the nineteenth century Herrick was usually regarded as a poet to be read in selections—as a poet, in fact, with less than a "century" of poems worthy of the name to his name.[3] This rapid reduction of over one thousand four hundred poems to less than one hundred was largely accomplished by applying standards of taste rather than those of criticism; and, with tastes generally inclining toward elegance and uplift, many of Herrick's poems were bound to be banished. So it was throughout most of the Victorian period and so it is still—to a limited extent—today.

The fact that some of his epigrams and erotic poems were offensive to several editors and critics contributed in part to their classification of Herrick as a "minor poet." Contrariwise, he was thus classified by many who found that certain of his lyrics and his country poems lent themselves to popular consumption in the magazines of the period. And the tag of "minor poet" has vexingly remained with him. It is vexing because its meaning is unclear and because it serves to inhibit or to distort a sound and appreciative reading of Herrick's poems. Finally, it is the tag that is read and occasionally remembered by the millions who briefly study those poems in their high school and college anthologies; and thus misapprehension and mis-appreciation are perpetuated.

Not all critics, however, have been deterred by old classifications. In the late Victorian period, for example, disagreements about Herrick's status and about the true nature of his poetry were as pronounced as they are today. Edmund W. Gosse, for instance, while acknowledging Herrick's "wonderful art and skill," failed to see him as anything more than a master-artificer, a poet-jeweler, "whose easy-going callousness of soul . . . makes it impossible for him to feel very deeply." [4] But another editor, Alexander Grosart, saw in the same poet "a deeper vein of thinking and feeling than is commonly suspected. . . ." [5] Taking cognizance of the poems on transiency and death, Grosart held that *Hesperides* reveals "an unlifted shadow of melancholy that must have lain broad and black over Herrick, a melancholy which was neither transient nor a mere concession to the fashion of the age." [6] Another editor, F. T. Palgrave, who supported Grosart, pointed out that "the light mask of classicalism and bucolic allegory" could conceal an essential seriousness of thought and feeling.[7] But these were voices in the critical wilderness, and neither Grosart nor Palgrave pursued their investigations further. It was to be over a half a century before the problems of Herrick's "seriousness" and pastoralism would receive more than token consideration.

In the interim, criticism of Herrick was largely confined to the reiteration of platitudes. Although Swinburne defied orthodoxy by defending Herrick's epigrams, suggesting that they performed the necessary function of providing contrasts to the more idyllic vein of *Hesperides*,[8] the majority report of Victorian criticism can be summarized in the adjective "superficial." For all his undoubted skill and charm, Herrick was held to be lacking in "high seriousness." Thus was perpetuated the paradox which has it that he was a superb craftsman who wrote junk. Today a variation of this view is still propounded by those who somehow are able to distinguish sharply between the well-wrought form of his poems and their supposedly insubstantial content (or who are content to repeat older critics and not to study what Herrick actually wrote).

Although the late Victorian editors and critics left a legacy of contradiction and confusion, they must be credited with helping to establish Herrick as one of those English poets with whom anyone with "literary" pretensions must at least be acquainted. Thus, after centuries of being at best a mere name, and after several decades of being an inconsequential minor poet, Herrick was at last confirmed as a "Literary Figure." He is so today. But if there is any validity to this study, it should be evident that he is more: he is a poet who can not only "delight" a modern sensibility but who can also "instruct" a modern mind. It matters little then whether he be labeled a "major" or a "minor" poet. Such terms are, after all, highly relative.

What is important is that Herrick is a major poet in the sense that Eliot uses the term: in the sense that his work has "a unity of underlying pattern" as well as variety; that it embodies a "continuous *conscious* purpose"; and that it must be read extensively, not merely sampled.[9] Certainly this statement is far truer of Herrick than it is of any of the "Cavalier Poets" with whom he is so frequently classified. While limitations of space will not allow for a thorough documentation of this assessment, its validity can at least be suggested. The risk involved in so doing is that the comparisons which must be drawn are bound to be somewhat invidious. Yet, if drawing them can help clear the critical air, the risk is worth taking.

Since quantitative measure does count for something in assessing a poet, it is worth noting that Herrick's canon is more extensive than those of Carew, Suckling, and Lovelace put together. Herrick also wrote in a greater variety of forms and employed a larger number of ancient and modern models. None of the three wrote more or better devotional poetry than Herrick, and they rarely equal and almost never surpass him in secular poetry. Only Carew—who wrote a magnificent elegy (*"An Elegie upon the death of the Deane of Pauls, Dr. Iohn Donne"*), one that is superior to any of Herrick's funeral poems, and an erotic masterpiece (*"A Rapture"*) that more than equals anything of Herrick's in the Ovidian vein—approaches him in stature.

Of the disciples of John Donne, only George Herbert excels Herrick in devotional verse—and Herbert wrote no secular poetry at all. (And the architectonic structure of Herrick's book bears favorable comparison with that of *The Temple*.) Though a few individual poems of Henry Vaughan, Richard Crashaw, and Thomas Traherne may be superior to anything of *Noble Numbers,* they too wrote little if anything that would compare with the best of what Herrick refers to as his "Humane Works." Indeed, only Donne himself clearly excels Herrick both as a sacred and as a profane poet. Yet *"Corinna's going a Maying," "The Apparition of his Mistresse . . . ," "A Country Life,"* the epithalamia, the "sack poems," and *"To live merrily"*—to name a few—are as successful as Donne's best. A similar situation obtains when Herrick is compared with Marvell. Marvell, of course, wrote considerably less than Herrick; but individual poems of Marvell in both the devotional and secular categories sometimes equal and occasionally surpass Herrick's best.

In short, Herrick is well-deserving of the accolade of Musgrove: "He was a poet of stature less only than the greatest . . ." of his age.[10] Herrick is indubitably the greatest of the "sons" of Ben Jonson, and a good case can be made for regarding him as a better poet—though not a greater literary figure—than his "father." In the four categories into which John Hayward classifies the poems of *Hesperides*—amatory, pastoral, epigrammatic, and occasional —Herrick has written more poems, and frequently more successful poems, than Jonson.[11] In the first two categories, for example, Herrick's supremacy can scarcely be questioned; in the latter two, Jonson seldom excels him.

Nevertheless, Ben Jonson is the source and fountain of Herrick's being as a poet—as Herrick readily and publicly acknowledges. And it is in the stream of the Neo-Classical impulse in English literature, a stream which runs parallel to and occasionally mingles with the stream of the Metaphysical impulse, that Herrick must be regarded as figuring importantly. His verse traces its beginnings to Jonson, but carries along toward Marvell and Milton, toward Dryden and Pope. While there is no evidence that he influenced any of these, or even that they read him, Herrick's poems (circulated in manuscript) and his published volume must have been palpable confirmations of the soundness of Jonson's theories of poesy and of the poet as maker.

None of these statements intend to suggest that Herrick as a poet is without limitations. Limitations are there—and he, more than anyone, was aware of them. Indeed, more than most poets, he followed the advice of one of his Roman mentors, Horace:

> Let poets match their subject to their strength,
> And often try what weight they can support,   50
> And what their shoulders are too weak to bear,
> After a serious and judicious choice,
> Method and eloquence will never fail.
>
> As well the force as ornament of verse,
> Consists in choosing a fit time for things,   55
> And knowing when a muse should be indulg'd
> In her full flight, and when she should be curb'd.
> (*Ars Poetica*, lines 38–45, Translated by the Earl of Roscommon)

Because Herrick knew his own artistic strength, exercised it constantly, and did not attempt to exceed it, he was one poet who never produced an ambitious failure. He attempted no verse tragedy, no epic poem. Yet each of his artistic successes is limited only by its conception, not by its execution. Understanding this without underestimating what can thereby be achieved is one of the keys to a judicious and rewarding appreciation of the poetry of Robert Herrick.

That we are at last well on the way toward achieving this goal is the sanguine opinion of L. C. Martin:

In the twentieth century Herrick has been appreciated with less rapture and more discrimination [than he was in the nineteenth], but his standing remains high. Better knowledge of Jacobean and Caroline poetry has revealed more clearly what he had in common with other writers and what he contributed of his own. The seriousness expressed or implied in much that he wrote has been brought more fully into light, and it is an advantage also that his work as a whole can now be seen to share in the complexity which belongs generally to Renaissance humanism, with its roots in classical literature, Christian doctrine, and medieval philosophy, symbolism, and superstition; for this composite inheritance, with its stimulating variety and contrasts, probably did more than the example of any single poet, Horace, Martial, or even Jonson, to make Herrick's poetry what it was.[12]

What Herrick himself is, essentially, may at least be suggested by the term, "poise." With a carefully cultivated intellectual and emotional poise he confronted the transiency of the world, the prospect of death, and the multiplicity of life; and with superb artistic poise he re-created his reactions to all three. He had the poise to perceive the way things are and were without losing sight of the way they might be. He had the poise to be serious without being melancholic, to be lighthearted without being trivial, to savor both the art of life and the life of art. This poise must, of course, have risen from his temperament as a man, yet his Neo-Epicurean cast of thought and his Neo-Classical artistic bent had to have been contributory factors. Though the art which exemplifies such poise has not always been in fashion, there can now be little doubt that Herrick is substantially correct when, in the poem which functions as preface to his *Hesperides,* he claims: "Full is my Book of Glories."

Notes and References

Chapter One

1. *The Poetical Works of Robert Herrick*, ed. L. C. Martin (Oxford, 1956), p. 446—hereafter cited as *Works*. All quotations from the poetry have been taken from this edition with the permission of the Clarendon Press, Oxford.

2. The Roman numeral in square brackets indicates that this is the third consecutive poem of *Hesperides* to bear this title. Identically titled works will be thus distinguished throughout this study. (N.B. Only Patrick's edition of the poetry—see footnote nine—accurately lists identical titles in the Index.)

3. *Songs by Roger Quilter* (Alexander Young, tenor; Gordon Watson, pianoforte). Argo RG 36 or Westminster XWN 18152. (Includes a "Song Cycle" of Herrick's lyrics to "Julia.")

4. *Revaluation* (New York, 1947), pp. 36, 39–41.

5. T. S. Eliot, *On Poetry and Poets* (New York, 1957), pp. 43–44 —hereafter cited as Eliot. John Press (see Bibliography) is another contemporary subscriber to this view.

6. For example, L. C. Martin (in pp. xvii–xxi of *Works*), Allen H. Gilbert, and Thomas R. Whitaker (see Bibliography).

7. S. Musgrove, "The Universe of Robert Herrick," *Auckland University College Bulletin* No. 38, English Series No. 4 (1950), 4—hereafter cited as Musgrove.

8. *Works*, p. xvii.

9. In his introductory remarks to *The Complete Poetry of Robert Herrick* (New York, 1963), pp. xi–xiii—hereafter cited as Patrick.

10. *Works*, p. xviii.

11. See *Works*, pp. xvii–xviii, and Patrick, pp. xi–xiii, for divergent opinions on this point.

12. *The Complete Works of Algernon Charles Swinburne*, ed. Sir Edmund Gosse and Thomas James Wise, XV (London, 1926), 261.

13. Musgrove, p. 6.

14. *Works*, p. 499.

15. Eliot, p. 44.

16. *Ibid.*, p. 45, p. 44.

17. *Ibid.*, p. 44.

18. *Ibid.*, p. 43.

19. Thomas R. Whitaker, "Herrick and the Fruits of the Garden," *Journal of English Literary History*, XXII No. 1 (March, 1955), 17—hereafter cited as Whitaker.

20. *"To* M. Leonard Willan, *his peculiar friend,"* line 6.

21. Eliot, p. 43.

22. *Works,* p. 522; Patrick, p. 148.

23. *Anatomy of Criticism* (Princeton, 1957), p. 194—hereafter cited as Frye.

24. Patrick, p. 5.

25. *"To his peculiar friend* Sir Edward Fish, *Knight Baronet,"* line 4.

26. Patrick, pp. 7–8.

Chapter Two

1. Frank Kermode, *John Donne* (London, 1961), p. 32.

2. *Idem.*

3. Allen H. Gilbert, "Robert Herrick on Death," *Modern Language Quarterly* V (1944), 67.

4. Note that Martin indexes all poems entitled *"Upon himselfe"* or *"On himselfe"* under the former title only.

5. Louis Untermeyer, ed., *The Love Poems of Robert Herrick and John Donne* (New Brunswick, N.J., 1948), p. 3.

6. Meditation XVII of "Devotions upon Emergent Occasions."

7. Patrick, pp. 40–41.

8. See *"Pride allowable in Poets."*

9. Epicurus x.125, in *Diogenes Laertius,* II, trans. R. D. Hicks, The Loeb Classical Library (London, 1925), 651—hereafter cited as Epicurus.

10. *The Communings with Himself of Marcus Aurelius Antoninus,* trans. C. R. Haines, The Loeb Classical Library (London, 1924), p. 235.

11. *English Literature in the Earlier Seventeenth Century: 1600–1660,* 2nd ed. rev. (Oxford, 1962), p. 4—hereafter cited as Bush.

12. Epicurus x.126, p. 653.

Chapter Three

1. Bush, p. 1.

2. *Ibid.*, pp. 35–36.

3. See *Works,* pp. xxxvi–xl, and unpublished dissertation (U. of Michigan, 1958) by Richard J. Ross, " 'A Wilde Civility': Robert Herrick's Poetic Solution of the Paradox of Art and Nature," pp. 180–276 —hereafter cited as Ross.

4. *Works,* p. 521.

5. See Morse Peckham and Seymour Chatman, *Word, Meaning, Poem* (New York, 1961), pp. 22–36.

6. *Works*, p. xxxviii.

7. The phrase, "a wilde civility," comes from *"Delight in Disorder"* (line 12), a poem separated from *"To* Dean-Bourn" in Martin's edition by only a page—enough to sharpen the contrast between the two concepts. (The former poem is analyzed in Chapter 6.)

8. Sam H. Henderson, "Neo-Stoic Influence on Elizabethan Verse Satire," *Studies in English Renaissance Literature*, ed. Waldo F. McNeir, Louisiana State University Studies, Humanities Series No. XII (Baton Rouge, 1962), 60—hereafter cited as Henderson.

9. *Ibid.*, pp. 63, 72–73.

10. Patrick, p. 142, paraphrases "some crosse the Fill-horse" as "some sit astride the shaft-horse," but "to cross" can also mean "to make the sign of the cross." Since the line is one of several describing semi-comic "devotions," the image Herrick intends to convey may be that of superstitious rustics making the sign of the cross over—and thus blessing—the faithful shaft-horse.

11. Henderson, p. 73.

12. *Works*, pp. 504–6.

13. Henderson, p. 79; see also Epicurus x.126–32, pp. 653–57.

14. Epicurus x.128, p. 653.

15. *Ibid.*, x.131, p. 657.

16. *Lucretius De Rerum Natura*, ed. Cyril Bailey, I (Oxford, 1950), 357.

17. "Fragment LXXVII" (Vatican Collection), *The Stoic and Epicurean Philosophers*, ed. Whitney J. Oates (New York, 1940), p. 44.

18. Epicurus x.125, p. 651.

19. *Works*, p. xxn.

20. Ross, pp. 93, 132–33.

21. *Ibid.*, p. 93.

22. Henderson, p. 66 (see also pp. 67, 70–71).

23. *Herrick* (London, 1961), p. 9—hereafter cited as Press.

24. *Idem.*

25. Ross, p. 93.

26. "Discoveries," *Ben Jonson*, ed. C. H. Herford and Percy and Evelyn Simpson, VIII (Oxford, 1947), 636—hereafter cited as Jonson.

Chapter Four

1. Press, p. 9.

2. *Ibid.*, p. 9; pp. 12–15, 17–18.

3. See, for example, E. M. W. Tillyard and C. S. Lewis, *The Personal Heresy: A Controversy* (Oxford, 1939), pp. 4–6, 44–48, 59–60; William Jay Smith, ed. *Herrick*, The Laurel Poetry Series (New York, 1962), pp. 21–26; *The Explicator* I (March, 1943); V (April, 1947); XIII (March, 1955); XIV (December, 1955).

4. "Herrick's 'Upon Julia's Clothes,'" *Modern Language Notes,* LXXIII (1958), 331.

5. See *Works,* pp. 517–19.

6. *The Well Wrought Urn,* Harvest Book edition (New York, 1947), pp. 67–69.

7. *Ibid.,* p. 70.

8. *Idem.*

9. Patrick (p. 100) suggests that the "Proclamation" may be "either a particular local proclamation of May Day festivities or possibly a reference to Charles I's 'declaration to his subjects concerning lawful sports,' 1633, which forbade interference . . . with 'having of May-games . . . and the setting up of May-poles and other sports therewith used.'" But Herrick's allusion need not be taken so literally. Tradition or even the day itself (because it is conducive to the celebration) can "proclaim" a holiday.

10. *Anatomy of Melancholy* 3.1.1.2.

11. "The Parsons Tale," 1.1086.

Chapter Five

1. In this chapter the title, *Hesperides,* will be understood to refer to Herrick's "secular" work—that collection of poems that comprises more than three-fourths of the 1648 volume—while *His Noble Numbers* will designate the collection of the remaining "devotional" poems. (There is still some confusion as to whether *Hesperides* and *His Noble Numbers* can legitimately be thus regarded as separate titles. The title page of *His Noble Numbers* does bear the date 1647, which seems to indicate an intended earlier or perhaps separate publication from that of *Hesperides.* And yet the main title of the 1648 volume is *Hesperides,* and its subtitle—*The Works Both Humane & Divine*—would appear to include *His Noble Numbers.*)

2. Frye, p. 97.

3. *John Milton: Complete Poems and Major Prose,* ed. Merritt Y. Hughes (New York, 1957), p. 728.

4. "Oberons *Feast*"; "Oberons *Palace*"; "The Beggar to Mab, the Fairie Queen"; "A Description of his [Oberon's] *Dyet.*" (The latter poem is printed for the first time by Patrick, pp. 163–64. He regards it as a variant and early version of "Oberons *Feast.*")

5. Bush, p. 115.

6. *Works,* p. 520.

7. *Revaluation* (New York, 1947), pp. 36, 39–41.

8. Whitaker, pp. 16–21.

9. See *"The good-morrow,"* line 19.

10. *Works,* p. 520: Ovid's statement (*Metamorphoses* xv.158) may be translated as "Souls are beyond death," that of Tacitus (*Agricola* 46) as "Noble souls are not extinguished with the body."

11. No satisfactory precedents for Herrick's use of "Tramplers" (line 10) are cited by the *Oxford English Dictionary*. It is most likely that the word is a misprint for "Tramples" or "wanderings."

12. See *"A charme, or an allay for Love"; "The Night-piece, to Julia"; "Charmes,"* and *"Another"* [I and II].

13. See, for example, *"A Panegyrick to Sir* Lewis Pemberton."

14. See *Works*, pp. xxxvi–xxxvii.

15. Miriam K. Starkman, *"Noble Numbers* and the Poetry of Devotion," *Reason and Imagination; Studies in the History of Ideas, 1600–1800*, ed. J. A. Mazzeo (New York, 1962), p. 17—hereafter cited as Starkman.

16. Press, p. 31.

17. Starkman, p. 9.

18. *Ibid.*, p. 3.

19. Cf. *"Love me little, love me long"* (line 3), *"Honours are hindrances,"* and *"The Welcome to Sack"* (line 8).

20. *The Poetry of Meditation* (New Haven, 1954).

21. *Ibid.*, p. 37.

22. Poem 745 ("Renunciation—is a piercing Virtue—"), *The Poems of Emily Dickinson*, ed. Thomas H. Johnson, II (Cambridge, Mass., 1955), 568.

23. Press, pp. 30–31.

24. *Ibid.*, pp. 30–35.

25. *Ibid.*, p. 35.

26. *Idem.*

27. Basil Willey, *The Seventeenth-Century Background* (New York, 1953), p. 50.

Chapter Six

1. See, for example, "TO THE KING, Upon his comming with his Army into the West"; "TO THE KING Upon his taking of Leicester"; "TO THE KING, Upon his welcome to Hampton-Court."

2. See, for example, *"To Sir* John Berkley, *Governour of Exeter"; "To Prince* Charles *upon his coming to Exeter."*

3. See, for example, *"A Dirge upon the Death of the Right Valiant Lord,* Bernard Stuart"; *"To the right gratious Prince,* Lodwick, *Duke of* Richmond *and* Lenox."

4. Ross, p. 1.

5. Harold E. Toliver, "Pastoral Form and Idea in Some Poems of Marvell," *Texas Studies in Literature and Language*, V, No. 1 (Spring, 1963), 83.

6. *Idem.*

7. Ross, p. 180.

8. *Religio Medici and Other Writings of Sir Thomas Browne* (New York, 1912), p. 19.

9. Jonson, VIII, 639.

10. Press, p. 10.

11. See *Oxford English Dictionary* s.v. "wanton" 2, 3.d.

12. Jonson, III, 170.

13. Dan S. Norton and Peters Rushton, *Classical Myths in English Literature* (New York, 1960), p. 170.

14. Jonson, VIII, 615.

15. *Ibid.*, p. 567.

16. *Ibid.*, pp. 638–39.

17. Patrick, p. 408.

18. *Works,* p. 517.

19. Patrick, p. 283.

20. *Ibid.*, p. 275n.

21. See *"Anacreontike"* [I and II] and *"Anacrontick Verse."*

22. *Works,* p. 489.

23. Patrick (p. 275) is doubtless correct in his comment on the phrase, "he one chiefe": "Martin changes *he one* to *be our;* but Herrick's mistress's shade would hardly call Jonson *her* chief." The phrase is awkward but its meaning is clear: Jonson is a chief among "Those Prophets of a former Magnitude."

24. See, for example, *"To his peculiar friend Master* Thomas Shapcott, *Lawyer"; "To the right Honourable* Edward *Earle of* Dorset"; *"To his Kinswoman, Mrs.* Penelope Wheeler"; *"To his deare Valentine, Mistresse* Margaret Falconbrige," *et al.*

25. *The Divine Science* (New York, 1940), p. 11.

26. *The Stoic and Epicurean Philosophers,* ed. Whitney J. Oates (New York, 1949), p. 30.

27. See *Oxford English Dictionary* s.v. "Plantonic" 3.b.

Chapter Seven

1. See *Works,* p. xvii (and Chapter 1 of this study).

2. *Works,* p. xviii.

3. Barron Field, Untitled review of Dr. J. Nott's selected edition of Herrick (Bristol, 1810) in *The Quarterly Review,* IV (Aug.–Nov., 1810), 168. See also Nathan Drake, *Literary Hours,* III (1804), 88.

4. "Robert Herrick," *Cornhill Magazine,* XXXII (July–Dec., 1875), 180.

5. *The Complete Poems of Robert Herrick,* I (London, 1876), clxxvi.

6. *Ibid.*, p. clxx.

7. *Chrysomela: A Selection from the Lyrical Poems of Robert Herrick* (London, 1877), p. xx.

8. In the Preface to *Robert Herrick, the Hesperides & Noble Numbers,* ed. Alfred Pollard, I (London, 1877), xxii.

9. Eliot, pp. 43–45.

10. Musgrove, p. 4.

11. *Robert Herrick: Poems from* HESPERIDES *and* NOBLE NUMBERS (Baltimore, 1961), pp. 10–11.

12. *Works,* p. xx.

Selected Bibliography

PRIMARY SOURCES

1. Editions of Herrick's Poems Generally Available

HAYWARD, JOHN. *Robert Herrick; Poems from* HESPERIDES *and* NOBLE NUMBERS. Baltimore: Penguin Books, 1961. A reasonable selection attractively printed. A minimum of explanatory notes. The critical introduction is of rather limited usefulness.

MARTIN, L. C. *The Poetical Works of Robert Herrick.* Oxford: The Clarendon Press, 1956. Based upon the 1648 volume but with additional poems from manuscript copies, this is the definitive edition. Includes an exceptionally informative introduction, extensive critical notes, a comprehensive commentary, and Herrick's extent letters. Indispensable to serious students of seventeenth-century poetry. Reprinted (but not revised) in 1963.

MOORMAN, F. W. *The Poetical Works of Robert Herrick.* Oxford: The Clarendon Press, 1915. This text, with a preface by Percy Simpson, but without Herrick's epigrams and without notes, was reissued in 1921 in the Oxford English Poets series (Oxford University Press) and again in 1935 (London, Humphrey Miller). The original edition has been superseded by Martin's edition and the reissue by Patrick's (see below).

PATRICK, J. MAX. *The Complete Poetry of Robert Herrick.* New York: New York University Press (The Stuart Editions), 1963. This text is also available in paperback in the Anchor Seventeenth-Century Series (Garden City: Anchor Books, 1963); it is identical in all significant respects to the Stuart edition. The best student's text because of its illuminating explanatory footnotes (which follow the individual poems), its selected and partially annotated bibliography, and its excellent index—the most accurate of any edition. Also has an introductory section. Useful to the serious student as well as to the casual reader of Herrick.

SMITH, WILLIAM JAY. *Herrick.* New York: Dell Books, 1962. A selected edition in The Laurel Poetry Series (in paperback). Contains a sensitive and provocative introduction, a brief bibliography,

a briefer chronology, a good selection of poems, and a few explanatory notes. A bargain.

2. Bibliographical Works

MACLEOD, MALCOM L. *A Concordance to the Poems of Robert Herrick.*
New York: Oxford University Press, 1936. Can best be used with
Moorman's edition (1915) or Martin's (1956).

TANNENBAUM, SAMUEL A. and DOROTHY R. *Robert Herrick (A Concise
Bibliography).* New York: Elizabethan Bibliographies, 1949.
Marred by inaccuracies, such as the listing of several articles as
treating Robert Herrick, the English poet, which in fact deal with
Robert Herrick, the American novelist.

SECONDARY SOURCES

AIKEN, PAULINE. "The Influence of the Latin Elegists on English Lyric
Poetry, 1600–1650, with Particular Reference to the Works of
Robert Herrick," *University of Maine Studies,* Second Series, No.
22 (1932). Informative on Herrick's models, but overstates and
oversimplifies his dependence upon them.

BROOKS, CLEANTH. *The Well Wrought Urn.* New York: Harcourt, Brace
& World, Inc., 1947. The fourth essay of this collection, "What
Does Poetry Communicate?", is one of the earliest demonstrations
of the depth and breadth of which Herrick is capable, and is still
the best study of "Corinna."

BUSH, DOUGLAS. *English Literature in the Earlier Seventeenth Century,
1600–1660.* 2nd ed., rev. Oxford: The Clarendon Press, 1962, pp.
114–19. A sometimes grudging but generally appreciative summary of Herrick's qualities and a judicious assessment of his place
in the age's literature.

CHUTE, MARCHETTE. *Two Gentle Men; The Lives of George Herbert
and Robert Herrick.* New York: E. P. Dutton & Co., 1959. Divert-
ing and historically informative, but tends to make the poems subservient to the life.

DELATTRE, FLORIS. *Robert Herrick: Contribution à l'Etude de la Poésie
Lyrique en Angleterre au Dix-septième Siècle.* Paris: F. Alcan,
1912. In French. Good chapter on Herrick's indebtedness, but
overemphasizes biographical aspect of poems and Herrick's lighter
vein. More sound than Moorman's study.

ELIOT, T. S. *On Poetry and Poets.* New York: Farrar, Straus and Cud-
ahy, 1957. The essay, "What Is Minor Poetry?", underestimates
the unity of *Hesperides,* but suggests a useful approach to its
study.

Explicator, The, I (March, 1943); V (April, 1947); XIII (March,

1955); XIV (December, 1955); XXI (December, 1962). Various interpretations of uneven quality of Herrick's "Upon Julia's Clothes."

GILBERT, ALLEN H. "Robert Herrick on Death." *Modern Language Quarterly,* V (1944), 61–67. Raises the question of Herrick's "seriousness" by pointing to his near-preoccupation with death.

JONAS, LEAH. *The Divine Science.* New York: Columbia University Press, 1940. Contains useful comments on Herrick's esthetic and its relation to other seventeenth-century views on poetry.

KERMODE, FRANK. (Review of Martin's edition). *Review of English Studies,* IX (Feb., 1958), 78–82. Has high praise for Martin's editing and rather less for Herrick's poetizing.

LEAVIS, F. R. *Revaluation.* New York: George W. Stewart, Inc., 1947. Cavalierly consigns Herrick to the limbo of poet-triflers.

LEITER, LOUIS H. "Herrick's 'Upon Julia's Clothes,'" *Modern Language Notes* LXXIII (May, 1958), 331. Still the most sensible of the many analyses of this short poem.

MCEUEN, KATHRYN A. *Classical Influence upon the Tribe of Ben.* Cedar Rapids, Iowa: The Torch Press, 1939. Views Herrick as more the master than the vassal of the ancients and calls attention to his "instructional" intent.

MOORMAN, F. W. *Robert Herrick: A Biographical and Critical Study.* London: John Lane, 1910. (Reissued by Russell and Russell, Inc., New York, 1962.) Informative on the history of the lyric, but treats poems impressionistically and superficially. Of limited use to the serious student.

MUSGROVE, S. "The Universe of Robert Herrick," *Auckland University College Bulletin* No. 38, English Series No. 4 (1950). Though it overstates Herrick's Christian orientation, this perceptive essay is essential reading.

PRESS, JOHN. *Herrick.* Writers and Their Work No. 132. London: Longmans, Green & Co., 1961. An uneven and uncertain monograph which, nevertheless, is worthwhile as a brief and general account of Herrick.

ROLLIN, ROGER B. "Robert Herrick and the Pastoral Tradition." Unpublished dissertation (Yale, 1959). Relates Herrick to the foreign and native bucolic tradition and analyzes (often accurately) his poems in that tradition.

ROSS, RICHARD J. "'A Wilde Civility': Robert Herrick's Poetic Solution of the Paradox of Art and Nature." Unpublished dissertation (University of Michigan, 1958). A sound, significant thesis unconvincingly presented at some length. Usually classifies rather than analyzes Herrick's poems.

STARKMAN, MIRIAM K. "*Noble Numbers* and the Poetry of Devotion." *Reason and Imagination: Studies in the History of Ideas, 1600–*

1800. Ed. J. A. Mazzeo. New York: Columbia University Press, 1962, pp. 1–27. The only extended exploration of *His Noble Numbers* and hence required reading. Shows *Noble Numbers* to be more representative of the age's devotional verse than was previously thought.

SWINBURNE, A. C. "Robert Herrick." *The Complete Works of Algernon Charles Swinburne.* Ed., Sir Edmund Gosse and Thomas James Wise. London: William Heinemann Ltd., 1926, XV, 260–63. A brief, overly rapturous appreciation.

TILLYARD, E. M. W. and LEWIS, C. S. *The Personal Heresy: A Controversy.* London: Oxford University Press, 1939. Herrick's "Upon Julia's Clothes" figures in a lively debate on a significant critical question.

WHITAKER, THOMAS R. "Herrick and the Fruits of the Garden," *Journal of English Literary History,* XXII (1955), 16–33. A difficult but very penetrating general analysis of Herrick. Though it underestimates the unity of *Hesperides,* it is still the best single essay on Herrick. Essential.

Index

(References to Herrick's poems are listed under his name.)

"Active Life" versus "Contemplative Life," controversy of, 73–75, 77, 127–28

Allegory, *see* Genres

Anacreon, 23, 51, 56, 94, 167, 185, 186, 195–96

Apollo, 55, 97, 154

Aristotle, 83

Art versus Nature, controversy of, 57–58, 79–81, 85, 87, 90, 106–7, 118, 165, 172–85, 205

Bacon, Sir Francis, 38

Baldwin, Prudence, 76

Beauty, 40–43, 57, 73, 80, 87, 92, 94, 105, 107, 175, 177, 205

Beaumont, Francis, 196–97

Bible, 68, 109, 111, 122, 134, 135, 136, 145, 157, 181, 189, 193, 202

Brooks, Cleanth, 96, 100

Browne, Sir Thomas, 32, 38, 126, 163–64, 173

Bunyan, John, 138, 143, 149

Burton, Robert, 71, 123, 175

Bush, Douglas, 46, 48, 131

Carew, Thomas, 105–6, 209

Carpe diem, theme of, 49–51, 69–70, 82, 94–96, 102

Cambridge University, 15, 177

Catullus, 45, 105, 111, 185, 187–88

"Cavalier Poets," 105–6, 107, 110, 208–9; *see also* as "Cavalier poet" *under* Herrick

Ceremony, *see* Ritual

Change, *see* Transiency

Charles I, 28–29, 165–69

Chaucer, Geoffrey, 124, 140

Christ, 129, 135–36, 143, 152–57, 202

Christianity, 33, 48, 99, 122, 127, 133, 134–64, 170, 172, 185, 190, 192, 200, 202, 203

Church of England, 127–28, 134–35, 142

Cicero, 48, 59

Civil war, in England, 17, 131, 165–169

"Cleanly-*Wantonnesse,*" 20, 24, 42–45, 69, 72, 75–76, 85–124, 139, 140, 168, 174, 194–95

"Contemplative Life," *see* "Active Life"

Contentment, ideal of, 69, 76–77, 151

Country Life, ideal of, 56–84, 123, 127, 160, 167, 169

Crashaw, Richard, 143, 163, 209

Critical approach, of this study, *see* Preface; *also* 18–31

Cromwell, Oliver, 39

Dean-bourn (Devon), 57–58, 175

Dean Prior (Devon), 17, 57, 137

Death, 20, 21, 22, 32–47, 49–50, 60, 69, 75–76, 93–96, 97, 102–3, 122, 132–33, 135–40, 142–43, 144, 149, 152, 153, 154, 155–60, 167, 171, 185, 192–93, 201–5, 207, 211

Decay, 21, 32–47, 79–80, 93–96, 136

Decorum, in poetry, 90, 136–37; *see also* his esthetic *under* Herrick

"Delight," as a function of poetry, 61, 82, 177, 197, 208

Devonshire, 17, 28, 29, 57–60, 63, 78, 81, 165, 169, 175

Dickinson, Emily, 162

Diction, 20, 21, 22, 34, 38, 39, 42, 53, 63–64, 67, 71, 78, 86–87, 88, 93–94, 95, 98, 103, 104, 106, 108, 109, 118, 119, 121, 123, 131–32,

145, 146, 148, 149, 156, 168, 171,
173, 175, 177, 200, 202
Donne, John, 17, 32, 35, 61, 87, 90,
97, 114, 125, 134, 143, 144, 157,
158, 163, 209
Drayton, Michael, 16, 130, 193, 201,
206

Elegy, see Genres
Eliot, T. S., 16, 25–26, 27, 28, 208
Elizabethan poetry and poets, 16,
60–61, 70, 80, 103, 120, 138
England, as context, 17, 28, 29, 56,
63, 149, 154, 165–69
Epicurus and Epicureanism, 40, 46,
50, 51, 72–76, 83, 150, 163, 201;
see also his Neo-Epicureanism
under Herrick
Epigram, see Genres
Epitaph, see Genres
Epithalamion, see nuptial verse under
Genres
Excess, or extremism, as error, 57–
58, 72, 74, 83–84, 91, 106, 127,
128, 139, 175; see also Moderation

Fairy poems, see Genres
Fame, see Glory
Fletcher, John, 196–97
Flux, see Transiency
Frye, Northrop, 29, 125

Genres, in Hesperides; allegory, 39–
40, 136–38, 144–46, 149, 167–69,
191, 200; apostrophe, 40–42, 51–
56, 155–57, 170; carol, 152–55;
ceremonial verse, 63–67, 120–22,
134–35, 184, 185–90; confession,
141, 142–43, 169; consolation,
139–41; didactic verse, 23, 26, 50,
63, 68–76, 93–94, 110, 160–62,
173–76, 202; dream-vision, 192–
199; elegy, 35–37, 178–80; epigram, 38–39, 79–84, 92, 110, 144–
145, 172–73, 178, 207–9; epitaph,
34–35, 180; fairy verse, 30–32,
170–71; invitation-to-love, 86–90,
95–103, 121, 170; love complaint,
90–92, 103–5; love lyric (general), 105–11; meditation, 158–
160, 203–4; "nature poetry," 37;

nuptial verse, 98, 111–20, 147;
occasional verse, 34, 135–36, 165–
167, 170–71; ode, 179–81, 191;
panegyrical verse, 28–30, 42–45,
58–59, 78–79, 122, 199, 200–201;
pattern-poem, 200, 205; prayer,
146–51, 176–77, 183, 190; satire,
57–58, 60–61, 127–32, 183; verse-
catalogue, 18–22, 76–77
Gilbert, Allen H., 33
Glory (literary fame), 15, 16, 17,
52, 178, 182–83, 189–90, 198–205,
206
God, 123–24, 135, 141–51, 152, 155,
157, 160, 161, 172
Golden Age, vision of the, 70, 166
"Golden Mean," the, see Moderation
Good Life, the, 24, 49, 51, 56, 60–
63, 67–79, 82, 84, 151; see also
Country Life
Gosse, Edmund W., 207
"Great Chain of Being," concept of
the, 23, 38
Grosart, Alexander, 207–8

Hayward, John, 209
Henderson, Sam H., 60, 70, 72, 80
Herbert, George, 125, 130, 143, 167,
206, 209
Herrick, Nicholas (father), 35–37
Herrick, Robert, as Anglican, 126–
129, 134–35, 142–43, 146; as
"Cavalier Poet," 23, 85, 105–6,
107, 122, 208; as "Christian poet,"
122, 125–64, 185, 192, 200, 202,
203, 211; his conception of the
art of poetry, 24, 30–31, 58, 82,
90, 138, 164, 167, 169, 171, 177,
179–92, 199–205 (see also Delight, Imitation, Instruction, Religion of Art); his conception of
himself as poet, 27–28, 30, 165–69,
181–85, 200–202 (see also as pastoral poet below); his conception
of his book, see Hesperides; his
craftsmanship, 16, 18, 71, 106,
129, 130–31, 134, 177–78, 181–
184, 186, 207–8; his "cynicism,"
38, 85, 105–6, 182, 183; as "Dionysian," 50–51, 56, 69, 82–83, 94,

185–99 (*see also* his sensuousness *below*); his eclecticism, 70–71, 97, 134–35; his esthetic, 31, 56–58, 79–84, 85, 112, 118, 163–164, 165, 172–77, 210, 211 (*see also* Art versus Nature, Beauty, Moderation, Religion of Art, Ugliness); his ethic, 20, 59–61, 63, 71–84, 85 (*see also* Good Life; *also* his Neo-Epicureanism, his Neo-Stoicism, his "world-view" *below*); his humanism, 46–47, 48, 141, 150, 163, 211; his "idealism," 27, 57–58, 63, 78–81, 85, 109–10, 165–67, 172; his lighter vein, 23–24, 26, 51–56, 65, 67, 79–80, 87, 92–93, 94, 98, 101, 102, 106–7, 109, 110, 114–19, 131–32, 149, 156, 161, 173, 177, 187–89, 191, 200, 208, 211; his lyricism, 15–16, 61, 85, 111, 123, 152–55, 165; his mythopoeia, 130, 170, 172, 191, 192, 199 (*see also* "Sacred Grove"); his Neo-Classicism, 35, 36, 38, 39, 45–48, 49, 50, 56, 59–60, 84, 90, 95, 161, 178, 205, 210, 211; his Neo-Epicureanism, 46–47, 49–50, 56, 72–77, 82–84, 85, 110, 118, 129, 150–51, 158, 162, 185, 201, 203, 211 (*see also* Pain, Pleasure); his Neo-Stoicism, 42, 49, 50, 60, 70, 72, 74–76, 80, 82, 129, 144; his "obscenity," 18, 79, 81, 92; his "paganism," 35–36, 125–27, 134–36, 138, 163; as pastoral poet, 19, 27–31, 56–58, 60–79, 87–92, 96–102, 149–51, 160, 165–72, 186, 192–95, 198, 200–203, 208, 209; his "poise," 97, 134, 211; his pride, 26, 39, 181; his rationality, 60, 71, 144–46; his realism, 38, 39, 55, 57, 63, 68, 78–81, 82, 97, 109, 111, 148–49, 156, 165, 166, 167, 172, 211; his reputation, 15–18, 126–27, 134, 152, 165, 206–11; as "ritualist," *see* Ritual; his Royalism, 17, 28–30, 57, 63–67, 105, 129, 155–57, 165–169; as satirist, 50, 51, 56–58, 60–62, 65, 76–77, 79–82, 127–32, 178; his sensuality, 20, 50–55, 69,

85–90, 92–93, 94–96, 98, 101, 106–11, 113–20, 121–22, 125, 168, 173–77, 192–96, 207, 209 (*see also* "Cleanly-Wantonnesse"; *also* as "Dionysian" *above*); his sensuousness, 20, 23, 49–56, 82, 83, 92, 94, 103, 108–13, 123, 173–75, 185–89, 192–95; sentimentality, his avoidance of, 53, 104, 200; his seriousness, 16, 23–24, 70, 80, 85, 92–93, 146, 173, 207–8, 211; his "triviality," 16, 17–18, 23–24, 70, 80, 107, 132, 207–8, 211; his verse-technique (*general*), 22, 37–39, 75, 78, 90, 105–6, 125–26, 131, 152, 182, 192, 210 (*see also* Diction, Genres, *Hesperides*, Imagery, Imitation, Irony, Metaphor, Metrics, Rhetorical effects, Ritual, Structure, Symbol); verse technique, lapses in, 43–45, 74, 83, 110, 129, 162–63, 176, 194; his "wit," 86, 94, 96, 103–4, 106, 107, 114, 116, 199; his "world-view," (*general*), 22–23, 45–47, 48, 50, 60–61, 70, 163–64, 165, 172, 205, 211 (*see also* Christianity, Death, Glory, Immortality, Life, Nature, Transiency; *also* his Neo-Epicureanism, his Neo-Stoicism *above*)

POEMS OF:
"All things decay and die," 39–40, 96; "Anacreontike," [I], 51; "Anacrontick Verse," 51; "Angrie God, To his," 148; "Apparition of his Mistresse calling him to Elizium, The," 192–98, 209; "Argument of his Book, The," 18–24, 27, 33, 37, 43, 85, 170; "Art above Nature, to Julia," 175–76; "Bad season makes the Poet sad, The," 165–167; "Best to be merry," 50; "Beucolick, or discourse of Neatherds, A," 78; "Blossoms, To," 40–41; "Booke, To his," [IV], 204; "Bradshaw . . . , To Mistresse Katherine," 200–201; "Caroll . . . , A Christmas," 152–55; "Changes to Corinna,

The," 92–94; "Child, Upon a," 34–35; "Choose for the best," 83; "Christian Militant, The," 127–29; "Comfort to a Youth . . ." 138–41; "Comforts in Crosses," 138; "Confession, His," 126, 141, 144; "Connubii Flores . . . ," 110; "Content in the Country, His," 76–77; "Corinna's going a Maying," 94, 96–103, 126, 163, 196, 209; "Country life: To . . . Thomas Herrick, A," 70–76, 83, 209; "Country life, To . . . Endimion Porter . . . , The," 77–78; "Creed, His," 142–43, 160, 201; "Crofts . . . , To his faithful friend, Master John," 200; "Cupid, Upon" [III], 92; "Daffadills, To," 40–41; "Dean-bourn . . . , To," 57–58, 59, 175; "Definition of Beauty, The," 175; "Delight in Disorder," 173–175, 176; "Departure hence, Upon his," 139; "[Detractor, the], Upon the same," 183; "Dirge upon the Death of . . . Bernard Stuart, A," 135–36; "Discontents in Devon," 169; End decreed, An," 82; Epithalamie to Sir Thomas Southwell . . . , An," 111–12, 209; "Evensong," 134–35; "Ever-loving God, To his," 148–49; "Excesse," 83; "Eye, The," [I], 90; "Fairie Temple . . . , The," 130–32, 133, 150; "Fame makes us forward," 182; "Farwell Frost, or welcome the Spring," 165, 167–69; "Fare-well to Sack, His," 51, 52, 126, 209; "Funerall Rites of the Rose, The," 132–34; "Generous Reader, To the," 26; "Glorie," 182–83; "God not to be comprehended," 146; "God, To" [XII], 146–47; "God, Upon" [I], 145; "Gods Anger," 145; "Gods Anger without Affection," 146; "Good death, A," 83; "Good Friday . . ." 155–157, 159; "Himselfe, On" [III],

51; [IV], 136–38, 148; [VI], 51; [VIII], 191–92; [IX], 33; [XIII], 83; [XVI], 123; "Himselfe, Upon," [I], 93; [III], 15–16; [VII], 201–2; "Hock-cart, or Harvest home . . . , The," 63–67, 78; "Hymne to the Muses, An," 190; "Impossibilities to his friend," 144; "Johnson, Upon Ben," 180, 191; "Johnson, Upon Master Ben," 178–79; "Julia, the Flaminica Dialis . . . , To," 120–22; "Julia's breasts, Upon," 92; "Julia's Clothes, Upon," 86–87; "Julia's haire . . . , Upon," 106–7; "Julia's Petticoat," 107–110, 175; "Julia's unlacing her self, Upon," 106; "KING, TO THE," 28–29, 142; "Lachrimae or Mirth, turn'd to mourning, His," 169–70; "Lawes . . . , To Master Henry," 152; "Letanie, to the Holy Spirit, His," 156; "Love, Upon, [VIII], 123; "Love me little, love me long," 110; "Love what it is," 123; "Lucie, Upon," 80–81; "Lyrick for Legacies," 184; "Lyrick to Mirth, A," 185; Man, Upon," 172–73; "Mattens, or morning Prayer," 134–35; "Meane, The," 84; "Meddow-verse or Anniversary to Mistris Bridget Lowman, The," 170–71; "Meditation for his Mistresse, A," 42–45; "Meditation upon Death, His," 158–60; "Mercy and Love," 145; "Mistresse objecting to him neither Toying or Talking, To his," 120; "Moderation" [II], 110; "Muse, To his" [I], 27; "Neglect," 92; "No fault in women," 106; "No Lock against Letcherie," 92; "Nuptiall Song, or Epithalamie . . . , A," 111–120; "Ode for him [Ben Jonson], An," 179–81, 191; "One who said she was alwayes young, Upon," 79–80; "Oulsworth, To . . . Master Michael," 199–200; "Painting sometimes permitted,"

81; *"Panegyrick to Sir Lewis Pemberton, A,"* 150; *"Paranaeticall, or Advisive Verse . . . , A,"* 67–70; *"Parcell-gil't-Poetry,"* 184; *"Parting from Mistresse* Dorothy Keneday, *His,"* 103; *"Parting verse, the feast there ended, The,"* 170, 171–72; *"Phillis to love, and live with him, To,"* 87–90; *"Pillar of Fame, The,"* 200, 204–5; *"Pleasures Pernicious,"* 83; *"Poetrie his Pillar, His,"* 203; *"Poetry perpetuates the Poet,"* 201, 202–203; *"Poets good wishes for . . . the Duke of Yorke, The,"* 28, 30; *"Posting to Printing,"* 17; *"Prayer for Absolution, His,"* 141–42, 144; *"Prayer to* Ben. Johnson, *His,"* 190–91; "PRINCE CHARLES, *To . . . ,"* 211; *"Proof to no purpose,"* 144; *"Protestation to* Perilla, *His,"* 144; *"Putrefaction,"* 38–39; "QUEENE, TO THE," 28–30; *"Request to* Julia, *His,"* 183–84; *"Request to the Graces, A,"* 176–77; *"Returne to London, His,"* 58–60; *"Reverend shade of his religious Father, To the,"* 35–37; *"Sappho, To,"* 94; *"Silvia, To,"* [I], [II], 122; "Soame, *To his worthy Kinsman, Master* Stephen," 200; *"Sorrowes succeed,"* 82; *"Sufferance,"* 138; *"Teare sent to her from* Stanes, *The,"* 103–5; *"Thanksgiving to God, for his House, A,"* 149–51; *"To be merry,"* 82; *"To enjoy the Time,"* 49–50; *"To finde God,"* 144–45; *"To live Freely,"* 82; *"To live merrily, and to trust to Good Verses,"* 185–90, 209; *"Transfiguration, The,"* 122–23; *"Verses,"* 199; *"Verses, Upon his,"* 181–82; *"Vertue,"* 83; *"Virgins, to make much of Time, To the,"* 49, 94–96; *"Wake, The,"* 61–63; *"Welcome to Sack, The,"* 51–56, 126, 209; *"What God is,"* 145;

"Wheeler, *under the name of the lost Shepardesse, Mistresse* Elizabeth," 90–92; *"When he would have his verses read,"* 23–24; *"Whips,"* 148; *"White Island, The,"* 160–62, 170, 192, 196; *"Winding-sheet, His,"* see Preface; *"Women, to hide their teeth . . . , To,"* 81; *"Women, Upon some,"* 106; *"Youth, To,"* 82

Herrick, Thomas (brother), 70–76
Herrick, Sir William (uncle), 15
Hesperides (general), 15, 18, 19, 21, 22, 58, 69, 70, 79, 82, 84, 97, 111, 126, 133–34, 138, 141, 143, 150, 158, 160, 163, 165, 172, 178, 185, 197, 199, 200, 203, 204, 205, 209, 211; design, 22, 49, 79, 84; persona, 27, 63, 158, 211; publication, 17, 30–31, 165, 183, 206; purpose, 16, 27, 31, 60–61, 63, 75, 160, 208; "texture," 22, 24, 28–31, 63, 92, 141, 146, 196; unity, 16, 22, 25–26, 27, 30–31, 47, 75, 79, 84, 141, 142, 169–70, 208; variety, 18–19, 22, 25–26, 27, 30–31, 47, 79, 141, 142, 146, 196, 208, 209; as a "world," an artistic microcosm, 25, 26–31, 60, 84, 167, 169–70, 172, 191, 192, 200
His Noble Numbers (N.B. See footnote 1 s.v. Chapter Five, p. 216), 125, 126, 133–34, 141–64
Homer, 26, 53, 187, 188, 195, 199
Horace, 46, 49, 50, 71, 167, 181, 184, 185, 205, 210, 211

Imagery *(general),* 28, 37–38, 55, 57, 112, 114, 130; amatory, 54, 55, 103, 104, 107, 113; agricultural, 64, 75, 78, 154; ceremonial, 98, 196; decay, 80, 94, 95; domestic, 149, 150, 156; mercantile, 74, 75, 104; mythic, 55, 78, 99, 113–114, 118, 204; nature, 28–30, 69, 91, 95, 108, 115, 116, 117, 160–62, 170, 193; religious, 129, 136, 179; supernatural, 108, 123, 170 *(see also* Diction, Metaphor, Symbol)

Imitation, theory and practice, 45–46, 51, 90, 173, 176, 177–78, 181–182, 209

Immortality, through Christian faith, 22, 129, 135–43, 146, 159–62, 172, 202; through poetry, 15–17, 37, 184, 185, 189–92, 195, 198–205, 206

"Instruction," as a function of poetry, 61, 63, 79–84, 93, 110, 177, 197, 208

Irony, 20, 21, 27, 37, 41, 45, 62, 94, 95, 102, 103, 104, 105, 127, 132, 154, 156, 183, 188–89, 203

Jonas, Leah, 201
Jonson, Ben, 16, 38, 39–40, 48, 70, 82, 105–6, 111, 129, 130, 135, 173, 176, 177–81, 186, 190–91, 197–98, 206, 209–10, 211
Juvenal, 58, 60, 178

Kermode, Frank, 32

Leavis, F. R., 16, 132
Leiter, Louis H., 86–87
Life, affirmation of, 46–47, 49, 70, 94, 103, 128–29, 149, 158, 162, 185; brevity of, 34–35, 41, 44, 158; improvement by Art, 58, 70, 79, 80, 81, 85, 87, 160, 167, 170, 171–72; values of, 45, 46–47, 56–57, 62, 63, 103, 128, 162, 204, 211
London, 17, 57, 58–60, 177, 180
Love, see "Cleanly-Wantonnesse"
Love poetry, see Genres
"Love's religion," see Religion, of love
Lovelace, Richard, 105, 106–7, 209
Lucretius, 50, 73

Magic, poetry as, 24, 138, 195
Marcus Aurelius, 42
Maria, Queen, 28–30, 166
Martial, 23, 185, 211
Martin, L. C., 16–17, 29, 30, 33, 79, 131, 136, 148, 175, 178, 187, 206, 210–11
Martz, Louis L., 157–60
Marvell, Andrew, 32, 94, 172, 193, 206, 209, 210

Meditative poetry, 142, 156, 157–60, 173, 175, 203

Metaphor (including Simile), 28–30, 34, 37–38, 42, 43–44, 51–52, 55, 60, 65, 82, 86–87, 104, 106–7, 108, 115, 126, 136, 137, 138, 148–49, 154–55, 170, 175–76, 177, 181, 202

Metaphysical poetry, 90, 96–97, 103, 107, 142–44, 210

Metrics, 41, 42, 97, 111–12, 139, 153, 169, 192

Milton, John, 22, 111, 127, 136, 143, 152, 153, 161, 182, 184, 185, 210

Moderation, 68, 69, 72, 74, 83–84, 85, 91, 110, 128, 150, 174, 175, 183

Moses, 109, 147
Musgrove, Sidney, 16, 22, 209
Myth, 21, 22, 51, 153, 170, 191, 192, 198; See also his mythopoeia under Herrick

Natural world, 19, 21, 23, 37–45, 56–57, 71, 84, 89, 95, 98–101, 172, 192; analogous to human world, 23, 37–45, 57, 58, 63–64, 69–70, 86, 91–93, 96, 98–102, 132–133, 175–76, 202; cycles of, 19–21, 37–45, 63–64, 67, 96, 153, 167–68, 171, 203

Nature, in its seventeenth-century sense, see Life, Art versus Nature
Nature poetry, see Genres
Neo-Epicureanism, see Herrick
Neo-Petrarchanism, 103, 105, 110
Neo-Stoicism, see Herrick
Norton, Dan S., and Rushton, Peters, 176
Nuptial verse, see Genres

Occasional verse, see Genres
Order, idea of, 48–49, 58, 77, 84, 91
Ovid, 105, 136, 185, 187, 188, 189, 193, 196, 209

Pain, 50, 56, 75, 85, 94, 103, 111, 162
Palgrave, F. T., 208
Panegyrical poetry, see Genres
Pastoral, theory, 19, 56–57, 62–63,

68, 71, 73, 88–89, 96, 100, 150, 172, 200; tradition, 19, 27–29, 31, 38, 62–63, 68, 70, 72, 74, 75, 77, 79, 87, 91–92, 136, 153, 155, 167, 185, 194, 201 (*see also* as pastoralist *under* Herrick); "antipastoral," 28, 58, 60

Patrick, J. Max, 17, 29, 30, 35, 184, 190

Persius, 50, 60

Plato and Platonism, 48, 122–23, 136, 161, 180, 202

Pleasure, 20, 33, 50, 56, 62, 75, 83, 85, 88, 94, 102, 103, 111, 118, 162, 185, 201

Pollard, A. C., 79

Press, John, 81, 85, 143, 162, 163, 173

Propertius, 45, 49, 105, 188

Prothalamion, *see* nuptial verse *under* Genres

Puritans and Puritanism, 127–30, 145–46

Religion, of Art, 24, 31, 37, 164, 179, 185, 189–91, 195, 198, 199–205; Christian, *see* Christianity; of Love, 54, 115, 120–24

Rhetorical effects, alliteration, 19, 34, 82, 107, 113–14, 118, 166, 178, 193–94; aphorism (*also* gnomic statement, sententia), 70, 75, 76, 77, 78, 82, 83, 110, 115, 121, 148, 177; catalogue, 18–22, 36, 42–45, 61, 76, 78, 87–90, 91, 92, 132, 144, 150–51, 195; compression (*also* foreshortening), 41, 82, 87, 107; conceit, 28–30, 90, 107, 114, 117, 132, 156–57, 199–200, 201; hyperbole, 52, 53, 54, 89, 114, 171, 181; paradox, 116, 145; pathetic fallacy, 88, 89; personification, 28, 89, 91, 97, 132–33, 166, 167–68, 174; pun, 106, 109, 128, 133, 137, 154, 170, 186, 188; rhetorical question, 68, 112; synechdoche, 73, 178

Ritual, 19–21, 34–36, 46, 63–67, 73, 78, 96–102, 120–21, 131–36, 142, 152, 155, 163, 186–89, 192, 194–195

Roman Catholicism, 128, 130–33

Ross, Richard J., 79, 81, 172

"*Sacred Grove*," as symbol, 29, 31, 44, 49, 63, 71, 79, 82, 87, 89, 91, 100, 134, 140, 149, 150, 154, 160, 162, 165, 168, 170–72, 186, 191, 193, 196, 204

Security, ideal of, 69, 73, 74, 127, 150, 160

Shakespeare, William, 17, 32, 48, 54, 71, 75, 110, 130, 162, 178–79, 181, 197

Spencer, Edmund, 48, 111

Starkman, Miriam K., 142, 146

Stoicism, 55, 128, 159, 163, 202; *see also* his Neo-Stoicism *under* Herrick

Structure, of poems, 18–22, 42, 78, 87–90, 97, 102, 107–9, 112–20, 130, 144, 152–55, 157–60, 185–90

Suckling, Sir John, 105, 106, 209

Swinburne, Algernon Charles, 17, 208

Symbol, and Symbolism, 38, 63–65, 74–75, 99, 107, 112, 123, 132, 169, 204

Tacitus, 136

Temperance, *see* Moderation

Tibullus, 49, 134, 185, 188–90

"*Times trans-shifting*," *see* Transiency

Transiency, 21, 33, 34, 37, 40–46, 49, 57, 69–70, 91–96, 102, 116, 128, 132–33, 169, 171–72, 184–85, 192, 198, 203–5, 207, 211

Toliver, Harold E., 172

Traherne, Thomas, 209

Ugliness, 79–81

Untermeyer, Louis, 33–34

Vaughan, Henry, 163, 209

Virgil, 71, 78, 166, 187, 196

Waller, Edmund, 17

Whitaker, Thomas R., 27, 133

Willey, Basil, 163–64

York, Duke of, 28, 30

Youth, 43, 93–96, 97, 101–2